Anyone who wonders why Republicans hardly ever mention the name of the most recent president from their party—or who might have been fooled into thinking that our economic and other problems were caused by the current president—should read The Reckless Presidency of George W. Bush. James Gannon clearly explains how and why this reckless presidency was anything but wreck-less. It is essential reading for the 2012 election year.

Robert S. McElvaine
historian & author of *The Great Depression*

"Liar, liar, pants on fire!" The old childhood taunt applies here when reflecting on the legacy of President George W. Bush. Reckless? Check. Lying? Check. Damage yet undone? Check. Gannon reminds us how the Bush dark shadow lingers in Obama-era politics. The former president may be ranch-sitting in his post-politics stage, but this book won't let him off that easily.

Nancy Snow
author of *Information War* and *Propaganda, Inc.*

...The Bush years are vividly portrayed as framed by disaster, with 9/11 and the 2008 housing crisis providing "bookends." In between came calamities: the Iraq war and the campaign to sell it to the world; Abu Ghraib; tax cuts that benefited the wealthy; and irresponsible deregulation of e~~~~ Gannon asserts that the 2001 invasi ied, but believes the country "lost it: Iraq in 2003." ... Few can quibble w t what-ever the final legacy of the .... might be, the Republican presidential candidates so far in 2012 "seem unable to escape the Bush shadow even as they try to ignore it."

from ***Publishers Weekly***

Other books by James Gannon:

Stealing Secrets, Telling Lies: How Spies and Codebreakers
Helped Shape the Twentieth Century
(Washington, D.C.: Brassey's, 2001)

Military Occupations in the Age of Self-Determination:
The History Neocons Neglected
(Westport, Connecticut: Praeger Security International, 2008)

Obama's War: Avoiding a Quagmire in Afghanistan
(Washington, D.C.: Potomac Books, Inc., 2011)

From the pages of *The Reckless Presidency of George W. Bush:*

The Race for the Republican nomination: You have to wonder if the Republican candidates for President in 2012 agree with the historians that George W. Bush was a failed president. Otherwise, why would they run like scared rabbits from the Bush record? ... It is as if they want the electorate to forget about Bush, fearful that if the voters were to remember, all but the die-hard radical right would run from any candidate with the same regressive agenda.

Selling the Iraq war: Most if not all politicians lie to some degree, and many lie egregiously and often. The things they lie about set the acts apart, and when you consider the disaster the Bush Administration promoted, sending American men and women to death and crippling injury in a costly and unnecessary war, they were not the little white variety. They were big black lies.

Torture: Conservative officials in the Bush Administration had turned a sensible program into disgraceful policy. What started as a procedure to train American military personnel to withstand the pain and embarrassment they might experience if captured by terrorists, the administration changed into a formula for the harsh interrogation (i.e., torture) of terrorists in American custody. ... Barbaric Chinese torture of Americans became barbaric American torture of Islamists.

Bush tax cuts: One other thing Bush promised was a broad-based tax cut that would apply to everybody. That was true on the face of it, but conditions were somewhat like George Orwell's famous allegory, *Animal Farm*, after the animals drove Farmer Jones off his land for his drunken, dictatorial treatment of them. In the immediate aftermath of the rebellion, the animal leaders issued "commandments," one of which read, "All animals are equal." After the pigs took control of the farm—they are said to be the smartest of farm animals—they began to look and act human. They even walked around on two legs and engaged in conspicuous consumption. The commandment on equality was revised to read, "All animals are equal, but some animals are more equal than others." In the same way, the Bush tax cuts benefitted all taxpayers, but they benefitted a few wealthy taxpayers a lot more than most. A sign in Bush's Oval Office should have been put up to read, "All taxpayers are equal, but some taxpayers are more equal than others."

SETTING DRUG PRICES: Although the new Medicare law was supposed to promote competition, the power to regulate was turned over to private insurance and pharmaceutical companies, leaving the private sector to perform a government function. The insurance companies would determine the list of drugs to be covered, and would set prices in negotiations with the drug companies. The government was expressly prohibited from being involved, even though the private parties were playing with the taxpayers' money. Prices set in this manner amount to additional taxes, as far as the consumer is concerned—taxation without representation, the same issue that helped to trigger the Revolutionary War and the birth of the nation. Where was Grover Norquist when this cockamamie idea was hatched?

ON 9/11: The American people could hardly have expected that President George W. Bush would understand the radical Islamic thinking that guided the 9/11 terrorists to the World Trade Center and Pentagon on September 11, 2001. Still, they have cut him too much slack for his failure to defend against the worst attack on America at least since the Japanese bombing of Pearl Harbor in 1941.

CLASS WARFARE: It is hard to imagine governance more dedicated than Bush's to the interests of the moneyed class. ... He was fighting the class war for sure, on behalf of the upper class.

REGULATION OF THE FINANCIAL INDUSTRY: Voters who wonder why repealing Dodd-Frank is so high on the hit list of

Republican candidates for president they need look no further than the [new Consumer Financial Protection Bureau]. They don't speak of it in public because they don't want the electorate to know the real reason for their opposition to the new [Dodd-Frank] law. After all, [the CFPB agency's] purpose is consumer protection, and no candidate for president would openly admit that he/she is against consumer protection.

THE TEA PARTY may have sprouted randomly from the grass roots of the American soil, but the far right has always cultivated it for its own purpose: to devour, like the meat-eating plant from outer space in the movie, "Little Shop of Horrors," the presidential flesh of Barack Obama.

BIG BROTHER IN THE WHITE HOUSE: Philip A. Cooney held the position of chief of staff for the President's Council on Environmental Quality (CEQ). The name itself—Council on Environmental Quality—had a certain Orwellian ring. It sounded environmentally friendly, but it functioned to discredit climate science. ... Cooney had come over to the Bush White House early in 2001 from the American Petroleum Institute (API), the oil industry's chief lobbying arm. ... He adhered to a 1998 internal API "Communications Action Plan," with a clearly defined mission that played out like a worm eating the apple from the inside. "Victory," the action plan declared, "will be achieved when ... average citizens understand uncertainties in climate science ... [and] recognition of uncertainties becomes part of the 'conventional wisdom.'"

SUBPRIME MORTGAGE-BACKED BONDS: Picture meat from many cows piled on a chopping block in the back room of your local supermarket being ground up into hamburger and sliced into patties. Customers could not know which, from where, or how many bovines were in the patties or whether the government had actually inspected them. Subprime mortgage-backed bonds were something like that. The jargon identifying them was very impressive, "collateralized debt obligations," but they were nothing more than financial hamburgers dressed up in AAA ratings and sold as prime beef—and buyers could be certain if they took the trouble to investigate that the government had not inspected them.

SOCIAL SECURITY: [Bush] wanted to privatize the system, but did not want to say so. He used the term "personalize" instead. Despite his protestations to the contrary, his goal was to destroy, not "reform" Social Security, by turning it over to Wall Street. He painted a grim picture of Social Security's future without "reform," which was disingenuous at best. He tried to cover up a trillion dollar dodge that would partially disembowel the Social Security trust fund.

DEREGULATION was a bi-partisan error committed over three decades in Republican and Democratic administrations. The nation would have been better served with re-regulation to adapt the system to financial innovation and technological change, but policymakers forgot the lessons of the Great Depression and fell for the siren song of the free market.

THE 2000 FLORIDA RECOUNT: The Miami-Dade counting began on Monday the 20th. ... On Wednesday, the 22nd, a large unruly crowd gathered at the board office on the eighteenth floor of the Metro-Dade Government Center. The Democrats sent their lawyers, of course, but Republicans, alarmed by the Florida Supreme Court decision to allow the recounts to proceed and fearing for the first time that Gore might win, deployed their shock troops. These included some neatly dressed, high-profile figures—Marc Racicot, governor of Montana; Representatives Lincoln Diaz-Balart and Ileana Ros-Lehtinen of Florida (Miami), John Sweeney of New York, and Rob Portman of Ohio—and about fifty Congressional staffers who had been dispatched from Washington. These were not Bolsheviks or Brown Shirts demonstrating for a dictator; they were organized Republicans rallying to shut down the vote count. They gained fame as the "Brooks Brothers mob."

The Reckless Presidency
Of George W. Bush

JAMES GANNON

Bärli,

Best wishes.

James Gannon

The Reckless Presidency
Of George W. Bush

JAMES GANNON

æon
ACADEMIC

Æon Academic Press • Seattle, WA

Published 2012

Printed in the United States of America

16 15 14 13 12   1 2 3 4

ISBN 978-1-936672-28-8

Library of Congress Control Number: 2012908972

For information, address:

Æon Press,
PO Box 2222,
Poulsbo, WA 98370.

Cover photo:
President George W. Bush makes remarks to military personnel and their families at Marine Air Corps Station Miramar near San Diego, CA on August 14, 2003. In thanking the troops for their service to the country, the President said, "Before you went in, Iraqis were an oppressed people, and the dictator threatened his neighbors, the Middle East and the world. Today, the Iraqis are liberated people, the former regime is gone, and our nation and the world is more secure." Photo by Paul Morse, Courtesy of the George W. Bush Presidential Library

Cover design by Sheila Cowley

To Regina and my latest grandchild, Dillon

Contents

Acknowledgements

I wish to thank relatives and friends—professionals in business, law, and journalism—for their help in the preparation of this book. My son, Kevin Gannon, read most of the chapters and contributed to my understanding of the convoluted Wall Street jargon that pervades the subprime mortgage-backed bond market. Paul Crawford read the chapter on class warfare and offered several pertinent comments. The title came out of conversations with Richard and Elizabeth Starkey, Mervin Block, Charles Coates, and Sheila Lamb over Sunday brunch and email exchanges. My thanks also to Randy Kuckuck, Publisher, and Trey Schorr, senior editor of PublishNext, for their advice and assistance in the publication and promotion of this book. Any errors of commission or omission are my responsibility.

The Reckless Presidency
Of George W. Bush

JAMES GANNON

Introduction

A Failed President

*In America any boy may become president and I suppose
it's just one of the risks he takes.*

—Adlai Stevenson

Even before George W. Bush had served out his first term, 338
of 415 American historians (81 percent) pronounced his presidency a
failure. Seventy-seven (19 percent) called it "successful." More than half
of the 338 had to go back before Nixon's time in office to find a more
inauspicious president. Fifty of the total (12 percent) judged President
Bush to be the worst in history. Eight of the seventy-seven who rated
the Bush incumbency successful used the term facetiously. As one put it,
"[The Bush] presidency has been remarkably successful in its pursuit of
disastrous policies." Seven said it was the most successful since Clinton,
his immediate predecessor.[1]

The History News Network of George Mason University published
the survey in May 2004, the fortieth month of his ninety-six-month
presidency. Robert S. McElvaine, chairman of the history department
at Millsaps College in Jackson, Mississippi, who conducted it, admitted that it was unscientific and too early for historical validity. But he
defended it because historians, he contended, "are in a better position
than others" to make judgments about current presidents.

The numbers grew even worse for Bush as he neared the end of his second term. In 2008 the same polling organization found that 107 of 109 responding historians (98.2 percent) considered the Bush presidency a failure and sixty-seven (61 percent) rated him the worst president in history.[2] Other president watchers waited until Bush had served out his second term, or nearly so. In one poll conducted for C-Span as Bush prepared to leave the White House, sixty-five historians put him in the bottom ten.[3] Another survey of 238 presidential scholars carried out by the Siena College Research Institute and published in July 2010 had him in the bottom five (thirty-ninth of forty-three to be exact) in the company of Andrew Johnson, James Buchannan, Warren G. Harding, and Franklin Pierce.[4]

Some of the historians' opinions of Bush (that McElvaine took from the survey without identifying the individuals who expressed them) were unflattering in the extreme. Here are just a few brief appraisals: "Glib, contemptuous, ignorant, incurious, a dupe of anyone who humors his deluded belief in his heroic self," one historian described him, and added, "No other president's faults have had so deleterious an effect on not only the country but the world at large." Another wrote, "When future historians look back to identify the moment at which the United States began to lose its position of world leadership, they will point—rightly—to the Bush presidency." "God willing," said another, "this will go down as the nadir of American politics." A colleague that McElvaine described as "one of the most distinguished historians" said, "Bush does only two things well. He knows how to make the very rich very much richer, and he has an amazing talent for f**king up everything else he even approaches. His administration has been the most reckless, dangerous, irresponsible, mendacious, arrogant, self-righteous, incompetent, and deeply corrupt in all of American history." In McElvaine's own opinion, Bush squandered the world's good will toward America after 9/11 with the unnecessary invasion of Iraq and its justification of torture, and transformed a budget surplus into "a massive deficit."[5]

It is not easy to understand why Bush's presidency could be so willfully bad. The late, perceptive Texas journalist, Molly Ivins, who knew Bush slightly from high school and studied him closely as governor of Texas, saw him as "shaped by three intertwining strands of Texas culture, combined with huge blinkers of class." These threads are religiosity, which she did not challenge; anti-intellectualism, which she thought was genuine, and machismo, which she believed to be a put-on. The class blinkers that closed off his vision beyond white, self-made men rendered him insensitive to the suffering of poor people. He denied there were pockets of hunger in Texas, but he never really looked for them. "It's not that he's mean," she wrote. "It's just that when it comes to seeing how his policies affect people, George W. Bush doesn't have a clue." She perceived his core problem as president to be living in denial. "When it comes to dealing with the less privileged," as she put it, "Bush's real problem is not deception, but self-deception."[6]

Class blinkers do not explain his miserable failure in foreign affairs, where he allowed his vice president, Dick Cheney, and Cheney's neoconservative cronies to guide his course of action. Some of Cheney's erstwhile friends remember the vice president as a loyal, competent, hard-working conservative who as Secretary of Defense followed orders from President George H.W. Bush, the father, and were surprised to see the aggressive, dogmatic, authoritarian Cheney who played such a dominant role in the early presidency of George W. Bush, the son. Brent Scowcroft served as the elder Bush's National Security Advisor while Cheney ran the Pentagon. He put it this way in an interview with Jeffrey Goldberg in the *New Yorker*, "I consider Cheney a good friend—I've known him for thirty years. But Dick Cheney I don't know anymore."[7]

Bush had an answer for his historian critics in an interview on Fox News Sunday in 2008: "I take great comfort in knowing that they don't know what they are talking about," said the president in his sometimes quaint English, "because history takes a long time for us to reach."[8] He was right to suggest that these polls are unscholarly because true history does not kick in until, perhaps, fifty years after the fact as the official secrets see daylight. McElvaine cheerfully agreed. He carried Bush's quote to introduce the article about the second survey he wrote for History News Network.[9]

You have to wonder if the Republican candidates for President in 2012 agree with the historians that George W. Bush was a failed president. Otherwise, why would they run like scared rabbits from the Bush record? Candidates for the 2012 Republican nomination for president speak reverently of Ronald Reagan, but hardly at all about the later Bush. It is as if they want the electorate to forget about Bush, fearful that if the voters were to remember, all but the die-hard radical right would run from any candidate with the same regressive agenda.

BUBBLE GUM POLITICS

Although Bush himself famously refused in his first term to admit that he had committed any errors as president, probably no man (or woman) is equal to the task of leading the world's most dominant nation in a time of relentlessly growing complexity. Success and failure are not absolutes; they exist on a continuum to a greater or lesser degree, and can be argued without end by observers who carry their own ideological and ethical baggage into the argument. So the purpose here is to emphasize the "disastrous policies." This book is about issues. But because irony begs illumination some note is taken of his biographical background.

As the saying goes, the child was father to the man. He spoke in later life with a Texas twang and proudly butchered the English language, as in pronouncing the word "nuclear" as "nuk-u-ler." But he had the knack for turning his malapropisms to his political advantage. His grammatical errors seemed to charm the Texas (and American) masses. He would sometimes mock his own verbal shortcomings in political speeches—usually evoking laughter and ovations. In college he made up sophomoric nicknames for his chums, a practice he continued with his supporters during his political career. Congressman John Kasich of Ohio, for example, a distant hopeful for president in 2000, he cheekily dubbed "Johnny Boy"; New Hampshire campaign advisor Tom Rath became "Rathbone"; communications aide Karen Hughes,

"Prophet"; campaign adviser Karl Rove, "Turdblossom"; Congressman Charlie Bass of New Hampshire, "Bassmaster"; his campaign manager Joe Allbaugh, "Pinky"; his campaign field director Barbara Russell, "Barbarini," and so on.[10] One nickname that he may have come to regret was that of Enron CEO Kenneth Lay, a significant contributor to his presidential campaign whom he christened "Kenny Boy" before the Enron scandal broke.

As a young adult and on into middle age, he drank too much, something that happens to a lot of people, including some in high office. But his binges led him into puerile episodes even in adulthood. In 1972 on a Christmas visit to the family home in Washington, he went out with his teen-age brother, Marvin, and came back drunk, knocked over the neighbors' garbage, and encountered his father glaring at him at the doorway to the house. "I understand you're looking for me," he said. "Ya wanna go mano-y-mano right here?" His father stood there without speaking, fixing him with a disapproving stare and the younger man backed away. He was a know-it-all twenty-six then and still young for his years. The son's drinking got him into a minor scrape with the law in 1976 near the family vacation home in Kennebunkport, Maine. After a social evening swilling beer at a local pub in the company of his teenage sister Dorothy and Australian tennis star John Newcombe, he was caught in a police speed trap, given a sobriety test, and arrested for drunk driving. His father later told the arresting officer that he had done the right thing.

His Christian rebirth put him outside the nation's political mainstream of the time, but, curiously, advanced his political career. One night in April 1984 he accepted Jesus "into my life as my Savior and Lord," as it says in the Sinner's Prayer, which Bush repeated after Jimmy Blessitt, former minister to Hollywood stars, who had turned himself into a world traveling Christian evangelist. Afterward, Blessitt told Bush, "Jesus has come to live within your heart.... You are now the child of God."[11] In Bush's autobiography, *A Charge to Keep*, ghostwritten by sportswriter Mickey Herskowitz of the *Houston Chronicle* for the 2000 presidential campaign, Bush attributed his conversion to the famous evangelist Billy Graham, advisor to many presidents and a friend of the Bush family who had visited their summer home in Kennebunkport in 1985. That is not what Herskowitz had written in the draft he submitted to the campaign staff headed by Communications Director Karen Hughes, but it came out that way in the book. Hughes must have decided that the widely admired Graham was a more politically correct agent of God than Blessitt. Graham never claimed to have had a part in the young Bush's Christian rebirth.[12]

It is fair to say, nevertheless, that the born-again experience had a profound impact on the young man's political career. The initial benefit redounded to his earthly father. In the 1988 presidential campaign, George H. W. Bush relied on his son as liaison to the Christian right. In the general election he won eighty-one percent of the evangelical vote, even though Christian leaders had no illusions that the elder Bush would further their cause. It was the son who spoke their language, and soon they would give him their votes as he climbed to the governor's mansion in Texas and, after that, to the White House.

Obviously, G.W. Bush was politically astute, even though—or, perhaps, especially because—he tolerated the hardball ethics of his chief political advisor, Karl Rove. In 1978 when Rove was on G.H.W. Bush's payroll and only a casual advisor to the son in a run for Congress in West Texas, the younger Bush told a reporter that he was pro-choice on the abortion issue. He lost that election. Later, in his campaigns for governor of Texas and president of the United States and with Rove as his campaign "architect" (as Bush later called Rove), he switched to pro-life. His inner circle indirectly denied that he was ever pro-choice, but his declaration was published in a Lubbock, Texas newspaper.[13] Whatever one wants to believe about the incident or the ethics of the issue, to be pro-life in Texas with its large religious right voting bloc was politically smart.

Bush hit a political home run with his venture as part owner of the Texas Rangers American League baseball team. His style with the

Rangers became a metaphor for his conduct in political office. He left the business of baseball to others in his group. He took no part in team finances or trades. He attended most, if not all home games and spent most of each game in a box seat near the home team's dugout. There, he could swap jokes with the players, heckle the umpires, or chat amiably with guests invited to join him or with youngsters who gathered near the dugout for autographs of their favorite players. He had cards made up with his own image and signature so that no kid would go away without an autograph. Sometimes he would call out to the batboy, "Hey, Bat, you got some bubble gum?" So the batboy whose indispensable task it is to supply balls to the umpire, took on the added responsibility of keeping a stash of bubble gum for Bush so the future governor and president could pass it around to the youthful fans on the unimpeachable presumption that their parents voted. Bush also did radio and television interviews in the broadcasters' booths. Before long, thanks in part to his "bubble gum politics," he was not just George H.W. Bush's son. He was a Texas celebrity in his own right.

NEOCONS AND FREE MARKET CONS

David Corn, the liberal journalist and author, begins his book, *The Lies of George W. Bush*, with a short declarative sentence: "George W. Bush is a liar."[14] He goes on from there to elaborate on the complexities of that simple assertion, filling 344 pages with stories of Bush lies while acknowledging that Bush is far from the only liar in the political universe. It would be absurd to think otherwise. In fact, lying is embedded in the American culture (more accurately, in the human culture), beginning at an early age when children hear from their parents the mythical story of Santa Claus presented as fact—a harmless, good natured lie that entertains parents and children alike, and provides a powerful seasonal stimulus to the economy. Most people would call it a good lie.

In politics lies are almost as common as the air we breathe.

Candidates lie to get elected. Office holders lie to promote an agenda or cover up mistakes. Bush lied, as Corn amply demonstrates, both as candidate and office holder. As president, he and his administration lied while advocating or defending disastrous policies—an unnecessary war in Iraq, a tax cut promised to all that primarily benefitted the rich, the quality of the air at Ground Zero, the effort to privatize the social safety net, etc., etc. These could be classified as bad lies, and it's the bad lies connected to disastrous policies like the war in Iraq that will define Bush's place in history.

Bubble gum politics helped to prepare Bush for the political chase, but did nothing to teach him how to govern. He was never much of a scholar at Exeter Academy, Yale, and later, Harvard Business School. He exuded a natural warmth and chattiness that made it easy for him to get along with fellow students—and in adulthood with professional allies. He possessed the political smarts to realize that he did not know much about certain issues and that ignorance of the issues was no way to get elected. Before he began campaigning for governor of Texas in 1994, he took stock of the political issues he wanted to emphasize: education, juvenile justice, welfare, and tort reform and enlisted experts on these subjects to tutor him on what he apparently had ignored in school. It was like cramming for a final exam. It worked very nicely. He followed up by campaigning on these issues and getting elected. When he set out to make good on his campaign promises that—pro forma for an ideologically driven Republican—also included tax cuts, he held regular breakfast meetings with key democrats whose support was necessary for passage. Thus, in his reelection four years later he could face the voters with a record of accomplishment and compromise that helped him win a second term.

A similar scenario played out in 2000 as he prepared for his presidential campaign. Again, he turned to experts to enlighten him about his major presidential deficit, foreign affairs. He had never given much thought about life beyond his own borders. Only this time, neoconservatives such as Paul Wolfowitz and Richard Perle whose ideas on foreign policy were outside the mainstream prominently answered the call. Perle described Bush as a *"tabula rasa"* (blank slate) and praised him for admitting his lack of knowledge. Neocons loved Bush because their idiosyncratic philosophy became etched on his barren *tabula*. Initially, as president, he adopted the neocon perspective on the Middle East as his own.

Two great calamities provide bookends for the G.W. Bush administration, the terrorist attack on America of September 11, 2001 and the collapse of the housing bubble in 2008 that nearly destroyed the U.S. and world economies. Conservative visions of America clearly affected these events and carried through in Bush's eight-year stint as president. One is the vision of imperial America struggling to secure the world in its own image, needing enemies to overcome, sending its armies to the far corners of the earth, and training allies to help fight its battles. Bush cannot be held personally responsible for all that went wrong. "Things happen," said Secretary of Defense Donald Rumsfeld in a different context, but they happened on Bush's watch: the failure to heed warnings of the threat posed by al-Qaida, the deceitful campaign to draw America into war with Iraq, the mindless torture of Iraqi prisoners, and the shameful cover-up of the administration's role in implementing its torture policy. The neoconservative agenda coincided with Vice President Dick Cheney's hawkish foreign policy views, and Bush usually went along with Cheney until the Iraq war went sour in the second term and public support for Bush plummeted.

The other conservative vision appears in Bush's domestic agenda. A blind faith in an essentially unregulated free market system generated the momentum for tax policies that favored the rich at the expense of the poor and middle class; widened the income gap between the classes, and paved the way for the housing bubble that led to the near collapse of the financial system. Ironically, to his personal dismay, Bush, the free market ideologue, seemed to turn his back on free market ideology when the recession hit. In his presidential memoir, *Decision Points*, he writes that after his financial advisors informed him that he was facing the worst economic calamity since the Great Depression, he told some close aides, "If we're really looking at another Great Depression, you can be damn sure I'm going to be Roosevelt, not Hoover."[15] But his actions did not exactly fit the analogy. He put up hundreds of billions of taxpayers' dollars at risk to buy troubled assets of desperately overleveraged banks and bail out the rich. But he did little or nothing to save minority homeowners whom he had enticed to take out mortgages they could not afford.

The Vast Right-Wing Crusade

The political conversation in America has changed since the presidency of Ronald Reagan. Before that, politicians with a left-wing agenda dominated. They wanted to close the gap between rich and poor and establish programs to help the underclass, like welfare, food stamps, and Head Start. The conservative Richard Nixon, reviled by the left, believed that the growing federal bureaucracy stifled economic progress. Yet he hired the liberal Daniel Patrick Moynihan as a White House advisor on urban affairs and pushed a radical left idea that featured direct federal payments to low-income families instead of taxing them. (He eventually dropped the idea because the reaction persuaded him that it was a political loser.) By contrast, voices on the right have generally guided the discourse since Reagan's time. The mildly liberal Bill Clinton, despised by the right, cooperated with conservatives in Congress to end the federal welfare program, and then made the laughable assertion that the era of big government was over. Dwight D. Eisenhower, the commander of allied forces in Europe during World II and in the 1950s the hero president of the United States, dismissed the radical right as an insignificant fringe group out of touch with reality. They wanted to eliminate Social Security, unemployment insurance, labor laws, and farm subsidies, he said, and they were doomed to disappear from public life. But they did not disappear.

They supported Barry Goldwater and then Reagan, and continue to struggle with the Wall Street Republican establishment for the heart and soul of the Republican Party.

Hillary Clinton used to speak of a vast right-wing conspiracy against her husband when he was the Democratic president. The evidence collected for this book suggests that there is a vast right-wing crusade—by this time, too open and too well known to be called a conspiracy—to reduce the size and power of the federal government, transfer power to the states, and give private industry a free hand to dominate the economy. The Bush record cannot be fully understood without reference to this movement, which finds accommodation in the Tea Party and other right wing groups. Shrinking the federal government seems to be the Nixon dream carried forward. In hands less skilled than his it could be a formula for disaster. Grover Norquist's famous quote sums up the idea: "I don't want to abolish government. I just want to reduce it to the size where I can drag it into the bathroom and drown it in the bathtub."[16] If the radical right takes power from the federal government, where does the power go? Who would fill the vacuum? Conservatives claim that the states would gain. Maybe that is true in some measure. But in the larger economic picture, the runaway winners would be the captains of industry, including Wall Street bankers, who already hold the reins of power through their lobbies and heavy campaign cash. Shrinking the federal government and its authority to regulate can only enhance the power of the wealthiest class in what is already a quasi-plutocracy.

Bush made it abundantly clear that he was fighting the class war on behalf of the upper class. In that context, tax cuts that primarily benefitted the rich created budget shortfalls that reduced funds for programs to help the needy even before the obsessive Norquist could get his hands on the government. In the same light, Bush's signature Medicare legislation that provided prescription drug coverage for seniors funneled hundreds of billions of taxpayers' dollars to private drug companies and health care insurers and thus weakened the financial underpinning of Medicare. Bush demonstrated the conservative objective of destroying the federal safety net for the elderly in a campaign to privatize Social Security during his second term. In what appears to be a deliberate strategy, Bush policies widened the income gap between rich and poor, and made America, where politicians often trumpet the lofty principle of equal opportunity, the most unequal advanced industrial society in the world.

As Barack Obama nears the end of his first term, Republican candidates who hope to replace him have engaged in a series of debates. They describe him as a failed President without explaining that George W. Bush left the American economy in a deep hole. In fact, they rarely even mention Bush. They promise to repeal "Obamacare," their contemptuous word for his health reform law, but don't reveal a plan of their own. They want to scrap the Dodd-Frank law to regulate the finance industry, which creates a consumer protection agency that promises to put a clamp on the industry's exploitation of customers. Beyond that, the conservatives promise further deregulation without regard to the fact that an absence of sufficient financial regulation was a major cause of the Great Recession. Even today Republicans refuse to raise taxes on the rich as the gap between rich and poor widens and the federal deficit climbs at near warp speed. They propose to reduce the deficit that Bush helped to create by privatizing or cutting back on the inaptly named "entitlement" programs: Social Security, Medicare, and Medicaid. Despite their willful blindness, the Republican candidates assert that any one of them will defeat Obama and be a better President. Whoever wins the Republican nomination will enjoy a larger share of corporate and other special interest donations. The Bush Supreme Court has ruled that big money campaign donations are protected by the First Amendment. SuperPACs with unlimited covert funds will swamp the television channels with vicious, negative advertising as the 2012 Election Day approaches.

A reader might wonder, why so one-sided? Why does this book cover primarily the dark side of the Bush presidency? And the answer is that this book is more in the nature of an indictment of wrongheaded governance, not a full-scale review of the administration. It comes not from an inside-the-beltway pundit, but from an outside observer trying to make sense out of what goes on in Washington. The reader is left to judge if the case is made. The point is not that Bush did everything wrong, only that he pursued several misguided policies that ill served the nation. He also did a few things right that will not actually be covered in this book. He went after al-Qaida by attacking Taliban-ruled Afghanistan, but the commander-in-chief failed to block Osama bin Laden's escape at Tora Bora and later erred grievously by invading Iraq. Because everyone is entitled to the best available health care, Bush should be applauded for pledging funds to eradicate AIDS, even if he did not attain the goal he set (politicians rarely do), but he should be called to account for the absence of a policy to provide health care to every American and the ideologically inspired restrictions he put on government support of stem cell research. Bush, like most Presidents (and people in every human endeavor), learned on the job, and his performance improved toward the end of his tenure, particularly with regard to the agreement negotiated with Iraqi leaders to withdraw American forces by the end of 2011 (that should never have been sent there in the first place). His successor, President Obama, kept his pledge for him. American troops have cleared out of Iraq. In the final two chapters the question arises whether America hit rock bottom in the Bush years, or whether things might get worse. With the birth of the Tea Party, that is an intriguing question.

Chapter 1

Tribal Politics

There is no act of treachery or meanness of which a political party is not capable; for in politics there is no honor.

—Benjamin Disraeli

THE CONCEPT OF "TRIBE" is used loosely here to describe any group with a certain kinship of interests whose members place the highest value on loyalty. Outside groups, contrary facts, inductive reasoning, compromise positions are minimized and often ignored. Over the centuries, tribes were a kind of stepping stone of cultural and political evolution from the family on up to the nation-state. History records the three primitive tribes of ancient Rome and the twelve tribes of Israel. Primitive tribes still exist deep in the Amazon forest and the jungles of southwestern Pacific islands and tribes remain a political force in nation-states around the globe. Vestiges of tribal activity turn up in even the most advanced societies including the United States.

Of course, American political parties are not actually tribes—they only act tribal often enough for it to be noticed. Not to put too partisan a face on it, the evidence is abundantly clear that the Republicans are more tribal than the Democrats. Hard-core conservatives, who seem to have gained a controlling influence in the Republican Party, display more in-group loyalty, are better organized, cling more to ideological substrates, launch more ad hominem attacks, more often distort the facts, and probe constantly for enemy weaknesses in a never-ending search for advantage. They are gritty, visceral, and can be mean spirited, spoiling for a fight with fire in the belly. Woe to those who break ranks; they could be ostracized—and some in the George W. Bush Administration actually were. Paul O'Neill, Bush's first Secretary of the Treasury, dared to think independently. He was dismissed for speaking out against preparations for the Iraq war and for advising higher taxes to close the budget gap. Lawrence B. Lindsey, an assistant to the president on economic policy, lost his job after estimating that the Iraq war would cost more than $200 billion, far above the figure Bush policymakers were peddling but far below what turned out to be the actual cost. Mike Parker, whom Bush appointed to head the Army Corps of Engineers, was fired for admitting publicly that budget cuts would hamper flood control. The exorbitant cost of excessive saving came to light when Hurricane Katrina struck New Orleans. In the second Bush term, eight federal attorneys were fired either for investigating Republicans or failing to pursue weak cases against Democrats.

Nothing of the sort happened to Democratic Senator Joseph Lieberman after he lost in the 2006 Democratic primary and won re-election as an independent, and then supported Republican John McCain for president in 2008. The Democratic leadership, hoping to achieve a filibuster-proof sixty-vote majority, treated him with kid gloves, giving him the chairmanship of the Homeland Security and Government Affairs Committees and the Air-land Subcommittee of the Armed Services Committee. Democrats are more likely to be practical, non-ideological, nerdy, wonkish, individualistic, conflicted, and indecisive–a pragmatic course under the circumstances. As Will Rogers once put it, "I don't belong to any organized party. I'm a Democrat."

The Republican qualities especially should be apparent as we trace in this chapter the political career of George W. Bush, his successes on the campaign trail, and in later chapters while in office, his aggressive use of campaign tactics to promote dubious policies.

LOW ROAD TO HIGH OFFICE

Despite their virtue as a non-violent, inclusive form of succession, American elections have always been rough and tumble affairs. The underside of politics can be traced all the way back to our revered founding fathers. Even then, character assassination found a place in the electoral process. In 1800, Thomas Jefferson secretly hired an attack dog, the writer James Callendar, to assail his opponent, erstwhile and future friend John Adams. Callendar dutifully ripped into Adams as a "repulsive pedant" and "hideous hermaphroditical character, which has neither the force and firmness of a man nor the gentleness and sensibility of a woman." At that time, criticism of the president was considered a violation of the Alien and Sedition Act, so Callendar spent nine months in jail for his effrontery. Since then, campaign decorum has not improved. In 1880, the Republicans inserted "Soapy Sam" into the campaign to save the election of James A. Garfield. "Soapy Sam" was the idiom of those days for the two-dollar bill, shamelessly passed out by the thousands in Indiana to stimulate the electoral fervor of otherwise indifferent voters. The money behind that effort came from the wealthy captains of industry. The Democrats tried to offset the Republican vote-buying advantage by sending in outsiders to cast multiple ballots. But Garfield won easily.[1]

The fervor short of violence did not abate in the twentieth century. While Democrats also engaged in exaggeration and misinformation— lies if you prefer, more passion seemed to emerge from Republicans. On the Democratic side, the 1964 campaign saw Lyndon Johnson's political guerrillas hammer Barry Goldwater by, among other devious ploys, printing up children's coloring books that showed the right wing Republican candidate wearing the robes of the Ku Klux Klan. (Goldwater was not a racist.) And who can forget Richard Nixon's CRP (Committee to Re-elect the President, CREEP) that carried out the 1972 Watergate break-in, or the notorious Donald Segretti who helped that year to drive Democrat Edmund Muskie out of presidential politics by forging Muskie papers. One phony document made it look as though Muskie had maligned the language and culture of French Canadians; others had him accusing certain fellow Democrats of sexual misconduct. Segretti served a mere four months of jail time for his misdeeds, less than half the sentence of James Callendar for vilifying John Adams.[2]

ROVE RISING

To understand George W. Bush's meteoric rise to the pinnacle of political power, it is important to know something about Karl Rove's zeal and character. In stark contrast to the dilettante he served, Rove is an extraordinary individual: vibrant, quick witted, a fast talker, consumed by politics, always conservative, well organized, creative, confident, fast to act out his schemes with a premium on winning above moral rectitude. He was a Christmas baby, delivered on December 25, 1950. He grew up in Nevada, the second of five children in a broken home. He never knew his biological father, and never realized until his teens that the man he grew up with was his stepfather who departed the family after admitting his homosexuality. A bright, nerdy youth, Rove possessed a flair for the dramatic. In high school he won an election for president of the student body senate after entering a candidates' assembly in the school gymnasium perched between two pretty girls on the backrest of a Volkswagen convertible wearing coat and tie and sporting horn-rimmed glasses, waving triumphantly to a cheering crowd. At that young age he knew already what it took to win elections.

Rove attended several colleges, but never bothered to get a degree. At the University of Utah, he became president of the school's College Republicans and plunged into their activities with alacrity. In 1970 he was dispatched to Illinois to organize campuses for the unsuccessful campaign of the conservative Republican Senator Ralph Smith. Rove's mind exploded with ideas, and not all of them involved Smith's run for office. He noticed that Alan Dixon, the Democrat running for state treasurer, had invited party officials, supporters, and the media to the formal opening of his campaign. Rove decided to disrupt it. He gained prior entry to campaign headquarters under an assumed name and stole some of Dixon's stationery. Then he wrote up an invitation promising free beer, food, girls, and a good time for all, and distributed a thousand or so leaflets to hippies, winos, rock concert fans, and the down-and-out at a soup kitchen. Hundreds of free loaders showed up at Dixon's party to mix with the Democratic hoi polloi. It must have been a funny scene worthy of a madcap Hollywood movie, but, understandably, Dixon was not amused.[3] As dirty tricks go, it was relatively harmless. At least in that instance, Rove did not sully innocent people as Segretti had done. (Later, the whispered smear of uncertain origins would be a hallmark of Rove-led campaigns.)

Rove continued to climb in the College Republican ranks and soon found himself as its executive director with an office in Washington and a salary of $9,200 (equivalent to $47,200 in 2009 dollars[4]). The College Republicans were an arm of the Republican National Committee, then chaired by George H.W. Bush. It was heady stuff for a young conservative in his early twenties, but, truth to tell, Rove started basically as a gofer. The job got more interesting in 1972 when he and a colleague, Bernie Robinson, went on a cross-country tour of campuses to instruct College Republican recruits on how to organize their chapters and deliver the conservative message. At one seminar, Rove jovially recounted the Dixon story as he and Robinson talked up the value of vulgar campaign techniques that also included going through opponents' garbage for useful campaign information.[5] These churlish antics would come back to bite Rove, but would not deter his spectacular rise in the Republican Party.

In 1973, tapped to run for chairman of the College Republican National Committee, he paired with another fast-rising political conservative, Lee Atwater of the University of South Carolina, for a week of politicking. With Atwater as his southern campaign chairman, they drove together in a rented car from campus to campus meeting with state College Republican chairmen, until they reached Lake of the Ozarks, Arkansas, site of the national convention. Once they arrived, they found that Rove was still behind Robert Edgeworth of the University of Michigan in the delegate count. Not to worry! Neither Rove nor Atwater, another Machiavellian on the rise, was willing to accept defeat. They enlisted the support of a group of rough-and-ready Chicago delegates who successfully challenged the credentials of many Edgeworth delegates. The furor, with Rove and Edgeworth supporters shouting epithets at each other, tied the convention in knots. Both men were nominated, and each declared victory. The convention was unable to settle it, so the problem was passed on to the RNC in Washington.

Before Chairman G.H.W. Bush announced his decision, Terry Dolan, future founder of the National Conservative Political Action Committee who had been a contender for the College Republicans' chairmanship before throwing in with Edgeworth, went to the media with damning evidence of Rove advising dirty tricks at his cross-country seminars. When the *Washington Post* ran the story, Bush went ballistic. The Watergate scandal was in full swing, and the *Post* was publishing a new angle about the story on a near daily basis. But the Committee to Re-elect the President, which engineered the break-in, was taking the rap, not the Republican Party. Bush was trying to save the party from bad ink. Disclosures of party seminars on dirty tricks were just what he did not need. Bush had ordered an internal investigation, but the findings were filed away. He knew what they said, but he was not willing to share them with the public. To put it simply, he covered them up. So when the story broke, Bush was disarmed. Putting party loyalty above full disclosure (tribal politics), he castigated Edgeworth for betrayal, even though Edgeworth had tried to talk Dolan out of going to the media. Bush then named Rove, the purveyor of dirty tricks, to head the College Republicans' national committee. (One trivial historical footnote: It was there, at the headquarters of the RNC, that Rove and George W. Bush first met.)

In 1976 Rove married a Houston socialite, Valerie Wainwright. Initially, they settled in Richmond, Virginia where he was raising money for that state's Republican Party. He learned the value of direct-mail fundraising and drew in more than enough donations to dig the party out of debt. But Valerie yearned for the social ambience of her Waspish roots, so they moved to Houston. Karl stayed close to the elder George Bush, fund-raising for his 1980 presidential bid and advising the younger George in his losing campaign for Congress in 1978. Karl traveled a lot, was rarely home, and in 1979 Valerie filed for divorce. Thereafter, Rove moved to Austin and hung out his shingle in an office that overlooked the Capital mall. He gained a lot of Republican clients, including ex-Democrats like Phil Gramm who won a U.S. Senate seat after switching to the Republican Party. Texas journalists James Moore and Wayne Slater say in their book, *Bush's Brain*, that Rove played a key part in altering the political landscape in Texas from predominantly Democratic to predominantly Republican. "In little more than a decade," they wrote, "every Democrat in elective statewide office was gone, replaced by Republicans—virtually every one a Rove client."[6]

One client, Bill Clements, is noteworthy for a bugging incident that speaks to Rove's winning-is-the-only-thing style of politics. In 1978, Clements had been the first Texas Republican in a century to be elected governor. Four years later he lost to Mark White after demonstrating under public scrutiny a prickly personality and a penchant for verbal gaffes. In 1986, the two men faced off again with Rove developing strategy for Clements who had started the campaign with a huge lead in the polls, but found by early October that White was fast closing the gap as the time approached for the only televised debate of the campaign.

Allegedly fearing that campaign secrets were being leaked to the other side, the Clements team hired a security firm to scan their offices for electronic bugs one day before the debate. A bug that could have picked up telephone conversations was found in a picture frame behind Rove's desk. There were no signs of entry and no conclusive fingerprint evidence. Rove called in print and TV reporters for a news conference and told them that only the White campaign could have benefitted from the bugging, and that is the way most reporters played the story. Although never brought up in the debate, the bugging story overshadowed any mention of issues in the news coverage that followed, and Clements went on to win the election. In some quarters, the suspicion lingered that Rove himself had planted the bug, but there was never any proof one way or the other.

EYES ON THE STATEHOUSE

After his important contribution as liaison to the religious right in his father's successful bid for the presidency in 1988, the young George, now a reborn Christian, moved back to Texas, his confidence buoyed and the thrill of politics coursing through his veins. He talked of running for governor in 1990 against the popular incumbent, the late Ann Richards. Part of him wanted to avenge that famous cutting remark she had uttered about his father's patrician background when she was the keynote speaker in the 1988 Democratic convention. "Poor George," she had declared, her words ringing out in the huge convention hall, "he can't help it. He was born with a silver foot in his mouth." But, reminded that a second defeat to begin his career might ruin his political future, George W. allowed himself to be talked out of running that year. Instead, he moved to Dallas and put together the syndicate consisting of his father's wealthy friends that bought the Texas Rangers. Clearly, he was in it not only for the love of baseball, but for the opportunity to enhance his political bone fides. His box seat near the home team dugout was his venue for political showmanship.

After his father's embarrassing defeat to Bill Clinton in 1992 he teamed with Rove and jumped into the political ring. Bush formally entered the campaign for governor of Texas in the summer of 1993 only eight percentage points behind Richards in the polls, a fairly insignificant margin that reflected his high public name recognition and a growing public unease in conservative Texas over Richards' stewardship of the governor's office. Bush was smart enough to realize that he knew next to nothing about key issues, so he enlisted prominent experts to tutor him on education, juvenile justice, welfare, and tort reform, and hammered Richards' alleged inability to solve these problems. He promised to cut taxes, get tough on crime, make schools accountable for performance, reform welfare, and, finally, to sign legislation to make it lawful for citizens to carry concealed weapons. Richards had upset the powerful gun lobby by vetoing such a gun bill. During the campaign she disparaged her opponent, taking up the image created by journalist Molly Ivans by calling him a "shrub," which seemed to imply that he was not big enough to be a bush, an image that Ivans disavowed.

One other thing: a damaging wedge issue reared up to smack Richards in the face—her appointment of homosexuals to public office. It began as a whispering campaign that spread like wildfire in the Christian east Texas countryside: she appointed homosexuals to office, so she must be a lesbian. Initially, Bush addressed the issue in code by warning that some of Richards' appointees had "personal" agendas. The conservative cognoscenti caught his drift. At the same time he pledged to conduct a positive campaign with no personal attacks. In the end, Bush pulled off the upset with a comfortable seven-percent margin, gathering fifty-three percent of the vote against forty-six percent for Richards. Four years later, he won reelection in a landslide with sixty-eight per cent of the vote.

The younger George Bush recognized his inadequacies, according to author Robert Draper, and compensated by surrounding himself with loyal people who knew how to run the business of government. As he positioned himself in the constitutionally weak office of Texas governor, he made it his priority to win the cooperation of two power-ful Democrats, Lieutenant Governor Bob Bullock and House Speaker Pete Laney, whom he needed to help him fulfill his campaign promises. They met weekly for breakfast during the legislative session of 1995, and laid the groundwork for legislation that met Bush's conservative goals (Conservative Texas Democrats don't think like liberal New

England Democrats). The bills wound through the legislature with the two Democrats doing the heavy lifting.[7]

The sweet smell of success made Bush a player in national politics. It transformed the governorship into a stepping stone to the presidency. Bush visited groups of wealthy conservatives to raise funds. He met with policy wonks from academe and right wing think tanks, asking for their comments on his views of national issues. Although he was running for reelection as governor, which he was assured of winning, in the public mind he became a player in the presidential sweepstakes. His national poll numbers shot up and contributions poured in for the anticipated run for national office. He showed a certain pro-forma hesitation about joining the larger race—mouthing the usual blather about family considerations, but these were overridden by his burning ambition and he allowed himself to be talked into it. In church on the morning of his second inaugural ceremony as Texas governor, he heard Pastor Mark Craig say that America was "starved for leaders who have ethical and moral courage." His mother, Barbara, whispered in his ear, "He was talking to you." As author Robert Draper portrayed it, Bush took it as a sign that God, speaking through Pastor Craig, wanted him to run for president.[8]

EYES ON THE WHITE HOUSE

Bush often spoke in code on the campaign trail. His use of the term "personal agenda" to signify perceived underlying aims of homosexuals appointed by Governor Richards to important state offices is one example. In that instance, people generally knew what he was talking about, especially his Christian conservative base who viewed homosexuality as a defiance of God's law. But another codeword was entirely misinterpreted by the general public, according to author Craig Unger. Early in his 2000 presidential campaign, he described himself as a "compassionate conservative," which seemed to indicate a caring outreach to the poor and underprivileged. When he took office, his policies were hardly compassionate for the poor, so people began to think that he had been a stealth candidate using soothing words to conceal a brass-bound right wing agenda. But to his Christian conservative base, the term was Bush's way of promising them a voice in the councils of power,[9] and he definitely lived up to that interpretation.

Bush had never given much thought to global problems. The neocons had been critical of Bush's father in 1991 for failing to push on to Baghdad after the U.S.-led coalition had destroyed the Iraqi army in retaking Kuwait. Ever since, they had urged President Clinton to pursue regime change in Iraq, by military force if necessary. Paul Wolfowitz, a leading neocon scholar from Johns Hopkins University, prepped George W. with the Orwellian idea of achieving peace through war in the region by striking a blow against so-called "rejectionist" states (such as Iraq, Syria, and Iran that rejected negotiations with Israel). Once the regime of Saddam Hussein was subdued, the neocons argued, the others would fall in line like dominoes. The road to Jerusalem, they said, is through Baghdad. By the time the younger Bush entered the White House his "tabula" was etched with neocon dogma.

2000 PRIMARY

Going into the primary season, Bush had the edge over Republican opponents in fund-raising and high-profile endorsements. He won in Iowa, the first stop, and then swerved into a ditch in New Hampshire and watched in shock as John McCain's "straight-talk express" sped by. The senator from Arizona received about forty-nine percent of the New Hampshire vote to thirty percent for Bush.

Then it was on to South Carolina where Rove opened his bag of dirty tricks and stopped McCain dead in his tracks. "Nothing was too low to rule out," said Dr. Nancy Snow, evoking the Bush team's negative campaigning as "the ghost of Lee Atwater on steroids."[10] (Snow mentioned Rove's friend Atwater as a reminder of the latter's low road during the 1988 presidential campaign of George H.W. Bush, the candidate's father.) Snow was then a professor of political science at tiny New England College in Henniker, New Hampshire and executive director of that state's chapter of Common Cause. A self-described Independent, she had been inspired by McCain's stunning victory in New Hampshire to observe and work for his campaign in South Carolina—and she was appalled by Bush's (i.e., Rove's) performance.

After New Hampshire, McCain spurted from nineteen points down in South Carolina to a five-point lead. But soon after his arrival the ground beneath him began to crumble. Bush first reiterated his "compassionate conservatism" in a speech at Christian fundamentalist Bob Jones University, which until that year had banned interracial dating. On the stage with him was a man Bush had never met before, J. Thomas Burch, Jr., a Vietnam veteran who headed an organization called the National Vietnam and Gulf War Veterans Coalition, which he funded with solicitations on behalf of Vietnam POW/MIAs, playing on widows' and close relatives' longing for their lost loved ones. Despite McCain's distinguished war record that included five years as a North Vietnamese prisoner of war, Burch had long accused him of abandoning the cause of Vietnam soldiers missing in action and Gulf War vets, and he did it again on Bush's platform. Bush then shook Burch's hand. It was an ugly scene, made uglier by the fact that Burch was not telling the truth. McCain had actually supported causes to help veterans of these two wars. He testified in favor of legislation to compensate victims of the Gulf War who came down with unexplained illness and had cosponsored the Agent Orange Act that was passed into law.[11] Asked by other veterans why he allowed Burch to speak at his rally, Bush replied with specious piety, "He's entitled to his own opinion." But to voice it on Bush's campaign platform left the impression that Bush endorsed it. McCain was incensed, which brought home the point of the Rove-Atwater modus operandi: get under the opponent's skin.

Dueling ads then took center stage. The ads were about taxes, but the subtext was credibility and the sitting Democratic President, Bill Clinton, reviled by South Carolina conservatives, became the measuring stick. Bush struck with an ad claiming that McCain had echoed Washington, D.C. Democrats by calling the Bush tax plan smaller than Clinton's. McCain shot back, saying that Bush was getting desperate with a negative ad that "twists the truth like Clinton." Bush took offense in his next ad at the comparison with Clinton: "Disagree with me, fine. But do not challenge my integrity."[12] McCain soon withdrew his ad, but Bush kept his running until primary day. McCain had turned the tables on himself and in the eyes of conservative South Carolina voters appeared to be the candidate traveling the low road.

Scurrilous rumors not directly traceable to the Bush campaign began to float around the state—similar to the rumors that circulated in Texas in 1994 about Ann Richards' sexual orientation. One rumor: McCain had conceived black children out of wedlock; another: his adopted Cambodian daughter who came out of Mother Teresa's Missionaries of Charity home for homeless children in Calcutta was one such illegitimate child; and another rumor: McCain was pro-abortion; and another: McCain was a "fag candidate" because he had met with gay members of the Log Cabin Republicans (Bush met with them, too, later in the campaign). The Bush staff reportedly conducted "push polls," in which the questions were loaded in a manner to elicit unavoidably negative opinions about McCain—a charge Bush spokesmen denied, saying all questions were based on identifiable facts.[13] In the end, McCain lost South Carolina by thirteen percentage points, and despite a subsequent McCain victory in Michigan with support from Independent voters, the Bush nomination was assured.

2000 GENERAL ELECTION

It remained in 2000 for the Republican attack machine to put Bush's Democratic opponent, Vice President Al Gore, through a gauntlet of assaults on his credibility. With the aid of unexpected media distortions, they devoted themselves to painting Gore as a man who would say anything to get elected, a portrayal that could easily be ascribed to Bush. The most damaging example revolved around the myth that Gore invented the internet, to which Gore himself contributed with words that could be misconstrued when he spoke of his own truly important role in its development.

The internet got its start as a project of the Defense Department's Advanced Research Projects Agency (DARPA) to help defend against a feared intercontinental missile attack on the United States after the Soviet Union became the first nation in space by launching Sputnik in 1958. The internet venture got off the ground a few years later with a concept proposed by J.C.R. Licklider of MIT for a "galactic network" of interconnected computers to exchange ideas and access data. With DARPA's funding, the internet became the collective project of an elite group of government, industry, academic and think tank scientists and engineers. The first small "Arpanet," as it was then called, materialized in 1969 with four western colleges, UCLA, Stanford, Utah, and UC Santa Barbara, participating. The project, enriched with email and enlarged with more stations, was demonstrated publicly for the first time at the International Computer Communication Conference in 1972.

Then-Congressman Gore heard about it, quickly grasped its huge potential, and introduced two bills in Congress to broaden the internet for civilian use. Later, during his campaign for President, Gore said in an interview with CNN's Wolf Blitzer, "During my service in the United States Congress, I took the initiative in creating the internet." In a real sense that was a true statement. He did not invent the internet—and he never said he did, but he had actually taken the lead in making the internet an "information superhighway" for public participation, to use his image. Perhaps the internet would have turned out the way it is without Gore, but the historical fact is that Gore was the catalyst that made it happen. Even former Republican House Speaker Newt Gingrich gave him credit for his initiative. But other Republicans seized on the word "create," subsequently used interchangeably with the word "invent." "If the vice president created the internet," blared

House Majority Leader Dick Armey of Texas, "I created the interstate highway system." Republican Congressman James Sensenbrenner of Wisconsin put out a press release headlined, "Delusions of Grandeur: Vice President Gore Takes Credit for Creating the Internet." Instead of getting the credit he deserved for his far-reaching perception, Gore was soon being cut up in the media for his "delusions of grandeur."[14]

Gore took another beating from the media after the first debate between the two candidates, this time not for anything he said, but for sounds he emitted while Bush was speaking. On several occasions as Bush was responding to questions posed to the two men, Gore let out audible sighs, as if to signal dismay at Bush's ignorance of the issues. Afterward, the Bush campaign team produced a tape of Gore's sighs and distributed copies to the media, which TV news programs repeatedly played for their entertainment value. (In TV news, they call it "show biz.") Instead of substantive evidence of Gore's better understanding of the issues, the voters were left with the image of a rude and arrogant man.

FLORIDA RECOUNT

Nevertheless, Gore won the election's popular count by more than half a million votes nationwide. The electoral contest was so close that it came down to the outcome in Florida, which in the initial count Bush won by fewer than 2,000 votes. Such a narrow margin triggered an automatic machine recount that changed nothing. The Democrats then sued for hand recounts, and so the election season was extended by thirty-six days in a furious struggle between the two political parties. It played out in state and federal courts, in the canvassing boards of four counties, and in the case of Miami-Dade County, in a boisterous rally of out-of-state Republicans to stop the limited manual recount.

The first sign of trouble came in Palm Beach County where hundreds of people who intended to vote for Gore came away from the voting booth wondering if they had actually voted for Pat Buchanan. They had. That's when the world learned of the "butterfly ballot," which carried the candidates' names in two columns with punch-hole marks in the middle. Voters were to indicate their preference by punching out the appropriate hole. The Palm Beach ballot was confusing. Bush and Gore were the first two names in the left column; Buchanan was the first name in the right column. But the marks between them were for Bush, Buchanan, and Gore in that order. Three thousand, seven hundred and four voters punched the second mark, and their votes went to Buchanan, almost double Bush's margin of victory in Florida and three-and-a-half times the number of votes Buchanan received in Miami-Dade and Broward (Fort Lauderdale) Counties combined. The conservative Buchanan admitted later that he could not possibly have received that many votes in the overwhelmingly liberal Jewish retirement community of Palm Beach County. But, short of a re-vote, it would be impossible to prove which or how many of the Buchanan votes were meant for Gore. Anguishing though it may be, those misshapen ballots determined the fate of the nation. Re-voting was not in the cards, but limited manual recounts were.

Closer examination of the ballots drew out still other language oddities: "hanging" and "dimpled" chads. Chads are bits of paper detached from the ballot when the stylus punches through. Some chads on the Florida ballots were left dangling at the punch hole, thus, hanging chads. The dimpled chads were not chads at all. Call them would-be chads, indentations at the punch-hole mark where the stylus did not penetrate the ballot, leaving either a tiny partial opening or no hole at all. Such imperfect ballots with hanging or dimpled chads were rejected in the machine tabulation, and as a group classified as the "undercount" or "under-vote."

In a close vote the margin of error for machines was such that Florida law allowed the candidates to request hand recounts in up to four counties. The Bush team wanted no part of hand counts. With their man ahead, they fought for the soonest possible certification to seal Bush's victory. It helped their cause that Florida's governor, Jeb Bush, was their candidate's brother, and the Florida secretary of state, Katherine Harris, the certifier of elections, an upwardly mobile Republican that put party above justice (tribal politics). Initially, she set a November 14 certification date, leaving county canvassing boards only one week after the election to submit their results, too short for time-consuming hand counts. That deadline was pushed ahead to the 17[th,] to allow for absentee ballots, and finally to the 26th by the Florida Supreme Court.

Then-President Clinton drew a simple but profound blueprint of the Florida recount competition: Gore, he said, treated it as a legal contest; the Republicans saw it as political war.[15] In other words, the Republicans played tribal politics; the Democrats relied on the rule of law drawn up by the founding fathers. As prescribed by Florida law, Gore's lawyers applied for hand counts in four Democratic strongholds along the Atlantic coast—Miami-Dade, Broward, Palm Beach, and Volusia (Daytona) Counties—where Gore was sure to get extra votes. Each county's canvassing board agreed to it, generally cutting the task down to size by deciding to scrutinize only the undercount. The result was mixed. Volusia, the least populous of the four counties, completed its work, but produced only a paltry twenty-seven more votes for Gore. Broward vote counters worked on Thanksgiving Day and managed to complete their review of the undercount and turned in 567 extra votes for Gore. A lackadaisical Palm Beach did not work on Thanksgiving, and did not finish the job, submitting only a partial list of additional votes.

In Miami-Dade, roughhouse Republican political action crushed the rational Democratic legal strategy. When Harris set a November 14 certification date, the Miami-Dade canvassing board voted, two to one, not to do a manual recount. She then stretched the date to Friday November 17. But on that day, the state Supreme Court ruled against her arbitrary action, and the following Tuesday set a November 26 deadline. Back on the 17th, the Miami-Dade board reversed its decision and voted for the manual recount. In fact, they decided to recount all 653,963 votes. They thought they could get the job done in two weeks. But when the state Supreme Court set a November 26 deadline, they lowered their sights to reviewing only the 10,750 ballots of the undercount.

The Miami-Dade counting began on Monday the 20th. The court-imposed November 26 deadline was announced the next day. On Wednesday, the 22nd, a large unruly crowd gathered at the board office on the eighteenth floor of the Metro-Dade Government Center. The Democrats sent their lawyers, of course, but Republicans, alarmed by the Supreme Court decision to allow the recounts to proceed and fearing for the first time that Gore might win, deployed their shock troops. These included some neatly dressed, high-profile figures—Marc Racicot, governor of Montana; Congress members Lincoln Diaz-Balart and Ileana Ros-Lehtinen of Florida (from Miami), John Sweeney of New York, and Rob Portman of Ohio—and about fifty Congressional staffers who had been dispatched from Washington. These were not Bolsheviks or Brown Shirts demonstrating for dictators; they were organized Republicans rallying to shut down the vote count. They gained fame as the "Brooks Brothers mob." They crowded into too small a space in the Canvassing Board's eighteenth-floor office.

Outside on the street an even larger, well organized crowd of Cuban-Americans, venting their rage against Clinton over the return in 2000 of the motherless child Elian Gonzales to his father in Cuba, also called for a halt to the recount. Republican operatives mingled with the street crowd, and Roger Stone reportedly communicated with his Republican associates by walkie-talkie from a building across the street. Stone is a former Nixon activist on the Committee to Re-elect the President who practiced hardball conservative politics well before Lee Atwater and Karl Rove appeared on the scene. The pushing and shoving, the bang-ing on doors and windows, the outcries of controlled rage with slogans such as "No justice, no peace!" and "Shut it down!" all disrupted the vote-counters' train of thought. After an effort to restore order by moving to a smaller space one floor up, and then moving back to the eighteenth floor for a formal meeting, the board stopped counting altogether.[16] For Gore to win with extra votes from the hand counts under severe time constraints was probably a long shot from the beginning, but with the sloth in Palm Beach and the chicken-heartedness in Miami-Dade it became impossible.

The die was cast. The Gore team's elegant legal arguments for Florida's electoral votes fizzled in the U.S. Supreme Court on five-to-four decisions that overruled two decisions of the Florida Supreme Court. The Bush team's nasty political war for the presidency triumphed in the halls of the faint-hearted Miami-Dade Canvassing Board. Bush remained above the fray. The Republican power play could not be traced directly to him or Rove, but the two of them must have shared a quiet smile or a hearty laugh behind the scenes.

2004 Election

Bush stood for re-election four years later, after America experienced the 9/11 tragedy and after the President launched wars in Afghanistan and Iraq. To Karl Rove, the dastardly terrorist attack and the Iraq war (ignoring the administration's pre-9/11 dereliction) were positive for Bush's re-election prospects, but to observers left and right as disparate as liberal Democratic Senator Russell Feingold of Wisconsin and archconservative Pat Buchanan, 9/11 and Iraq were tragic setbacks for America. The wars were surely on the public's mind, but two underhanded activities, the attacks of the Swift Boat Veterans for Truth (SBVT) on Democratic nominee John Kerry's Vietnam War record and a wedge issue on gay marriage, very possibly played a larger part in tipping the election in Bush's favor.

As Senator Kerry of Massachusetts, another Iraq war dissenter, stepped to the podium at the Democratic National Convention to accept his place at the head of his party's 2004 ticket he abruptly stiffened, executed a snappy salute, and solemnly declared, "I'm John Kerry, and I'm reporting for duty." Then he stood triumphantly smiling and waving at the crowd, soaking in the deafening roar of the party faithful.

Without specifically mentioning it, he was at that moment pitting his war record—service in Vietnam as a river boat commander and recipient of a silver star and a bronze star for bravery in action and three purple hearts for non-life-threatening wounds suffered in combat—against that of Bush who dodged the Vietnam War by jumping to the head of the line over many prior applicants to join the Texas Air National Guard, thanks to influential friends of his daddy, then a congressman. The combat records stood out because the nation was at war (against Iraq, Afghanistan, and al-Qaida). Who was better qualified to lead the nation under those circumstances? Anyone familiar with the Republican attack machine has to know that Karl Rove could not let Kerry's distinguished service stand on its own merit. Something would have to be done to undermine this major Kerry strength, and although Rove was running the show, it must be handled so that it would not reflect directly on his candidate. George W. Bush would merely float above the fray like a Snoopy balloon in the Thanksgiving Day parade.

INVASION OF THE SWIFTEES

At ground level the fight was down and dirty, no holds barred. Suddenly the Swift Boat Veterans for Truth came out of nowhere like a mushroom after a summer rain. The Swiftees' mushroom proved to be poisonous. The founders and brain trust for the group called Kerry, the man who would be commander-in-chief of the armed forces, a liar, a coward, a traitor to his comrades in arms, and unfit for command. It couldn't get more down and dirty than that.

The SBVT was a Section 527 organization, a classification taken from its place in the Internal Revenue Code. It was tax exempt, not directly affiliated with a candidate, and free of regulation by state and federal election commissions. Such 527 organizations existed at both ends of the political spectrum to flay the opposition. SBVT had rich Republican roots. Gazillionaires Bob J. Perry, a Houston home builder and longtime donor to Bush, former House Majority Leader Tom

DeLay, and other Republican office seekers, donated $4.45 million to SBVT in 2004; Harold Simmons of the Contran Corporation, a Texas practitioner of the leveraged buyout, $3 million; and T. Boone Pickens, founder and chairman of the hedge fund, BP (for Boone Pickens, not British Petroleum) Capital Management, $2 million.[17] The $9.45 million from these three donors represented more than half of all the money donated to SBVT for the 2004 presidential campaign. Of course, it was perfectly legal. That's what some wealthy people and corporations do with some of their money; they invest it in political causes that serve their interests. The use to which the money was put created tensions.

Originally, membership in the SBVT was limited to veterans who served in Vietnam in a swift boat unit like Kerry's that patrolled the coast and rivers of South Vietnam. But the vast majority of about 250 Navy veterans that signed on did not serve at the same time or place as Kerry. One of fifteen founding members of SBVT was a former commander of the Swift Boat forces, Rear Admiral Roy Hoffman (ret.). Another, John O'Neil, the group's chief spokesman, served as commander of Swift Boat PCF 94, which had been Kerry's boat, but O'Neil possessed no first-hand knowledge of Kerry's service.

Part of the context for the Swiftees' denunciation of Kerry was his testimony against the Vietnam War after his return to civilian life. On April 22, 1971, he testified before the Senate Foreign Relations Committee representing Vietnam Veterans against the War in a devastating indictment of American activities in Vietnam. According to Kerry's testimony, more than 150 honorably discharged veterans, some highly decorated, had previously told his organization of crimes they committed on a day-to-day basis with full knowledge of their officers. Here's how Kerry summed it up:

> They told the stories of times they had personally raped, cut off ears, cut off heads, taped wires from portable telephones to human genitals and turned up the power, cut off limbs, blown

up bodies, randomly shot at civilians, razed villages in fashion reminiscent of Genghis Kahn, shot cattle and dogs for fun, poisoned food stocks, and generally ravaged the countryside of South Vietnam in addition to the normal ravage of war, and the normal and very particular ravaging which is done by the applied bombing power of this country.[18]

It's easy to understand how career officers who have invested their lives in military service would be upset at Kerry's testimony, which on its face seems captious. It turned many veterans against him regardless of any acts of bravery written into the record. The SBVT considered it a pack of lies, accusing him of "grossly and knowingly distorting" the service of military personnel serving in Vietnam.

But the Swiftees went further. They charged him with distorting his own service. They ran attack ads on television and published a book called *Unfit for Command* written by O'Neil and Jerome Corsi that disputed the award of medals to Kerry as based on exaggerations or outright prevarications.[19] Neither author served with Kerry (Corsi never even served in Vietnam), but the officers and men who actually witnessed the events in question, including Army Lieutenant Jim Rassman whom Kerry plucked from the water during a firefight, backed Kerry's side of the story. In an op-ed article in the *Wall Street Journal*, Rassman said Kerry's accusers were "people without decency" who are "lying" and "should hang their heads in shame."[20] Senator John McCain, a victim of out-of-party slurs during the South Carolina Republican primary and a war hero in his own right, also came to Kerry's defense. He condemned the first TV ad as "dishonest and dishonorable," and asked Bush, whom McCain formally supported, to denounce it. Bush answered by urging Kerry to join in an effort to outlaw all 527 organizations, a classic ploy to dodge the issue. Bottom line: Bush did not disapprove the SBVT slur.[21] Kerry supported his record by releasing relevant documents, while the SBVT made patently untrue allegations from veterans who falsely claimed to have served with Kerry. Still, the argument that raged from August to the November election over which side was telling the truth could not have helped Kerry's chances.

So what Rove wanted, Rove got—the diminution of Kerry's distinguished war record while the President continued to hover in a virtual state of benign levitation above the political conflict. As noted, attack ads and dirty tricks have always been a part of the American electoral scene. It is as certain as anything can be that they will continue to play a role because, though repugnant, they are effective.

THE WEDGE ISSUE

A wedge issue draws voters who might not otherwise vote to cast ballots in support of an initiative and a like minded candidate. In 2004, an initiative to ban same-sex marriage appeared on ballots in eleven states, with the presidential candidates on the same ballot. Bush stood to gain from the arrangement because, in general, people opposed to gay marriage would be inclined to vote for him. In each of the eleven states Bush increased his voting percentage over that of the 2000 election. Even so, he carried only nine of them and lost two, the same results in the same states that he registered in 2000. So it would seem that in the big picture the wedge issue had no practical effect.

But a closer look might lead to a different conclusion. In 2000, Bush's narrow margin in Florida assured his Electoral College victory. In 2004, the pivotal state was Ohio, one of the eleven states that carried a gay marriage ban on the presidential ballot. An ad hoc conservative group calling itself the Ohio Campaign to Protect Marriage gathered 575,000 signatures for the initiative, almost double the number needed to get it on the ballot. The initiative carried easily in all eleven states. In Ohio it picked up 61 percent of the votes. Bush also won Ohio, but he won with only 51 percent, which was 1 percent better than the 50 percent he registered in 2000.

Breaking the Ohio vote down, the gains for Bush were much larger than 1 percent among certain groups that opposed gay marriage: 17

percent higher for frequent churchgoers, 12 percent among the elderly, and 7 percent among blacks.[22] It may well be that the gay marriage issue gave Bush the edge he needed to carry Ohio and provide the electoral votes needed nationally. These figures don't prove it; they only give rise to significant conjecture. But Tony Perkins, president of the Family Research Council, took it as Gospel. Gay marriage, he said, "was the hood ornament on the family values wagon that carried the President to a second term."[23] It serves no credible purpose to dispute Perkins— or to accept his conclusion.

THE PERMANENT CAMPAIGN

As president, George W. Bush followed a management pattern not too different from his joyride with the baseball Texas Rangers. He would be the figurehead; others would attend to the business of state. If they should disagree on a policy matter he would hear them out and determine what course to follow. He was "the decider." Enter Dick Cheney, a veteran politician with exceptional skills for bureaucratic infighting. Cheney had been the Secretary of Defense for the elder Bush during the Gulf War in 1990-91, and, long before that, history's youngest White House chief of staff in the Gerald Ford Administration of the 1970s. Initially, Cheney rebuffed inquiries about his availability as the younger Bush's running mate in the 2000 election, pleading his heart condition, the constitutional prohibition against residents of the same state running on the same ticket, and his possible conflict of interest arising from his ties to the oil industry. He did agree to compile a list of candidates for consideration. Bush interviewed them, only to find that none of them fit his comfort zone. Cheney did fit, and finally, the roadblocks to his availability notwithstanding, Bush told him that he was "the solution to my problem."[24] While Cheney may have solved Bush's problem, in the ensuing eight years he created many problems for America that even after his departure from the vice presidency he did not acknowledge.

Readers who see the White House as one of the sacred symbols of American democracy might take another look. It is more than that. Candidates and staff plotting hardball politics and spinning lies on the campaign trail to get elected often continue these activities while in office in the pursuit of policy goals. Politicking from the White House is a bipartisan activity performed by whichever party is occupying it, but when it came to political warfare, the Bush Administration that included hardball players like Vice President Cheney and political advisor Rove were in a league of their own.

In the Bush White House, far right conservatives led the nation to disastrous outcomes. They put America in a large financial hole with the passage of two big tax-cut bills that reduced revenues by about $1.7 trillion over ten years, and then dug the deficit even deeper with a $1 trillion-plus outlay to fight wars in Afghanistan and Iraq; a Medicare prescription drug bill with a price tag of about $720 billion.[25] Not to be overlooked is the anti-regulation persuasion that contributed hugely to the onset of the Great Recession. These initiatives are treated in subsequent chapters. Suffice it to say here that these policy efforts were sold to Congress and the American people with a process some scholars are calling the "permanent campaign." Calling it that is a nice way to describe rough and tumble campaign tactics used to deceive Congress and the public into accepting signature legislation and war authorization.

Chapter 2

Money Politics

The flood of money that gushes into politics today is a pollution of democracy.

—Theodore H. White

KARL ROVE, George W. Bush's campaign strategist who has been called "Bush's Brain," greatly admires Mark Hanna, who steered William McKinley's ride to the White House in 1896 and often gets cited in the history books as the originator of modern political campaigning. Hanna—make that "McKinley's brain"—once quipped, "There are two things that are important in politics. The first is money and I can't remember the second."[1] He spoke before television was invented. The flow of money in the television age with its power to communicate and the concomitant crush of reporters might shock him beyond quotable words.

One thing is certain. In the twenty-first century Hanna would never get away with the laid-back campaign tactics he employed to elect McKinley. While the Bible-thumping Democrat, William Jennings Bryan, traipsed the countryside to give fiery speeches condemning the gold standard, McKinley campaigned casually from his front porch in Canton, Ohio. Hanna, using his connections to the railroad industry, arranged free excursions to Canton for carefully selected groups of McKinley supporters. The night before meeting the candidate they would be asked to submit written questions. When they gathered at his porch next day, McKinley would answer them reading from scripted notes. Imagine McKinley in the twenty-first century in a nationally televised candidates' debate. This man with his wooden personality would be turned into sawdust. Hanna used the money saved on the candidate's aversion to campaigning to print McKinley leaflets, plaster roadside billboards with McKinley advertizing, and send out McKinley surrogates to speak on his behalf. Hanna worked from a campaign chest at least three times larger than Bryan's. Money talked and McKinley won.[2]

CAMPAIGNING

Bush may have dreamed stirring images of pioneers while running for President in 2000, but they were not the pioneers who won the West. They were the Pioneers—with a capital "P"—taking part in a scheme to help win the White House by pledging to hustle up at least $100,000 for the presidential campaign. With individuals limited to $1,000 donation, 241 fundraisers out of 550 who tried, actually reached or surpassed the one-hundred-grand goal in 2000. Nineteen of the top Pioneers cashed in with cushy ambassadorships. Six were convicted of crimes related to their political activities. All told, the Bush campaign raised $211 million for the 2000 general election. Vice President Al Gore, his Democratic opponent, was not far behind. His campaign collected $199 million. Both received $67.6 million in public funds.[3] Campaign revenues keep going up. Like the Mississippi River in spring absorbing heavy rains and melting snow, the cost of campaigning is high and rising.

In the 2004 election Rove built an expanded playing field. With the individual donation limit doubled to $2,000 by the McCain-Feingold reform act, fundraisers or "bundlers," as they are called, who collected $100,000 were still Pioneers. At $200,000 they became Rangers, and at $300,000, Super Rangers. Rove established a fourth level for fundraisers under the age of forty who brought in at least $50,000.[4] They were designated "Bush Mavericks," something, perhaps, in the fundraising game equivalent to cub scouts. Bundlers of all ages in many walks of life provide a service that most politicians would rather avoid. Many are good at asking for money because they are situated in political, business, or social positions that allow them to pressure potential donors, or they might be employers who give their employees money to donate. Some, like twenty-three-year-old Nate Morris of Jefferson County, Kentucky did it out of idealism and a talent for networking. Morris may have been the youngest Bush Maverick in 2004.[5] Campaign funds collected in this manner leave the candidates more time to schmooze with voters. The Democrats showed similar skills appealing to their core of constituents.

But where there is money and power, there are sure to be shady characters looking to peddle influence. Approximately one-sixth of 940 Bush bundlers in two election campaigns came from the ranks of lobbyists and other well connected political operatives. The lobbyist and convicted felon Jack Abramoff was a Bush Pioneer in 2004. A Texas non-profit group, Texans for Public Justice, put Abramoff at the top of an alphabetical list of Pioneers and Rangers who bundled more than $100,000 and $200,000 respectively in Bush donations.[6] The *Austin American-Statesman* reported in 2006, after the Abramoff scandal broke, that the Republican National Committee gave $6,000 of it to charity, money that allegedly had come directly from Abramoff, his wife, and an Abramoff client, the Saginaw Chippewa Tribe of Michigan, and kept the rest.[7] The "rest" reportedly consisted of more than $100,000 and it is not credible that Abramoff would have an arm's length relationship with the people who gave it. The donors most probably popped out of the Abramoff rolodex. The law did not require that they be identified. Bush has denied that he knew Abramoff, but Secret Service logs show that the disgraced lobbyist visited the White House at least six times while Bush was in office. Abramoff claimed that he occasionally conversed with the President.[8] If it can be argued that Bush bears no responsibility for this corruption of democracy, it can also be said that he did nothing to stop it. In fact, he fed his political ambitions off of it.

HOW THE MONEY IS SPENT

There is no shortage of new, indispensable political products to spend the money on, chief among them television. More than half of the money drawn in from fundraising goes out for television commercials, most of which aim at tearing down an opponent. The first campaign ads on television appeared in 1952. They were bought by the Republican Dwight D. Eisenhower team. Adlai Stevenson, his Democratic opponent, disdained the new medium in 1952. But four years later, both sides resorted to television advertising, and from that time on, the practice has grown and the money spent has grown exponentially. Fast-forwarding to 2000, all candidates, political parties, and independent groups combined spent $771 million on large market TV advertising. In 2004, the total more than doubled to $1.6 billion; in 2008, it rose to $2.1 billion, and in 2012 it is expected to surpass $3 billion.[9]

It was a TV ad that actually baited Democratic Sen. John Kerry into committing probably his worst blunder of the 2004 Presidential campaign. The ad was hastily pieced together before Kerry's appearance in Huntington, West Virginia to burnish his credentials on security. It accused him of voting no on an $87 billion supplemental bill to fund the wars in Iraq and Afghanistan, which the Bush campaign played as tantamount to non-support of the troops, the ridiculous assertion that has a way of popping up in every presidential campaign when U.S. troops are fighting and dying in foreign wars. Kerry explained to his audience that he had proposed an amendment to offset the steep cost by getting allies to help pay for the wars or by repealing tax cuts for the rich. Then he said, "I actually did vote for the $87 billion [bill] before I voted against it." The Bush campaign had been trying to pin Kerry with the "flip-flopper" label. But with that outburst, nobody did it better than Kerry himself. Later Kerry explained his goof as "one of those inarticulate moments."[10]

Public opinion polling, another reflection of the changing political market place, has also become common. Much of it is conducted independently by the media and polling organizations, but some of it is also commissioned by well heeled campaigns. Modern practitioners of the art do not forget the disaster of 1948 when the polls predicted that Republican Thomas E. Dewey would handily defeat the incumbent Democratic President Harry S. Truman, only to see Truman triumph and his detractors eat crow. But pollsters today have learned from their mistakes and the findings of the political and social sciences. They are better prepared, more attentive to the questions they ask and the way they ask them, and careful to hedge their predictions by creating a "margin of error" for close calls. Polling is still not perfect, and probably never will be. But the candidates usually know whether they are winning or losing, and act accordingly. When they are ahead they try to convey an air of confidence to the electorate. When they are behind, they try to reassure the voters that they will close the gap and come out on top. How many times is it said by losing candidates in the heat of campaigning, "The only polls that count are those on Election Day"?

Focus groups, another useful tool in campaigning, emerged in the mid-twentieth century as a way for advertisers to measure product appeal with consumers. They caught on later in politics so that candidates would know what issues fly or fall flat with voters. When you stop to think about it, selling candidates is a lot like selling soup. The Bush campaign used focus groups while the *faux*-macho candidate pretended that he did not need them. Early in the 2000 campaign at sessions in California, Michigan, and South Carolina, a Bush speech was played for small groups that were asked to respond to points he made. If a respondent liked what Bush was saying, a knob could be turned one way; if not, it could go the opposite way. This produced a computer-generated graph line over the video of Bush speaking in which the permutations would indicate how the audience responded on particular issues. Bush and his staff would then know which opinions expressed in his speech played well and which did not. Guided by the focus groups, the candidate's chief speechmaker, Michael Gerson, submitted sixteen versions of the stump speech. Yet Bush tried to leave the impression that he was his own man on the campaign trail. "I don't get coached," he said in an interview. Toward the end of the campaign Bush reportedly used focus groups routinely.[11]

Lobbying and Earmarks

During the eight years of the George W. Bush Administration lobbyists spent $18.84 billion plying their K Street trade. Lobbying expenditures increased every year from $1.65 billion in 2001 to $3.3 billion in 2008 (and continued to edge up in the first two years of the Obama Administration). The number of lobbyists rose, too, starting with 11,842 in 2001, going up to 14,861 in 2007, before tapering off slightly to 14,185 in Bush's final year (and scaling back further in 2009 and 2010).[12] So many lobbyists spending so much money in representing special interests to influence the nation's policymakers, legislators, and regulators get in the way of honest democracy.

Lobbyists do their damage under the shield of free speech and the right to petition embedded in the First Amendment. The Supreme Court ruled in a 1975 case involving campaign finance, *Buckley v. Valeo*, that money in effect equals speech, making America's modern political system a virtual Tower of Babel. Then in 2010, the highest court ruled in *Citizens United V. FEC*, that corporations are persons, overruling key parts of the McCain-Feingold law enacted in 2002 regulating corporate television advertising before an election and giving license for the rich to speak louder than the poor.

Lobbyists of one kind or another have been around ever since the nation was founded. They cozy up to legislators and regulators wherever the democratic system exists, in federal, state, and local jurisdictions, and foreign nations. But in Washington, D.C., at least, the practice has undergone fundamental change since the late 1970s. Before that, lobbyists were tucked away in larger organizations like law firms or hidden from public sight with euphemisms like "consultant." About that time firms whose principal or only business was lobbying began to appear in Washington and kept growing over the next three decades. Robert G. Kaiser, a reporter for the *Washington Post*, documents the rise of one such firm in his book, *So Damn Much Money*. The firm's success story—originally it was called Schlossberg-Cassidy & Associates and later, Cassidy & Associates—is historic because it originated the practice of using earmarks to activate programs benefitting clients, ultimately at a cost of billions of dollars to taxpayers.

Gerald Cassidy, a lawyer, met journalist Kenneth Schlossberg when they worked together in the early 1970s for the Senate Committee on Nutrition and Human Needs, chaired by Sen. George McGovern. After helping to generate positive publicity for the boss with hearings in Florida on the disgraceful living conditions of migrant laborers, they got caught up in McGovern's run for the Presidency in 1972. Despite his decisive defeat, McGovern entertained the idea of running again in 1976, but Cassidy and Schlossberg, by this time fast friends who were never enthusiastic about McGovern's Presidential ambitions, left their Senate employment and went into business together.

Schlossberg-Cassidy & Associates started in 1975 as a "consulting" firm working out of Schlossberg's townhouse basement three blocks from the Capitol. The two friends provided a wide range of research and advisory services that did not include directly influencing lawmakers. They specialized in nutrition and food, which reflected their detailed knowledge from working on the nutrition committee. They sent out hundreds of letters to friends and potential clients announcing their new enterprise, but received no response. After several months of zero income, their first client was a California food company seeking payment from the Department of Agriculture for services provided on a federal school lunch program. Schlossberg knew the person to call at Agriculture, and after extracting a $10,000 retainer from the client, arranged for payment.

Business gradually picked up, and soon they boasted a roster of clients that included Pillsbury, Nabisco, and General Mills paying monthly retainers. They moved to an office in L'Enfant Plaza south of Independence Avenue. Three years later they hit it big. They became lobbyists and discovered an entirely new legislative procedure for spending and inflating the use of taxpayers' money that came to be known as "earmarks."

The late Jean Mayer, President-designate of Tufts University outside Boston, wanted to build a national nutrition center in Boston and sought federal funds to make it happen. He had a personal relationship with Schlossberg and turned to the young consulting firm for guidance. Schlossberg-Cassidy bent to the task. Cassidy, the lawyer, found the necessary precedent, legislation already on the books that had authorized a nutrition center in North Dakota. A key appropriation had approved federal funds to build a particular facility for a single university, exactly what was needed for Tufts. It turned out that Tip O'Neill, then-majority leader and soon to be Speaker of the House, represented the district where Tufts was located. Even better, fond childhood memories influenced his actions. O'Neill grew up in the Tufts neighborhood and as a kid he and his pals used to sneak onto the Tufts athletic field to play ball. O'Neill had attended Mayer's inauguration as president of Tufts in July 1976, and at the reception offered his help for anything Mayer might need.

The O'Neill connection was manna from heaven for Schlossberg-Cassidy. They started by persuading the Department of Agriculture to request $2 million for a feasibility study. Then they used their connections to drum up support in Congress for what was obviously a worthy project. It was not a hard sell. Politicians who work under the Capitol dome readily perceive the value of bringing home the bacon to their state or district and in those days of old fashioned comity, also engaged in logrolling, the practice of trading favors with colleagues, even across party lines. In fiscal year 1978 Congress appropriated $20 million to the Department of Agriculture to build the Tufts nutrition center in Boston's Chinatown and an additional $7 million to fund the center's initial operation. Congress did the funding with earmarks, created and smoothly managed by the outside firm, Schlossberg-Cassidy, working on a $10,000-a-month retainer from Tufts. Its success added to the bottom line. Schlossberg-Cassidy continued to perform services for Tufts, but its retainer climbed to $125,000 per month. Suddenly they were big-time players in the lobbying business.

The business grew. The firm took on more university clients and then corporate clients, all paying monthly retainers. It expanded its employee base mostly by attracting knowledgeable Congressional staffers whom it paid incomes in salary and bonuses three or four times higher than what they had earned on the Hill, and moved their office to spacious new quarters at 700 13th Street in the business district north of Pennsylvania Avenue. But the more successful the firm became, the more Schlossberg acquired a sense of unease. He did not like the influence peddling that became part of the business. In 1984, after nearly ten years in business together, the partners split. Cassidy bought out Schlossberg for $812,600, and went on to become fabulously rich. The firm, renamed Cassidy & Associates, prospered enormously in the late 1980s. When the break-up came, each partner was taking home about half a million dollars a year. In 1987, with Schlossberg gone, the firm earned $18.8 million. Throughout the late 1980s Cassidy paid himself $3 million to $5 million per year. Having lived his childhood in a working class Catholic family, he became a conspicuous consumer, riding in a chauffeured Lincoln Town Car, buying expensive antiques, taking vacations abroad, and acquiring a large suburban home and a country estate on Maryland's east shore. As the practice of earmarks spread, the lobbying field became more crowded. The Cassidy firm's income dipped somewhat from its halcyon days in the late 1980s, but it was never bad. Jerry Cassidy held the firm together, paid his associates and employees extremely well, maintained good relations with influential Senators and Congressmen on Capitol Hill (mostly with generous campaign contributions), and kept coming up with new clients and new ideas to pad the bottom line.[13] Kaiser used Cassidy & Associates as the proto-type for the rise of the reviled lobbying business in Washington.

THE K STREET PROJECT

Only a few of the lobbyists in the nation's capital work on K Street, but K Street is another way of expressing the lobbying activity, just as Wall Street says global investment. "Wall Street" is a powerful symbolic term. It represents high finance in America and around the globe. When the so-called "Occupy" movement took shape in New York's financial district, it had struck at the heart of the capitalist system. When the movement spread out across the country, it took on another powerful symbol in Washington: K Street, the vital nexus between capitalism and government that exercises a corrupting influence on democracy. Lobbyists lavish so much money on Congress these days that it disposes many members to minimize the interests of the states and districts that sent them to do the people's business.

In the 1990s, earmarks became a political weapon in a Republican-crafted war between the parties. Like the fictitious war between the worlds, the war between the parties has inflicted severe damage on the nation. It has brought gridlock to the balance of power among the executive, legislative, and even judicial branches of government handed down by our founding fathers. It threatens to plunge the nation into a crisis whose consequences no one dares to contemplate.

For forty years Democrats ran Congress like a bi-partisan old boys' club with favors traded across friendly party lines. It was a hypocriti-cal system that required compromise and often the abandonment of core values. In 1994 Newt Gingrich engineered a revolution that gave House Republicans a majority. With Republicans in control, every-thing changed. Peaceful accommodation took a back seat. Uppermost in the minds of Republican leaders was an obsession for holding onto power. Gingrich became Speaker and seized upon the idea of using earmarks to achieve that end. Unlike most legislative business in the new age of partisan warfare, however, the House retained the old system on earmarks. The leaders split the earmarks with Democrats, about sixty-forty, making sure that any Republican member facing a serious challenge on Election Day got his needed share. Members lined up for their freebees in such numbers that the price of earmarks had to be trimmed—fewer $20 million projects like the Tufts nutrition center; instead, many earmarks cost less than $1 million. Of course, none was subjected to hearings. The government had to borrow to pay for them. The leaders simply passed them out like free tickets to a town fair. Earmarks helped to grow the ever-growing national debt.

Easy money has a corrupting influence, and the Republicans did not go unscathed by it. Gingrich proved to be an erratic Speaker, expressing brilliant but often contradictory ideas and was prone to outbursts of pique that rubbed colleagues the wrong way. After the House Republicans lost ground in the 1998 midterm elections, the conservative leadership team that included Majority Leader Dick Armey of Texas, Majority Whip Tom DeLay of Texas, Republican Conference Chairman John Boehner of Ohio, and Republican Leadership Chairman Bill Paxon of New York pressured Gingrich to step down. Gingrich went them one better; he resigned his seat in Congress. Power, it is said, abhors a vacuum, and the one created by Gingrich's departure was soon filled by DeLay, a tough-minded street fighter who enforced a rigorous party discipline. While still majority whip, he engineered the election of Deputy Whip Dennis Hastert of Illinois to the Speakership in 2001, and when Armey gave up his House seat in 2003, DeLay won the election to replace him as majority leader. Essentially, it did not matter whether DeLay held the position of whip, leader, or speaker; he was what they once called in show biz the top banana in the Republican House after Gingrich left.

Before DeLay entered politics, he ran a pest control firm, which later earned him the sobriquet, "The Exterminator." When the government impacted his pre-congressional business in Texas by banning DDT, he turned into a crusader against regulation. As majority whip, he became known as "The Hammer," for the ruthless efficiency with which he maintained party discipline. Members crossed him at their peril. He controlled the distribution of money and earmarks that could improve or weaken incumbents' chances for reelection, depending on how well they toed the party line. He wallowed in money with few scruples about fundraising and disbursements. His reckless behavior led to his downfall.

As early as 1995 in his career as Republican whip, DeLay kept an account of donations by corporate public action committees (PACs). Those PACs that over the preceding two years donated more to Republicans were listed as "friendly," while the heavy Democratic donors in the same time period were "unfriendly." DeLay would meet with the friendly lobbyists, but not the unfriendlies, and that tactic was meaningful to lobbyists now that Republicans were in the majority. He placed the donors list contained in a plastic covered folder on a table in the ante room of his Capitol office just off the floor of the House chamber where any visitor could look at it. Lobbyists were left to draw their own conclusions. Donations that found their way to Republican candidates soared that year, although Republicans already had a sizable fundraising lead on Democrats. An early payoff for Republican corporate donors was an invitation from DeLay to join in writing a bill to impose a thirteen-month moratorium on regulations.

DeLay forged close professional ties to a couple of controversial non-government persons, conservative ideologue Grover Norquist and lobbyist Jack Abramoff. Norquist, founder of Americans for Tax Reform who had locked in most Republican lawmakers to a pledge against raising taxes, came up with the idea for the notorious K Street Project. It called for the Republican majority in Congress to badger K Street firms into hiring Republican staffers over Democrats, "or else"—and "or else" meant that DeLay would not give Democratic lobbyists the time of day. Firms that employed lobbyists began hiring more Republican staffers. Over a decade, twenty-nine came from DeLay's staff out of the "revolving door" in DeLay's office. Even entry level lobbyists could earn six-figure annual incomes. To stay in business, Cassidy & Associates (Cassidy, the Democrat) lured a Republican leadership insider, Gregg Hartley, with an offer of just under $1 million a year, plus a percentage of retainer fees from clients he brought to the firm. Cassidy gave Hartley carte blanche to run much of the Cassidy operation, and Hartley hired a number of Republican staffers.[14] Whereas in the past, lobbying activity had usually centered on a piece of do-good legislation for an incumbent's Congressional district, the Republican leadership now focused on retaining power. It used earmarks to keep members in line and expected lobbyists to contribute heavily to Republican campaign chests. For their cooperation, DeLay allowed the lobbyists to review, or even write bills from scratch pertinent to their corporate employers.

THE ABRAMOFF SCANDAL

The power-hungry Republican leadership had already corrupted the political process. Jack Abramoff took it beyond corruption to villainy. Abramoff, dubbed "Casino Jack" by Hollywood,[15] was a paradigm of excess. He could not have succeeded without his connections to power brokers like DeLay in Congress and Rove in the White House, the latter an old pal from college Republican days. Abramoff's close partner in crime, Michael Scanlon, came from DeLay's staff where he had handled public relations, and Abramoff's personal secretary, Susan Ralston, moved over to Rove's staff in the White House. Other notables who collaborated with Abramoff included Ralph Reed, founder and director of the Christian Coalition, and Grover Norquist.

Abramoff wined and dined powerful people from Congress and the executive branch at his Washington restaurant, Signatures. The signatures on the restaurant's walls were those of historic figures like Czar Nicholas, Winston Churchill, Rocky Marciano, Thomas Edison, and Meyer Lansky on framed portraits, photos, and letters. Abramoff also spent more than $1 million a year for skyboxes at four different arenas in the Washington-Baltimore area to entertain his celebrity friends at professional sports events. Sometimes politicians used a skybox for a fundraiser.

He treated his special benefactor, DeLay, to lavish free trips abroad, which DeLay took pains to camouflage because House ethics rules forbid members from accepting free trips from lobbyists. One of Abramoff's clients, the Commonwealth of the Northern Mariana Islands, a United Nations protectorate administered by the United States, played host to the textile business, with sweatshops that employed low-wage workers from western Pacific and Asian nations. A U.S. government investigation found that employees on Saipan were paid less than the minimum wage and lived in substandard conditions, suffering malnutrition and health problems. In 1998 Abramoff sponsored a DeLay visit to Saipan. DeLay, House majority whip at the time, traveled first class and stayed at a beachfront hotel. It is not clear that he saw any sweatshops or shantytowns where the workers lived. He came away cynically calling Saipan, "a petri dish of capitalism."[16]

In 2000 DeLay traveled to the British Isles on a trip that included talks with British Prime Minister Margaret Thatcher and a golf outing at world famous royal St. Andrews in Scotland. The National Center for Public Policy Research, a conservative non-profit group, sponsored the trip, but Abramoff who served on the board of the National Center arranged it and persuaded two of his clients, the Mississippi band of Choctaw Indians and eLottery, to each contribute $25,000 of the $70,000 cost. ELottery provides internet service to state lotteries. The Mississippi Choctaw, eLottery, and the National Center all said they were unaware that the donations were meant to help finance DeLay's trip. DeLay denied knowledge of Abramoff's involvement, but two months later he voted in line with Choctaw and eLottery interests to defeat a bill to criminalize certain kinds of betting over the internet.[17]

An early link between Abramoff and DeLay in the 1990s came through the U.S. Family Network, supposedly a nationwide grassroots organization funded almost entirely, according to the *Washington Post*, by corporations with close ties to Abramoff. The Family Network had little or nothing to do with families or moral issues, and everything to do with money. Organized by DeLay's chief of staff, Edwin A. Buckham, it brought in $2.5 million to Buckham's firm, Alexander Strategy Group, during its five-year existence. Buckham did not disclose the donor list, but $1 million may have come through a London law firm from Russian oil and gas executives hoping for DeLay's support on legislation passing through Congress that would lead to a bailout of the Russian economy through the International Monetary Fund. DeLay who traveled to Russia in 1997—a trip arranged by Abramoff and Buckham—denied through a staff spokesperson that the contributions influenced his voting on the legislation. There was no evidence that any of the donations went directly to DeLay, but Buckham employed DeLay's wife, Christine, and paid her $3,200 a month, which would come to more than $115,000 over three years. Her job, or at least one of her jobs, was to supply Buckham with lists of lawmakers' favorite charities, which is useful information for lobbyists.[18]

The Indian scams by which Abramoff is best remembered began with the Mississippi Choctaw. The tribe contacted Abramoff in 1995 when he worked in Washington as lobbyist for the Seattle law firm of Preston Gates Ellis & Rouvelas Meeds. Republicans had gained control of the House and were considering legislation to tax Indian enterprises. Abramoff with help from Grover Norquist of Americans for Tax Reform (ATR) contributed to the defeat of the House bill in the Senate. The Choctaw paid Preston Gates and the ATR for their services. Subsequently, other issues arose including a sales tax that Abramoff helped to head off.

In 1999 Abramoff engaged Ralph Reed as a Preston Gates subcontractor. Reed was looking for business after having founded a "consulting" firm called Century Strategies. Abramoff asked him to use his old Christian Coalition rolodex to round up opposition from Evangelicals at the grassroots level to stamp out potential competitors to the Choctaw casino business. The Choctaw paid Reed through conduits that included ATR so Reed could hide his work for gambling interests. Over time, the payments added up to millions of dollars. Norquist, who had earned a decent paycheck for helping to beat back tax legislation, kept a relatively small share of the Reed pass-through.[19]

In 2001 Abramoff's eyes grew bigger as saw the prospect for profits in the millions of dollars. He brought Scanlon into the Choctaw business in a scheme they called "Gimme five." "Five" referred to $5 million a year in grossly inflated fees for Scanlon's firm, Capitol Campaign Strategies. Abramoff did not tell the Choctaw that he would get kickbacks from Scanlon that amounted to half the profits. All told, the Mississippi Choctaw spent more than $19 million for the services of Abramoff, Scanlon, and their various subcontractors and phony charities that Abramoff or Scanlon controlled.[20]

As far as the Choctaw knew, Abramoff and his fellow scammers performed well, which helped them to negotiate contracts with other tribes, starting with the Louisiana Coushatta. Scanlon signed on for $534,500 to operate under the radar as the tribe negotiated a 25-year compact with the state to renew the tribe's casino license. Meanwhile, Abramoff, working on a fat $125,000 monthly retainer, found a way to pressure the Texas legislature to bar casino gambling and keep Coushatta competitors from opening casinos in eastern Texas. Again, he enlisted Reed to exploit the moral opposition to gambling in the Christian grassroots and, again, they arranged to pay Reed through conduits to obscure his work on behalf of Coushatta gambling interests. In the final analysis, Abramoff and Scanlon managed to pry loose $32 million from the Louisiana Coushatta, the most money extracted from any of the Indian tribes they served.[21]

Abramoff made his most aggressive move in his approach to the Ysleta del sur Pueblo Tribe (Tigua) in Texas. After helping while in the service of the Louisiana Coushatta to smooth the way for the state to close the Tigua casino near El Paso he went to the Tigua expressing indignation about this bad turn of events without letting on that he had a role in it. He offered with Scanlon's help to pull strings in Congress to get an earmark that would allow the Tigua to reopen the casino. (By this time he had severed his employment with Preston Gates and moved over to Greenberg Traurig, a top Florida law firm with an office in Washington that had represented the Bush campaign team in the 2000 Florida ballot dispute. But Greenberg Traurig dropped him in the midst of his dealings with the Tigua after the *Washington Post* printed a series of articles about his shady business.) The Tigua casino, about as far from Louisiana as you can get in Texas, was never a threat to the Coushatta, but as rumors circulated that another tribe wanted to open a casino in eastern Texas, Abramoff convinced the Coushatta that if the El Paso casino remained open, the state would also allow casino openings in eastern Texas that would cut into their customer base. In his double-dealing presentation to the Tigua, Abramoff promised to work pro bono, but he asked them to hire Scanlon for $5 million (and settled for slightly less). He failed to mention that he would share Scanlon's profits. The pair actually did try to insert language favorable to the Tigua casino project in an election reform bill in Congress, but it never made the final cut. Rep. Robert Ney of Ohio inserted it in the House version, but Sen. Christopher Dodd of Connecticut kept it out of the Senate bill, and the Tigua earmark died in conference. The failed Abramoff/Scanlon effort cost the Tigua $4.2 million.[22]

Abramoff carried on for about a decade, from the mid-1990s to the mid-2000s. Scanlon rode with him for the last three or four wild years. The scope of the "Gimme Five" operation was large, the chutzpah breathtaking. In addition to the three tribes mentioned above, Abramoff and Scanlon scammed three other tribes: the Saginaw Chippewa of Michigan, the Agua Caliente Band of Cauhilla Indians of Palm Springs, California, and the Sandia Pueblo of New Mexico. All told, the tribes doled out about $85 million to Abramoff/Scanlon, their subcontractors, fake charities they controlled, and favored lawmakers. The Tigua and Saginaw Chippewa helped pay for another golf outing in Scotland for a group of Abramoff's friends that included Congressman Ney. Abramoff quietly intervened in tribal elections of the Saginaw

Chippewa and Agua Caliente to elect candidates who would further his and Scanlon's interests.

The wheels of justice have turned slowly in the Abramoff scandal. Abramoff pleaded guilty to defrauding the Indian tribes, but his conviction came in a separate case of bank fraud in Florida in the purchase of a casino cruise ship company. He served three-and-a-half years of a six-year sentence in that case. Scanlon pled guilty in the Indian fraud case, and received a twenty-month sentence in a minimum-security federal prison and 300 hours of community service, plus restitution of more than $20 million. Most of the restitution, nearly $18 million would compensate Abramoff's former law firm, Greenberg Traurig, which had already repaid four of the tribes. Congressman Ney pleaded guilty to corruption and served about a year of a thirty-month sentence. Rep. John Doolittle of California, and his wife, Julie, were investigated for their ties to Abramoff, but never prosecuted. He resigned his seat in the House and became a lobbyist. Kevin Ring, Doolittle's former chief of staff who went to work for Abramoff, has appealed his conviction for corruption. The Justice Department investigated DeLay for several years and decided not to bring charges against him. But a Texas jury convicted him on two charges of violating state law against corporate donations to candidates. He was sentenced to three years in prison and ten years probation, but remained free while appealing the conviction. Two members of the Bush Administration were caught in the Abramoff net. David Safavian, former chief of staff of the General Services Administration, was convicted of obstruction of justice and lying to investigators and sentenced to a year in prison. J. Steven Griles, former Deputy Secretary of the Interior (number two) pleaded guilty to obstruction of justice and received a ten-month sentence.

SLIM CHANCES FOR REFORM

You have to hand it to Cassidy and Schlossberg. They went from the government payroll to the private sector where they brought innovative technological change to lobbying. They rate as heroes of free enterprise. On the dark side, their unregulated innovation led to political corruption deleterious to democracy. Earmarks are only one tool in the lobbying trade, but a powerful one that needs to be regulated. In the Bush years, lobbyists swarmed over Congress like a plague of locusts in a wheat field, not just advising members about their clients' needs, but actually writing special interest legislation—until Congress took action against the plague that did not go far enough.

There is a qualitative difference between the Abramoff/Scanlon use of earmarks and that of Cassidy/Schlossberg. The latter pair started out advancing a beneficial cause—the nutrition center—with no idea of the unintended consequences that would follow, and when the unseemly side of lobbying began to take shape, an uneasy Schlossberg opted out. Cassidy went on to become a multi-millionaire and a big spender with a high life style. Abramoff and Scanlon had no purpose other than to fleece the Indians for whom Abramoff expressed deep contempt by repeatedly referring to them in e-mails to Scanlon as "monkeys," "troglodytes," or "morons." Overall, lobbying usually falls somewhere in the legal loopholes short of fraud. It badly needs to be regulated.

The scammers covered here were remarkable people. Abramoff, Norquist, and Reed all came from the same conservative culture as Karl Rove. All four were active in the College Republican National Committee. If they learned anything from their youthful leadership experience, it was not about ethics. Philosophically, Abramoff, Norquist, and Reed strived for the conservative ideal of smaller government; but with greedy eyes fixed on riches for the taking, they thrived in the mundane reality of corrupt government. Reed turned into a pious fraud, covertly taking gambling money from one tribe to engage evangelical Christians against the tribe's gambling competitors. Norquist, the taxman's worst nightmare, was a hands-on witness to the flimflam. Abramoff, in his dealings with the Indian tribes, was demonstrably criminal (as was Scanlon). Rove, the "architect" of sometimes marginally malapropos Bush campaign maneuvers, knew what Abramoff was up to, and managed to keep the President out of Abramoff's cesspool. It is hard to believe, however, that the President was not clued in—unless he didn't want to be. Four members of Bush's administration either were convicted or pleaded guilty in the scandal. One served prison time.[23] As noted above, Bush also received Abramoff campaign donations.

Obviously, something needs to be done. But it is not so simple. It was already against the law for a public official to accept payment, favors, or expensive gifts for decisions favorable to a lobbyist's client. That is what landed Congressman Ney in jail and sent Congressman Doolittle into retirement. But a lot of political positioning has been taking place. In the aftermath of the Abramoff scandal a Democratic Congress in 2007 passed rules requiring transparency and justification for an earmark.[24] President Bush issued an executive order a year later forbidding agencies to act on earmarks "unless included in the text of bills voted on by Congress and presented to the President." But the order left it up to the Republican-controlled agencies to decide if the Democratic earmarks had merit[25]—a hole big enough to drive a Republican earmark through. In November 2010 President Obama called on the Democratic Congress to pass earmark reform to cut back on federal expenditures at a time of deficit crisis when Republicans had won a majority in the House but had not yet taken control. With the parties then at dagger points, Republican leaders responded by demanding that the President veto any bill that contained earmarks, and this he did.[26]

Congress tried but failed to fix the problem of the "revolving door" through which members of Congress, their staffs, regulatory officials, and others from the Executive Branch can magnify their incomes by going into the lobbying business. A proposal doubling the waiting time from one year to two years for a retired public official to engage in lobbying had to be abandoned because members anticipating a prosperous retirement as lobbyists rebelled against it. Former Senator John Breaux of Louisiana put the issue on a personal basis, "I have been in government my entire life. What do you expect me to become, an auto mechanic?"[27] In other words, Breaux is saying that his welfare should come before the public interest, which goes to show that people accustomed to privileged have a hard time giving it up. So Congress needs to fix the revolving door, i.e., to reduce the attractiveness of the lobbying business.

Chapter 3

The 9/11 Sleep

We, with God's help, call on every Muslim who believes in God and wishes to be rewarded to comply with God's order to kill the Americans and plunder their money wherever and whenever they find it.

—Osama bin Laden

THE AMERICAN PEOPLE could hardly have expected that President George W. Bush would understand the radical Islamic thinking that guided the 9/11 terrorists to the World Trade Center and Pentagon on September 11, 2001. Still, they have cut him too much slack for his failure to defend against the worst attack on America at least since the Japanese bombing of Pearl Harbor in 1941. It was clear within a few years after the event how the attack was plotted and carried out—the careful, long-range al-Qaida planning; the central role of Khalid Sheikh Mohammed, the infiltration of outside Islamists into the United States, their flight training in America, the failure of American intelligence to "connect the dots," the ease with which the terrorists boarded the airliners, their violent takeovers, and the fiery denouement. Less has been said about what was going on in the high sanctum of American power in the months leading up to 9/11.

The disinclination to question the president's performance is understandable, especially after his stirring words to rescuers and demolition workers amid the wreckage of the World Trade Center four days after the tragedy. As Bush started to speak, a worker shouted, "I can't hear you!" "I can hear *you*," the President shouted back, "and the people who knocked down these buildings will hear all of us soon." The deafening roar of the crowd accentuated a pinnacle moment of the Bush presidency. It was enough to make a shaken nation forget to ask how the administration failed to keep the horror of 9/11 from happening in the first place. At the very least, it remains an unresolved question.

To be sure, the President and his top advisors did not set a high standard for securing the commonwealth, despite a stern warning from Director of Central Intelligence George Tenet and the CIA's deputy director for covert operation, James L. Pavitt, that al-Qaida was a "tremendous" and "immediate" threat to attack the United States. In a meeting with Bush and Dick Cheney five days before their inauguration, Tenet and Pavitt described bin Laden and his network as one of three top threats facing the United States, the other two being the proliferation of weapons of mass destruction and the growing power of China.[1]

The exhaustive 9/ll Commission Report fixed the tone for evaluation of that tragic event by declaring at the beginning that the commission did not embark on their study to assign individual blame—as if that would be politically incorrect—and then reminding the reader that hindsight is always clearer than foresight—which is indisputable.[2] "Did [the government's leaders] understand the gravity of the threat?" the report asks, and in response to its own question, it went on to spread the blame, or at least, to obfuscate accountability for the disaster. "As best we can determine, neither in 2000 nor in the first eight months of 2001 did any polling organization in the United States think the subject of terrorism sufficiently on the minds of the public to warrant asking a question about it in a major national survey. Bin Laden, al-Qaida, or even terrorism was not an important topic in the 2000 presidential campaign. Congress and the media called little attention to it."[3] That conclusion is a cop-out. The President is the chief executive officer. His job requires, not that he follow public opinion or popular babble, but that he lead the nation. He and a small circle of aides, who are privy to the latest intelligence, know more than anyone else in the country about vital threats to security, and are in a unique position to make decisions in the best interests of the United States.

The report's language is a prime example of groupspeak. The bi-partisan commission—five Republicans and five Democrats—was anxious to present a unanimous, non-controversial document that every member could sign. But it hardly squares with Tenet's testimony before the commission that in the summer of 2001 "the [intelligence] system was blinking red," or the heading in the August 6 PDB (President's Daily Brief) that warned, "Bin Laden Determined to Strike in the US."[4] The PDB prepared by the CIA from all available government intelligence sources is distributed to a select number of high-ranking officials—confined to six in the Bush administration at that time. They had to know during the summer of 2001 that al-Qaida was up to something big. The President in his smug overconfidence responded to the growing number of reports of al-Qaida terrorist threats by telling his National Security Advisor, Condoleezza Rice that he was "tired of swatting flies." He wondered why the CIA could not just go out and eliminate the troublemakers.

The administration's defense of its inaction has been to say that the reports lacked specificity. No one predicted that on a certain date fanatical Islamist terrorists on a suicide mission were going to hijack commercial American airliners loaded with highly flammable fuel and use them as weapons by plunging them into the twin towers and the Pentagon, although there had been some speculation within government about airliner hijackings for suicide missions.[5] Intelligence is never that simple; it is compiled from bits and pieces of information and usually presented to intelligence consumers with a measure of nuance and/or equivocation. But the warning signs were out there and all of the many threats considered credible were duly reported up the chain of command. It was the commander-in-chief's responsibility to be prepared for the worst.

THE DANGER SIGNS

Ominous terrorist threats that summer of 2001 peaked in the month of June,[6] and stirred alarm in the American intelligence community. They seemed to indicate attacks on Israel or friendly Arab states on the Arabian Peninsula, but they were sufficiently vague to create anxiety anywhere on earth, including the United States. On June 12 a CIA report contained a line saying that Khalid Sheikh Mohammed was recruiting people to travel to the U.S. for the purpose of conducting suicide attacks. On June 22 the CIA warned its station chief of a possible al-Qaida attack on a U.S. embassy. About that time a terrorist threat advisory spoke of near-term "spectacular" attacks that would cause numerous casualties. The U.S. Fifth Fleet moved out of its port in Bahrain, the Marine Corps halted an exercise in Jordan, and the State Department temporarily closed its embassy in Yemen.

Richard Clarke, a carryover from the Clinton Administration as National Coordinator for Counterterrorism, was the White House expert on all things related to terrorism. He chaired the Counterterrorism Security Group (CSG) composed of top counterterrorism officials throughout government, including the CIA, Defense Intelligence Agency, National Security Agency, and the State Department. He notified his immediate superior, National Security Advisor Condoleezza Rice, and her deputy, Steven Hadley, that al-Qaida personnel were boasting of "important surprises" in the coming weeks that would affect Israel and the U.S. Clarke predicted on June 28 in concert with his CSG colleagues that a major attack or series of attacks would come in July. A message, reportedly from al-Qaida, declared that something "very, very, very, very" big was about to happen. On June 30, a PDB notice was headlined, "Bin Laden Planning High-Profile Attacks."

In July American agencies took steps to protect U.S. assets abroad, and twenty friendly countries launched operations to disrupt al-Qaida and affiliated terrorist cells. Special precautions were taken in late July to safeguard the G-8 economic summit conference in Genoa, Italy. Domestically, Clarke asked CSG agencies to cancel vacations and go on full alert. He called together senior security officials of the Federal Aviation Administration, Immigration, Secret Service, Customs, and the Federal Protective Service to warn them of the danger. In particular, he asked the FAA to issue a security warning to airlines and airports, with special scrutiny at ports of entry. The FBI warned federal agencies and state and local law enforcement of the growing volume of threats but downplayed the threat of a possible attack in the U.S.[7] All of this occurred in the month of July. In mid-month word came through the U.S. spy network that the "spectacular" event was on hold for at least two months, but had not been cancelled. (As it turned out, that report was spot on.) Clarke recommended continued vigilance, but the moment of maximum alert had passed. The alarm in July 2001 two months before the al-Qaida terrorist attack has an eerie precedent in the Pearl Harbor attack of 1941. Two weeks before the Japanese struck, Pacific Fleet Commander Admiral Husband E. Kimmel ordered an exercise north of Oahu to test defenses against a possible surprise attack in the area from which the Japanese carriers launched their planes on the morning of December 7. The exercise was no accident. A justifiably alarmed Kimmel was looking for the Japanese fleet two weeks early.[8]

What seems to be missing in the 9/11 Report is any sense of urgency among Bush and his highest policy advisors before the disaster hit. The President acknowledged as much to Bob Woodward, telling him in an interview, "I knew [before 9/11 that Bin Laden] was a menace, and I knew he was a problem.... But I didn't feel that sense of urgency, and my blood was not as boiling [as after 9/11]."[9] The absence of urgency penetrated deep into the bureaucracy. Rice spoke to the 9/11 Commission in 2004 of "systemic problems" with government intelligence that required "structural reform." "But structural reform is hard," she testified, "and in seven months we didn't have time to make the changes that were necessary. We did them almost immediately after 9/11."[10] In the great sweep of governance, it usually takes a major crisis to bring about major reform.

The event presupposes an inescapable lethargy prior to the crisis, and produces a period of uncertainty afterward as to whether the reform was effective. Another significant drag on Bush terrorism policy showed up in the neoconservative thinking that permeated the high echelons of the Defense Department. Deputy Defense Secretary Paul Wolfowitz belittled the al-Qaida threats based on his pet theory that al-Qaida could not carry out a major attack without state sponsorship, especially from Iraq. In a more speculative vein, the Bush policymakers suffered from an overbearing, ideologically inspired disdain for the previous administration: it seemed that whatever the Clinton team did, they would do differently. Clinton took al-Qaida seriously, but played a weak hand in Bush's eyes; Bush would wait and see about al-Qaida and act vigorously when necessary. He did act vigorously—after the horse was out of the barn.

At least the President—even though strongly influenced by aides with solid conservative views, Wolfowitz, Rumsfeld, and Cheney—repeatedly asked the right question: whether any of the threats pointed to an attack on the United States. That prompted the CIA's August 6 PDB that contained the eye-catching headline, "Bin Laden Determined to Strike in the US." The meat of the warning, however, was not as dire as the headline suggested. It cited historical facts, not current intelligence. It did not come close to the bar that one of America's great unsung heroes, Lt. Cdr. Joseph J. Rochefort, set for himself. He commanded the top secret codebreaking station at Pearl Harbor early in World War II that broke the Japanese naval code, leading to the American victory in the Battle of Midway, June 4-6, 1942, an early turning point of the Pacific War. The self-effacing Rochefort blamed himself for the surprise Japanese attack on Pearl Harbor of December 7, 1941. It is an intelligence officer's duty, he later recalled, to tell his commander today what the enemy is going to do tomorrow.[11] In that light, the CIA's August 6, 2001 PDB did not tell the commander exactly what, when, and how the enemy was going to attack the United States. But it did offer a scenario that should have put the commander on edge.

Ramzi Yousef's 1993 bombing of the World Trade Center, the

PDB rationalized, did provide an incentive that bin Laden would like to emulate. The deadly American missile strike on an al-Qaida training base in Afghanistan following the terrorist bombings of American embassies in East Africa would inspire bin Laden to honor the ancient Arab principle of vendetta by attacking Washington. The failed millennium plot to bomb Los Angeles International Airport was mentioned as another al-Qaida operation on American soil (it had al-Qaida's financial support for what was essentially a free-lance exercise). The brief also warned that bin Laden pursues his terrorist projects over the long term and that sleeper cells were lodged like computer viruses in the United States. Finally, it called attention to an uncorroborated report that bin Laden wanted to hijack a U.S. aircraft and hold passengers as leverage to gain the release of the "blind sheikh," Umar 'Abd al-Rahman, imprisoned in the U.S. for plotting terrorist attacks in New York City.[12]

Put those pieces together, and you have elements of the 9/11 attacks: the references to the 1993 attack on the twin towers, a revenge attack on Washington, long term planning, and airplane hijackings, with the major difference that the 9/11 hijackers were not home grown, but had infiltrated from the outside. As presented, in the absence of solid intelligence, it would have required a transcendent genius to have drawn a coherent picture of the 9/11 plot as it actually happened, but with the information from the PDB of August 6 and the many prior threat warnings it would also have been hard to ignore imminent danger. At the White House, however, President Bush and his coterie of foreign policy advisors could see only dimly what was happening on the ground. They focused largely on the issues of rogue states, China rising, and WMD proliferation that generated a "gee whiz" missile defense and an unnecessary war on Iraq.

Heads above the Clouds

It cannot be said that the administration buried their heads in the sand like an ostrich; rather they held their heads above the clouds looking for incoming missiles, intent on preparing for a high-tech war in space. They needed someone to tell them that al-Qaida lacked the weaponry to fire missiles on the United States, just as Rochefort informed his commander that the Japanese did not have the capability to attack the American mainland in June 1942, as some intelligence bureaucrats in Washington were warning. On January 26, 2001, less than a week after his inauguration, Bush renewed his campaign pledge to build an unproven and very expensive missile defense system. A little more than three months later and a decade after the end of the Cold War with the Soviet Union, he formally committed the United States to an anti-missile defense even more advanced than the Strategic Defense Initiative first proposed by President Reagan in 1983.

In a speech at the National Defense University in Washington, D.C. on May 1, he framed what he considered to be the nation's primary post-Cold War threat. "Unlike the Cold War," he said, "today's most urgent threat stems not from thousands of ballistic missiles in the Soviet hands, but from a small number of missiles in the hands of [some of the world's least responsible states], states for whom terror and blackmail are a way of life."[13] He was referring to states like North Korea, Syria, Iran, and Iraq, but he did not single them out by name, and of those nations only North Korea had any semblance of a nuclear arsenal. He might also have had China in mind, but China was too big for America to challenge without raising global tensions. Notably, he ignored al-Qaida, which was known to covet nuclear weapons that would have to be delivered by stealth on the earth's surface, rather than through space. The 9/11 attacks were a little more than four months away, but scattered reports of al-Qaida's threats had already been brought to his attention. Not that he should necessarily have put al-Qaida front and center, but only that bin Laden's terrorist group was hardly in his thoughts as he identified his major policy objective for national defense. The WMD issue gained traction after 9/11 when it became the main false pretext for invading Iraq.

BUREAUCRATIC STAGNATION

Richard Clarke experienced the Bush team's mishandling of al-Qaida in the netherworld of bureaucracy. At his first meeting with his new boss, the Sovietologist Condoleezza Rice, he detected a look of skepticism as he briefed her on al-Qaida. "[H]er facial expression gave me the impression that she had never heard the term [al-Qaida] before...," he wrote in his memoir.[14] After he spoke to her about terrorism, she spoke to him about shedding some of the functions of his office, although she allowed him to keep his staff of twelve intact. More damaging to his operation, she lowered the CSG's standing. When Clarke asked to brief a "principals meeting" of Cabinet heads on the al-Qaida threat, Rice put him off. First, he should brief Cabinet deputies, she told him.

The first such deputies meeting, chaired by Steven Hadley, was delayed until mid-April—another sign of the Bush team's weak response to the al-Qaida threat. The meeting did not go smoothly. Clarke clashed with Wolfowitz, the neocon defense deputy, who told him he was making too much of al-Qaida and argued his theme that state-sponsored terrorism from the likes of Iraq was the greater menace. Clarke pushed back, with support from John McLaughlin and Richard Armitage, the deputies at CIA and State respectively, sticking to his position that al-Qaida posed a lethal and imminent threat to American interests. Caught in the middle, Hadley put the issue on hold. He decided the group would start by focusing on al-Qaida and then turn to other forms of terrorism, including Iraq's. They would have to wait for general policy positions on Afghanistan, Pakistan, and India to be drawn up. He urged in the interim that more papers be prepared on the response to terrorism and more meetings be held to discuss the papers, thus showing strong bureaucratic skills but scant urgency on combating terrorists. Frustrated, Clarke proposed, in a memo requested by Rice to streamline the CSG, that a new White House cyber security unit be created and that he be assigned to head it. In other words, he wanted out. That took Rice by surprise, but she agreed to it and prevailed on

Clarke to stay at CSG until October 1, the beginning of the new fiscal year. That departure date was delayed by 9/11.[15]

At the CIA, Tenet shared some of Clarke's frustration. Like Clarke, Tenet was a holdover from the Clinton Administration. As Clinton's days in the White House were winding down prior to the Bush inauguration, outgoing National Security Advisor Sandy Berger asked Tenet to draw up a proposal on how to deal with al-Qaida based on the hypothetical supposition that no policy or resource constraints would apply. Tenet turned the project over to Cofer Black, head of the CIA's Counterterrorist Center (CTC), which recommended, among other measures, the covert disruption of al-Qaida in its Afghanistan sanctuary, support for the anti-Taliban Northern Alliance, and assistance to neighboring former Soviet Muslim states to help them fight their own homegrown terrorists. They called it the "Blue Sky" project. Tenet sent it to Clarke on December 29, 2000. Clarke, according to Tenet, took ideas from it and added some of his own in a memo to Rice. In the main, Clarke added a role for the military services to attack al-Qaida and Taliban command and control targets, which would appear to put the struggle against terrorism on a footing of full-scale war. When Tenet heard about Clarke's memo, perhaps thinking that Clarke was playing bureaucratic games, he dropped by Hadley's office one day in early March and left him Cofer Black's Blue Sky paper. He characterized it as a "draft," so it had no formal status, but he wanted the NSC to know the CIA's position. A month or so later, at about the time Clarke presented his counterterrorism plan to the deputies meeting, the NSC called Tenet's office and asked that someone pick up the Blue Sky paper. The NSC was not prepared to deal with the al-Qaida issue in the absence of a general policy formulation for South Asia.[16] It should come as no surprise that most, if not all of the recommendations on counterterrorism from both the CIA and CSG were implemented after 9/11. In other words, in the wake of that horrendous event, the U.S. went from defense to offense against the terrorists. There could be no assurance, though, that even if these forceful measures had been in place beforehand, that 9/11, or some similar tragedy, could have been averted.

Clarke asked Condoleezza Rice for the principals meeting to brief agency heads about the al-Qaida threat on January 25, five days into the Bush Presidency. He finally got his opportunity on September 4, eight-and-a-half months later and one week before the devastating al-Qaida attacks on New York and Washington. He described the meeting as "largely a non-event." He and Tenet spoke out for a strong anti-al-Qaida policy. Secretary of State Colin Powell urged a diplomatic effort to get Pakistan to side with the U.S. against the terrorists. Rumsfeld struck a somewhat discordant note by following the Wolfowitz line. He reminded his colleagues that they would also have to deal with terrorism from other sources. Rice wrapped things up by directing Clarke to prepare a broad National Security Presidential Directive for the President's signature.[17]

It would be hard to believe from what they recalled years later that Clarke and Rice were at the same meeting. He said it was a non-event; she said, in effect, that it was an affirmation of a forceful anti-al-Qaida policy. In her testimony before the 9/11 Commission in 2004 she painted a picture of a President alert to the problem. Strategy to combat al-Qaida, she said, was developed over the spring and summer of 2001, and approved by the President's national security officials on September 4. It embraced recommendations from the various agencies that included a diplomatic push to end al-Qaida sanctuaries, CIA covert activities, and military action against al-Qaida and the Taliban. "The President understood the threat and he understood its importance," Rice declared. "He made it clear to us that he did not want to respond to al-Qaida one attack at a time. He told me he was 'tired of swatting flies.'"[18]

Rice's version seems suspiciously like a politically motivated remake of history in the Karl Rove mode. In the final analysis, the President's reference to "swatting flies," as if the al-Qaida terrorists were mere pests, sticks in his craw. Was he speaking disdainfully as the leader of the world's most powerful nation? Or did he not realize that the fight against al-Qaida was a difficult, long-term project? Either way, it was a poorly chosen expression. Even when one acknowledges the difficulty of deducing beforehand the evil genius of the 9/11 plot, it can be said that the top Bush policymakers all the way up to the man occupying the Oval Office were asleep at the gate. In the years after the disaster, Bush apologists proudly boasted that the nation averted further terrorist catastrophes in America. Bush deserves thumbs up for that. But on the same level of reasoning, he should also accept responsibility for probably the worst man-made disaster in American history.

Chapter 4

Big Black Lies

Political language... is designed to make lies sound truthful and murder respectable.

—George Orwell

AMERICA, JUSTIFIED IN ATTACKING AFGHANISTAN IN 2001, lost its moral compass by invading Iraq in 2003. The campaign to sell the Iraq war was one of the most shameful episodes in the history of the American democracy. The ad hoc White House Iraq Group (WHIG) guided the campaign from inside the White House. Karl Rove, Bush's chief political strategist, chaired WHIG meetings attended by top aides to the president and vice president. They scheduled speeches and media interviews and released or leaked information that was often twisted or dead wrong.

When one considers the sheer iniquity of WHIG's mission, it is little wonder that Rove would try to run away from it, as he did on a promotional tour in early 2010 to pitch his $1.5-million memoir called *Courage and Consequence*. On one of his stops, the courage to answer a consequential question about his role as chairman of WHIG was notable for its absence. In an interview on the NPR program, "Fresh Air," he dodged a question from his interviewer, Terry Gross.

She read him a discerning passage from a book by Scott McClellan, former G.W. Bush White House press secretary, who had written his own memoir, *What Happened*, published two years earlier. In it

McClellan criticized WHIG's "political propaganda campaign to sell the [Iraq] war," which began in late summer 2002. "A pro-war campaign might have been more acceptable had it been accomplished by a high level of candor and honesty, but it was not," McClellan wrote. "[A]s the campaign accelerated, caveats and qualifications were downplayed or dropped altogether. Contradictory intelligence was largely ignored or simply disregarded. Evidence based on high confidence from the intelligence community was lumped together with intelligence of lesser confidence. A nuclear threat was added to the biological and chemical threats to create a greater sense of gravity and urgency. Support for terrorism was given greater weight by playing up a dubious al-Qaida connection to Iraq. When it was all packaged together, the case constituted a 'grave and gathering danger' that needed to be dealt with urgently."[1] (The quote here is extended beyond what was read on "Fresh Air.")

Rove's answer was patently untrue. He told Terry Gross that he recalled the meetings beginning in the summer or fall of 2003 to prod military and embassy officials in Baghdad into spreading the word about the troops' good work in Iraq.[2] Not so! The WHIG meetings began in August 2002, as McClellan reported, several months before the Iraq war was launched—a simple fact that anybody can Google. Spreading the "good news" may have been the goal in the autumn of 2003 long after the invasion, but in 2002 WHIG managed a campaign carried out by high-level White House officials to convince the American people of the red herring that Iraq actively supported al-Qaida, the perpetrators of 9/11, and threatened to attack America with weapons of mass destruction.

So what if Rove forgot the date? He was a busy man. Could it not have just slipped his memory? That would be hard to believe, because he chaired the WHIG meetings, and their date and function were not minor details. Even if he lied to Terry Gross, what was the problem? It seemed like a simple little white lie. No harm done. To the contrary, by misstating the timing, Rove could avoid talking about the most disgraceful performance of the Bush Administration: the campaign of lies perpetrated by the White House and sham intelligence units in the Pentagon to guide America into a dishonorable war of aggression.

President Bush put America's young men and women in harm's way to wage the unnecessary war in Iraq, which snuffed out the lives of more than 4,000 American troops and disabled thousands more. The direct and indirect costs will add up to trillions of dollars. The truly compassionate will not forget, either, that the war left more than 100,000 Iraqi civilians dead and from 2,000,000 to 4,000,000 homeless. It is a record that Bush and Rove would rather the nation forgot. WHIG's role, as McClellan correctly points out, was to sell the Iraq war to the American people and the U.S. Congress with a propaganda campaign that made false and exaggerated claims. WHIG drew support for its campaign from a body of questionable intelligence collected by neoconservative ideologues and lies from anti-Saddam Iraqi émigrés.

Bush's standing in history is at stake, and the truth will consume him. Neither Bush nor Rove was burdened like the neoconservatives with a deep philosophy about America's global role. But Bush, heavily influenced by hardliners like Cheney, Rumsfeld, and a coterie of neocons, chose to go to war, and Rove applied his considerable skills to the task of gaining public support for it. As the American people begin to understand the truth, Rove and other Bush loyalists will inevitably do their best to disavow it. Lying is not really the problem. Most if not all politicians lie to some degree, and many lie egregiously and often. The things they lie about set the acts apart, and when you consider the disaster the Bush Administration promoted, sending American men and women to death and injury in a costly and unnecessary war, they were not the little white variety. They were big black lies.

TROTSKY'S WAYWARD CHILDREN

To take a step back, the neocons were the major catalysts of the Bush team's broken logic. They were, and still are a small but energetic group of super hawks that gained a chokehold on American foreign policy during the Bush years. The roots of the neocon movement took hold in the 1930s when a small group of New York Jewish intellectuals inspired by the democratic socialist ideas of Leon Trotsky made names for themselves in literature and political opinion. Prominent among them in the political sphere were Irving Kristol and Norman Podhoretz who worked together as editors of the monthly journal, *Commentary*, after World War II. Their views turned sharply right in reaction to the anti-war sentiment of the 1960s that was taking hold in the Democratic Party. That marked the beginning of the modern neoconservative movement. Kristol and sociologist Daniel Bell founded the quarterly journal, *Public Interest*, which published many articles by leading intellectuals of the time, Jewish and non-Jewish, critical of Lyndon B. Johnson's presidency.

Little or nothing remains of liberal foreign policy thought in the neocon movement. Some of its leading figures today, including Richard Perle and Douglas Feith, got their start on the staff of the late Senator Henry M. "Scoop" Jackson, Democrat of Washington state, a liberal on social issues and a cold war hawk. Paul Wolfowitz did some work for Jackson on anti-ballistic missiles.[3] Within the latter-day group of foreign policy hawks, however, such as Cheney and Rumsfeld, many individuals held traditional conservative values across the political spectrum. Although it would be a stretch to label Cheney and Rumsfeld as neocons, for the sake of simplicity they are lumped together as American imperialist dreamers, blinded by faith in the false god of U.S. world dominion. They believed, as two leading neocon theoreticians put it, that America should adopt a policy of "benevolent global hegemony."[4]

The neocon philosophy of America as a global Leviathan surfaced briefly in 1992 in the draft of a biennial Pentagon policy declaration called "Defense Planning Guidance." Wolfowitz, then the undersecretary for policy planning, supervised the project. He assigned the job to I. Lewis "Scooter" Libby, a Wolfowitz protégé, who asked Zalmay Khalilzad, another prominent neoconservative, to write the draft. The ideas it contained—an aggressive world posture, unilateral military action, the suppression of potential rivals for world supremacy, and the protection of the West's oil interests in the Middle East—were suppressed after being reported in the *New York Times*, but they became policy a decade later in the administration of George W. Bush.

In the 1990s, Laurie Mylroie, a Harvard-educated scholar and dogged researcher bursting with unproven theories, which are harmless enough until commingled with power, developed a hypothesis of Iraqi responsibility for al-Qaida terrorism. In the late 1980s when Iraq enjoyed America's support in its war with Iran, so much did she trust Saddam Hussein that she tried, naively, to broker a back-channel peace deal between Iraq and Israel,[5] but when Iraq invaded Kuwait in 1990 she turned 180 degrees and saw him as something akin to a reincarnated devil (closer to reality because Saddam, like Stalin, murdered his own noncompliant people). In her book, *Study of Revenge*, first published in 2000 and updated in 2001, Mylroie charged that the plague of terrorist acts against America, starting with the first bombing of the World Trade Center in 1993, was part of *"a new kind of war*—an undercover war of terrorism, waged by Saddam Hussein"* (Milroie's italics).[6] The terrorist campaign, she argued, was too big and sophisticated to be carried out by a small crowd of al-Qaida renegades without state sponsorship, words that Wolfowitz would echo as he promoted war with Iraq. She alleged that Ramsey Yousef, the central figure in the 1993 bombing whose real name was Abdul Basit Karim, was an Iraqi agent that had stolen Basit's identity. Several neocons embraced her theory (later refuted by British intelligence with fingerprint evidence) after lobbying for regime change in Iraq. Wolfowitz, serving then as dean of the School of Advanced International Studies at the Johns Hopkins University, enthusiastically endorsed her book, calling it "provocative and disturbing." Wolfowitz had coauthored with Khalilzad of the Rand Corporation (and future ambassador to Afghanistan, Iraq, and the United Nations) a 1997 article in the conservative *Weekly Standard* advocating the use of military force to "liberate" Iraq.[7] Shortly thereafter, Irving Kristol's son,

William, the *Weekly Standard's* publisher and co-founder with Robert Kagan of the neocon think tank, Project for a New American Century (PNAC), sent a letter to President Clinton urging that America remove Saddam, with military force if necessary. Kagan coauthored the letter and several other conservative hawks signed it.[8]

After Bush won the 2000 presidential election, neocons walked the corridors of power. Vice President Cheney, the president's most influential advisor at the time, anchored the hard-liners' network from the White House. The old warrior Rumsfeld, who taught Cheney the ropes of bureaucratic infighting in the Nixon/Ford years, ran the Pentagon. Neocons Wolfowitz and Feith held the numbers two and three positions in the Defense Department. Libby was Cheney's chief of staff. These men made up the inner circle of foreign policy hawks in the Bush Administration. Hadley, the deputy national security advisor, was privy to their contrivances and eager to accommodate them. The like-minded John R. Bolton was positioned in the State Department as undersecretary for arms control, where Secretary Colin Powell sometimes offered a dissenting voice to Cheney's and bore neocon tread marks on his back for his mostly losing efforts. Both Hadley and Bolton were Cheney allies. Perle, the top neocon power broker known as the "prince of darkness" for his hard line during the cold war against negotiating arms control with the Soviet Union, led the Defense Policy Board, a civilian advisory group lodged in the Pentagon. From there, Perle had access to America's deepest military secrets, but he soon gave up the chairmanship over an apparent conflict of interest uncovered by *New Yorker* correspondent Seymour Hersh.[9]

Conservative hawks never forgave Bush's father for ending the 1991 Gulf War at the Iraqi border when the way was open for total conquest and the removal of Saddam Hussein from power. Ironically, Cheney, secretary of defense at the time, sided with his president, George H.W. Bush, saying "it would be a mistake to get bogged down in the quagmire inside Iraq."[10] He went back on these words when he advised Bush, the son, a decade later to invade Iraq. Cheney had actually shown his true colors in 1997 when he signed on with PNAC.

Wolfowitz brought with him into his powerful new office the Mylroie theory that Iraq was behind the al-Qaida terrorist network. At the first meeting of the President's National Security Council eight months before 9/11, Wolfowitz argued for an attack on Iraq. Bush did not dismiss the idea out of hand. Wolfowitz had been one of his foreign policy tutors during the presidential campaign. So the new president was very much in synch with neocon thinking. He merely said, according Treasury Secretary Paul H. O'Neil, "Go find me a way to do this."[11] The terrorist attack of 9/11 opened the way. Wolfowitz impatiently called for war on Iraq the day after 9/11. That same day Mylroie, prior to her downfall, wrote an op-ed article in the *Wall Street Journal* blaming Saddam Hussein for the attack. This time Bush was on the case. He asked Clarke, his counterterrorism czar, to see if Iraq was complicit in the act. Clarke had previously reviewed possible operational Iraqi ties to al-Qaida and found no evidence of them. He dutifully checked again, and again came up empty.[12] Clarke, along with most of the intelligence community, had no doubt that al-Qaida had carried it out on its own.

Bush at least held onto the appropriate response of first going after the actual perpetrators in Afghanistan. The Iraq folly came later. Bush claimed that war with Iraq was a last resort, but he ordered Rumsfeld to begin planning for it sixteen months in advance of the invasion date—just in case.[13] In the meantime, the neocons kept trying to confirm their deduction that Iraq was behind 9/11. In late September 2001, Wolfowitz enlisted James Woolsey, former CIA director and a neocon true believer, to head a team from the defense and justice departments to explore in London the Mylroie theory that Ramsi Yousef, the 1993 World Trade Center bomber, was actually an Iraqi agent. (The trip was taken without the knowledge of the CIA or the State Department, until the British government asked the American embassy if the Woolsey team were on official business.) Yousef had spent time in the United Kingdom (including school in Swansea, Wales), and if his fingerprints on file with MI5 in London did not match those of the 1993 WTC bomber, it would support her argument. But the fingerprints did match, and the Mylroie theory crashed.

Cooking the Intelligence

Undeterred, the neocons took another approach. Deep in the bowels of the Pentagon, while the military professionals drew up the war plan, conservative ideologues sanctioned as the Counter Terrorism Evaluation Group (CTEG, also known as the Policy Counterterrorism Evaluation Group), combed the raw intelligence in the darkest secrecy for scraps of information to prove the Iraqi connection to al-Qaida. CTEG started as a secret two-man operation, with David Wurmser and Michael Maloof sitting for hours in front of powerful computers. They worked in the section headed by Feith, the undersecretary of defense for policy planning. Feith had been Perle's aide in the Reagan Administration when Perle was an assistant secretary of defense. Maloof had also been on Perle's staff then as an investigator. In the interim, Feith and Wurmser had collaborated with Perle in 1996 on a policy paper for newly elected Israeli Prime Minister Binyamin Netanyahu entitled, "A Clean Break: A New Strategy for Securing the Realm," which advised Netanyahu to seek strategic alliances with Turkey and Jordan to counter hostile countries like Syria and Iraq. One of its recommendations was the removal of Saddam Hussein from power.[14]

Feith and Wolfowitz were utterly without doubt about the connection between Iraq and al-Qaida, but the CIA and other agencies in the broad sweep of the government Intelligence Community (IC) did not buy into it. Years later, Feith was dismissive of the CIA in a book review for the *Wall Street Journal* of Tenet's memoir, *At the Center of the Storm.* "The CIA's assessments," said Feith, "were incomplete, nonrigorous and shaped around the dubious assumption that secular Iraqi Baathists would be unwilling to cooperate with al-Qaida religious fanatics, even when they shared strategic interests."[15] In other words,

Feith seemed still to cling to the ideologically inspired assumption that Iraq supported al-Qaida without a shred of evidence to prove it. The Wurmser/Maloof team would find the evidence. They set out to show the connections between terrorist organizations and support systems that included sponsoring states. According to Maloof, they found many scraps of information in the raw material already reviewed by the CIA that "suggested these linkages."[16]

Neocon mistrust of the CIA was not made of whole cloth. The agency had found Saddam Hussein's Stalinist dictatorship very hard to penetrate. So it lacked solid in-country assets and knew little more than what its experts read in the newspapers and technical journals. Vice President Cheney shared the neocons' disenchantment dating back to the Gulf War in 1990-91 when he was secretary of defense. The CIA had said then that Iraq was five years away from acquiring a nuclear bomb. His own staff shortened the timeline to eighteen months, and after post-war inspections the nuclear expert David Kay reported that Iraq could have had an A-bomb within six months. In his later role as vice president, Cheney no longer trusted the bland, finely analyzed assessments coming from the CIA. But he did not directly contradict the intelligence reports that he reviewed on an almost daily basis. Rather, in trips to the Langley, Virginia CIA headquarters, he would draw out the analysts by making them confront their conclusions: How do you know this? What's the source of that? Have you considered this other possibility? Of course, Cheney had his own dark suspicions about Hussein that made it difficult to accept anything less than the Iraqi dictator's most dire intentions. Consequently, the vice president would eventually come to err on the side of exaggeration.

Wurmser and Maloof pieced together a broad unity of disparate terrorist organizations in a common organized war against the U.S and its allies. The idea of such ties among separate entities in the Muslim world was not entirely far-fetched. Bin Laden's al-Qaida and Ayman al-Zawahiri's Egyptian Islamic Jihad had already come together as the "World Islamic Front for Jihad Against the Jews and the Crusaders" (the International Islamic Front, IIF), which the two terrorist leaders announced jointly in 1998. Free lancers and other terrorists more focused on local issues trained in al-Qaida camps. In the 1980s, the secular Baathist regime in Syria had cooperated with the Shia theocracy in Iran in support of what became Shia Hezbollah in Lebanon, years before al-Qaida existed. But the idea of an operational alliance between Hussein's Iraq and al-Qaida was rejected by the intelligence professionals. Furthermore, as the scholar John Prados points out, "The thesis of an alliance between Saddam and bin Laden required overturning the whole logic of the al-Qaida religious argument, which was that states should be forced to convert to the fundamentalist 'way.'"[17]

Wurmser and Maloof also looked for signs that Iraq participated in the 9/11 attack, but for proof the neocons had to settle for some very shaky evidence. First, there was the disputed meeting of April 2001 in Prague between 9/11 terrorist pilot Mohamed Atta and an Iraqi intelligence officer, Ahmad Khalil Ibrahim Samir al-Ani, that the bipartisan 9/11 study group later shot down.[18] Second, an Islamist prisoner held in Egypt, Ibn al-Shaykh al-Libi, told his captors that Iraq trained al-Qaeda terrorists in the use of chemical and biological weapons. Wurmser and Maloof embraced the report despite warnings from the DIA that Libi might simply be telling the Americans what he thought they wanted to hear. Later, Libi recanted.

The pair represented their findings on a large map hung on the wall with intersecting lines connecting various terrorist organizations with each other, their supporters, and state sponsors. Maloof said it looked like a spider web.[19] Many lines led to Baghdad. They reported weekly in writing on their progress to Stephen Cambone, Feith's top aide and a member of the neocon think tank, PNAC. Feith and Cambone would review the reports and pass them upstairs to Wolfowitz and Rumsfeld. They might also "stovepipe" (bypass the CIA and other agencies) what they considered important enough to Scooter Libby and Stephen Hadley. Wurmser and Maloof exceeded their research mandate to the point of seeking input from Ahmad Chalabi, the leader of the exile group, Iraqi National Congress (INC). They shared the information with the intelligence agencies, but the professionals, who considered the Iraqi exile community unreliable, simply filed it away. In any case, it meant Wurmser and Maloof had gone beyond the *review* of existing files to the *collection* of suspect raw intelligence.

Chalabi, a friend of Perle's, was a political wheeler-dealer and controversial figure. Born in 1944 into a prominent Iraqi Shia family, he earned a Ph.D. in mathematics from the University of Chicago and later taught at the American University in Beirut. He founded the Petra Bank of Jordan in 1977, and as its chairman was convicted in absentia of bank fraud by a Jordanian court that left a twenty-two-year prison term hanging over him if he should set foot again on Jordanian soil. His conviction did not keep him from wheedling millions of taxpayer dollars out of U.S. agencies. After the Gulf War of 1990-91 the CIA set him up in the Kurdish north of Iraq, outside Saddam's control, to foment insurrection against the regime. But in 1995 the revolt fizzled. The CIA sent a troubleshooter to find out what went wrong. The agent found Chalabi living high on the hog in Kurdistan in a large house with several limousines in the driveway. In London, he discovered an INC newspaper that did not publish and an INC radio station that did not broadcast. Worse than the waste of money, the CIA also learned that Chalabi had close ties to Iran. One of his INC aides exchanged information with Iranian intelligence. The CIA concluded that he might have been an Iranian agent. The CIA cut its ties with Chalabi in 1996. Two years later Congress passed the Iraq Liberation Act and appropriated $97 million to foster regime change in Baghdad. Most of the money was doled out to Iraqi opposition groups, and the INC received $33 million of it under a contract with the State Department from March 2000 to September 2003.[20] Chalabi and some of his prized exiles were the sources of dubious intelligence that helped make the case for war.

Wurmser and Maloof finished a 150-page report by early 2002 claiming that al-Qaida carried out the 9/11 attack, assisted by Hezbollah, funded by the Saudi royal family, and sponsored by Iraq.[21] Then the team broke up. Wurmser transferred to the staff of John Bolton at the State Department and later switched to Cheney's office in the White House. Maloof lost his security clearance over allegations of unauthorized contact with a foreign agent, a Georgian woman who eventually became his wife. After they left, Chris Carney, a Penn State political science professor, and Tina Shelton, a DIA analyst, took over their duties.

Shelton was a conscientious researcher. She bored in on the task assigned to her of finding closer Iraq-al-Qaida ties than the CIA suspected, and put her results on paper in a report to Feith. After Feith presented it to Rumsfeld and Wolfowitz, Rumsfeld urged him to show it to Tenet at the CIA. On August 15, 2002 Feith made a power point presentation to Tenet and other top CIA officials, alleging that the CIA missed some important contacts between Iraq and al-Qaida. One slide stated that "intelligence indicates cooperation on all levels, a mature symbiotic relationship" between Iraq and al-Qaida, including signs of possible Iraqi coordination with al-Qaida in the 9/11 attack on America. In this presentation the reported meeting between Mohammad Atta and the Iraqi agent in Prague, downplayed by the intelligence community and later dismissed by the 9/11 Commission, was accepted as a "known contact." Tenet acknowledged that the session yielded some information that the CIA had not previously focused on, but it still did not rise to the level of a cooperative relationship. Feith withheld one of his slides that suggested fundamental problems with the CIA's assessment of the raw data. A month later, the same lecture was given to staff in the White House with Scooter Libby and Stephen Hadley in attendance, only this time the slide critical of the CIA was left in. Years later, the Pentagon's Inspector General, Thomas Gimble, found after investigating Feith's office that this ploy "undercut" the CIA.

THE PROPAGANDA MILL

When Feith added another, more muscular unit to his domain, the Office of Special Plans (OSP), it strengthened Vice President Cheney's pipeline through Scooter Libby to the neocon boiler room in the Pentagon. William Luti, a former Navy captain, came over from the vice president's office to work for Feith as deputy undersecretary of defense. He had formerly served in the speaker's office as a military aide to Newt Gingrich. Under Feith, he ran the bureau of Near Eastern and South Asian Affairs (NESA).

Karen Kwiatkowski, then a career U.S. Air Force lieutenant colonel doing a three-year tour of duty in the Pentagon and contemplating retirement, remembered a meeting at which Luti pressed his staff to finish a report that he felt compelled to "get over to Scooter right away."[22] Kwiatkowski had to ask a colleague who Scooter was. Obviously, she was not a neocon. She had been "volunteered," as she put it, to join Luti's NESA to handle the North Africa desk. A fellow staffer warned her on her first day that if she wanted to succeed in her new post she had better not say anything positive about the Palestinians. (Many neocons openly sided with Israel's right-wing Likud Party, the intellectual heir of Vladimir Jabotinsky who early in the last century envisioned a greater Israel from the Nile to the Euphrates.)

Among her new colleagues was Abram N. Shulsky, soon to take over the new OSP. Shulsky would fold both the Iraq desk and whatever was left of the CTEG intelligence unit under his wing. (By this time CTEG was moribund, but it was not officially disbanded until 2004. When word got out about the work of Special Plans, Rumsfeld revealed the existence of CTEG.) Shulsky was a well connected neocon, having roomed with Wolfowitz in college at Cornell and Chicago, worked on Perle's staff in the Reagan Pentagon, and collaborated with Libby on a study of American global strategy after the cold war. Kwiatkowski, who took well to office schmoozing, described him as a mild mannered, scholarly man willing to engage in conversation. But he and the more irascible Luti, she reported, shook up the NESA bureau. Civil servants who did not agree with the neocon philosophy were kicked upstairs or pushed into retirement. New people were brought in as the OSP gobbled up vacant office space. When Kwiatkowski arrived in May 2002, the Iraq desk was located in the same office with the rest of NESA; by August, the Iraq desk was gone and Shulsky's OSP had new quarters, but she followed its output as one of many Pentagon staffers on the distribution list of its "talking points" on Iraq policy.

In all, she spent about ten months in NESA from May 2002 to February 2003 during OSP's birth and rise to fame. So, if not an insider, she certainly had a front-row seat to the neocons' act. With a high security clearance, she was well versed on the intelligence coming out of the DIA. When President Bush spoke to the nation in prime time in the first week of October 2002 about the alleged Iraqi threat, she found many of his statements at variance with the facts as she knew them. So she asked a DIA analyst on Luti's staff, who fed the president "all the bull" about Saddam's links to terrorists and possession of weapons of mass destruction? The analyst, John Trigilio, replied, "Karen, we have sources that you don't have access to."[23]

The sources Trigilio referred to were Iraqi exiles filtered mostly through the Iraqi National Congress. OSP continued to cultivate the relationship with Chalabi that Maloof had begun through Perle. Kwiatkowski learned that Bill Bruner, newly occupying the Iraq desk, had formerly served as a military aide alongside Luti in the speaker's office under Newt Gingrich. He came to NESA about when Luti did. She wondered why he always wore civilian clothes since he was a military officer on active duty. "He's Chalabi's handler," she was told, and often attended meetings in hotels in downtown Washington.[24] Michael Rubin, a neocon who actually did serve in OSP, denied that Bruner was Chalabi's handler. "Chalabi did not have a set handler," said Rubin.[25] (He did not deny that Chalabi was being "handled.")

Rubin wrote an article devoted primarily to attacking critics of the OSP for the conservative journal, *National Review Online*. The greatest share of his volleys was aimed at Kwiatkowski who wrote damaging reviews from inside and outside her NESA perch. From August 2002 on, during the months that remained to her in the Air Force, she contributed anonymously to a blog, "Soldiers for the Truth," run by the late Colonel David Hackworth, a legendary, highly decorated Army officer who became a critic of the Vietnam war and, later, the Iraq occupation. Her columns were published under the heading, "Insider Notes from the Pentagon." After retiring she went public. She wrote a lengthy article for the online magazine, *Salon*, gave speeches, and submitted to an interview with *LA Weekly*. *Mother Jones* featured her in an article about OSP headlined, "The Lie Factory." For neocons, she posed a serious problem: she was not your familiar liberal muckraker like Seymour Hersh or a freelancer writing for *Mother Jones* or *The Nation*. Kwiatkowski was a conservative career military officer who voted Republican but got fed up with neocon tactics. She described herself as a "soldier for the truth."

In the midst of his harangue against the neocons' enemies, Rubin managed to give a brief account of the OSP's overall mission and his own duties on the staff. "My job," he wrote, "was that of any desk officer: Writing talking points for my superiors, analyzing reports, ..., and drafting replies to frequent letters from [Democratic] Congressmen John Dingell and Dennis Kucinich." The OSP's Iraq team, he added, "produced Power Point slides on a variety of issues" and "made them available to Pentagon desk officers not proficient in Iraqi affairs." Talking points, he explained, "are a standard way to provide information throughout the military." For the most part, the talking points were not related to new intelligence findings, but were restatements of unclassified U.S. policy, "updated because policy is fluid and is dictated by events."[26]

It looked perfectly innocent as Rubin painted the picture, but Kwiatkowski had a different slant: "propaganda," she called it. "They pushed an agenda on Iraq, and they developed pretty sophisticated propaganda lines, which were fed throughout government, to the

Congress, [to Libby and Hadley in the White House, Bolton in the State Department], and even internally to the Pentagon to try and make this case of ... severe threat to the United States." The OSP also kept certain outside neocon sympathizers in the know, such as the American Enterprise Institute, the Center for Security Policy, and media outlets that included the *Weekly Standard* and columnist Charles Krauthammer of the *Washington Post.* The talking points were not intelligence-driven, said Kwiatkowski; they were politics-driven based on the "expansionist, imperialist policies" of the neocons.[27] (The neocons argue that the OSP output was policy-driven.)

DOD Inspector General Thomas Gimble's two-year study of OSP released in February 2007 criticized Feith for developing "alternative intelligence assessments" on the Iraq-al-Qaida relationship because, he said, it drew "inappropriate" conclusions "inconsistent with the consensus of the Intelligence Community." Gimble also found that Feith's briefing to the White House "undercut the Intelligence Community." Feith reacted with unresponsive, hair-splitting answers that he was not drawing conclusions about ties between Iraq and al-Qaida, but simply leveling criticism at the intelligence community for not paying enough attention to them. He said he accepted the conclusion of the 9/11 commission report that no operational relationship existed between Iraq and al-Qaida. "Nobody in my office ever said there was an operational relationship," Feith argued.[28] He also denied undercutting the CIA. His office, he said, was not involved in intelligence. Rather it dealt with policy and exercised "good government" for calling attention to intelligence errors. Ultimately, he expressed satisfaction that his efforts were successful, because Tenet sent a document to the chairman of the Senate Intelligence Committee that contained many points of agreement with Feith's version of the Iraq-al-Qaida relationship shortly before the Senate approved a war-enabling resolution.[29] In other words, Cheney, Rumsfeld, Wolfowitz, Feith, and their neocon colleagues succeeded in browbeating and whipsawing Tenet to the point where he fell in line with them.

SPREADING THE TAINTED WORD

By the summer of 2002, polls showed that the American public was not buying the White House argument for war against Iraq. Even the revered conservative and Republican Party loyalist Dick Armey, the House majority leader from Texas had spoken out against an unprovoked invasion as an act of aggression contrary to American values (Armey later voted under strong White House pressure for the war-enabling resolution, an example of tribal politics where party loyalty trumps moral rectitude). Brent Scowcroft, who had served Bush's father as national security advisor, condemned it as a strategic mistake for diverting America from the war against al-Qaida. Some observers have speculated that Scowcroft was carrying a message from the president's father, former President George H.W. Bush, who scrupulously avoided public comment on his son's management of the presidency. In any case, the younger Bush did not like what he heard, and his chief of staff, Andrew Card, responded to the boss's pique by creating an ad hoc group to sell the Iraq war to Congress and the American people. This was the ultimate indefensible act that left the Bush administration wallowing in the political muck. It became known as the White House Iraq (or Information) Group (WHIG) and held weekly meetings in the Situation Room chaired by Karl Rove. Also involved, among others, were Rice, national security advisor; Hadley, her deputy; Karen Hughes, the White House communications director; Michael Gerson, the chief White House speechwriter; White House Press Secretary Ari Fleischer, and from the vice president's staff, Scooter Libby and Cheney's communications specialist, Mary Matalin, who soon left her White House job to take care of her two young children.

For Rove to run the show raises the specter of subverting national policy to political calculation. Rove is, above all, a political animal. Politics is his passion. His handling of policy is about as far-sighted as the next election. That's why authors James Moore and Wayne Slater considered Rove's appointment as a White House policy advisor a tragedy for America. As chairman of WHIG, he perceived the "war on terror" to be a political issue that favored his client, the president, and he played the role with all the force of an intense political campaign. It did not matter to Rove that Iraq had no provable part in the 9/11 attacks; WHIG would make it look as though Saddam Hussein was leading the charge by accusing him of creating programs for weapons of mass destruction and of training al-Qaida fighters to use the weapons. These charges turned out to be untrue, but Rove was not interested in the facts, only in the image of war as a burning necessity. He plays to win. He got his war—and his desired political issue.[30]

Richard Dearlove, chief of MI6, the British counterpart to the CIA, neatly capsulated the Bush drill to Prime Minister Tony Blair in the summer of 2002 upon his return to London after meetings with American intelligence officials in Washington. "Bush," he said, "wanted to remove Saddam through military action, justified by the conjunction of terrorism and WMD. But the intelligence and the facts were being fixed around the policy."[31] In this context WHIG's eager staff produced a number of papers with derogatory titles such as, "Apparatus of Lies: Saddam's Disinformation and Propaganda, 1990-2003," "A Decade of Deception and Defiance," and "What Does Disarmament Look Like?" One paper called "A Grave and Gathering Danger: Saddam Hussein's Quest for Nuclear Weapons" went through five drafts before Rice finally rejected it because it was "not strong enough." Gerson, by the way, saved some of the language ("a grave and gathering danger") for insertion into a Bush speech before the United Nations. To scholar John Prados, an analyst with the National Security Archives, the WHIG enterprise, "shows that the stream of exaggerations, half-truths, and outright lies purveyed to Americans...were not by accident or misunderstanding but were elements in a purposeful political program."[32]

WHIG swung into action in early September 2002. The *New York Times* published an article on Sunday morning September 8 about Iraqi efforts to reconstitute its nuclear weapons program, coauthored by two of its star reporters, military correspondent Michael Gordon and Judith Miller who had shared a Pulitzer Prize with others on the *Times* staff for a series on the global terrorist threat. Miller had also coauthored a book with Laurie Mylroie, *Saddam Hussein and the Crisis in the Gulf,* and as might be imagined, enjoyed excellent access to the neocons and the INC. Prominently featured in the September 8 article was news of a shipment of aluminum tubes destined for Iraq that had been intercepted in Jordan. Gordon reported that the tubes were to be used in centrifuges for enrichment of uranium, information leaked to him by the White House. In fact, the intended use of the tubes was disputed within the government—for enrichment, said the CIA; for conventional rockets, not enrichment, argued the Energy and State Departments—a fact not leaked by the White House. On this subject, the Energy Department had the most knowledgeable experts.

Cheney appeared on NBC's *Meet the Press* that Sunday and said the tubes were meant for uranium enrichment. There was no mention of the alternate view, which would have undermined the intended message. In an act of sheer deviousness, Cheney declined to discuss "classified material," but referred his host, Tim Russert, to the *New York Times* story without letting on that the *Times* got its information from the White House. The same day, Condoleezza Rice said on CNN's "Late Edition with Wolf Blitzer" that the aluminum tubes were suitable only for nuclear weapons programs and added what became the Bush team's blockbuster mantra put forward by speechwriter Gerson, "We don't want the smoking gun to be a mushroom cloud." Powell rounded out the WHIG's performance that day with the assertion on "Fox News Sunday" that Saddam undoubtedly "has chemical weapons stocks."

The neocons thought they had another piece of evidence of an Iraqi nuclear program in a report from an Italian freelance spy that Niger had made a deal in the late 1990s to sell five hundred tons of yellowcake (uranium oxide) to Iraq. Within the IC the idea was considered absurd. Iraq, indeed, had a lot of yellowcake, but lacked the machinery to process it. Besides, such a large quantity of bulky uranium ore would be very difficult to transport undetected. The French who controlled the mining consortium in Niger considered the report bogus. Documents offered as proof of the deal were later exposed as forgeries. But early in 2002 when the neocons learned of it without actually seeing the paper, they took it as another piece of solid evidence. Vice President Cheney demanded that the CIA check it out. On the recommendation of Valerie Plame, who worked undercover in the agency's Counter Proliferation Division, her husband, Joseph C. Wilson, IV, was sent to Niger in February 2002 on a fact-finding mission.

Wilson was an experienced diplomat who served there in the 1970s and as ambassador to neighboring Gabon in the 1990s. As deputy chief of mission in the Bagdad embassy in 1990, he was the last American official to talk to Saddam Hussein before Iraq overran Kuwait. Wilson made the trip to Niger, conferred with Ambassador Barbro Owens-Kirkpatrick, spent eight days "drinking sweet mint tea and meeting with dozens of people," and reported back that he found no evidence to support the yellowcake story.[33] That, of course, did not satisfy the vice president or the neocons.

The September 8 media blitz marked the beginning of the administration's effort to make the case for aggression against Iraq. According to a House minority report released by Democratic Congressman Henry Waxman (not an unbiased source, to be sure, but one with a reputation for accuracy), five top administration officials (Bush, Cheney, Rumsfeld, Powell, and Rice) made sixty-four misleading or false statements in sixteen public appearances between September 8 and October 8, 2002 in which they alleged, based in large part on dubious intelligence, that America was imperiled by an Iraqi buildup of weapons of mass destruction and that Iraq had undercover ties to al-Qaida.

On October 7 Bush addressed the nation with a speech in Cincinnati that the major broadcast networks and cable news channels carried in prime time. Like a prosecutor building the case against a criminal defendant, he ticked off a lengthy list of alleged crimes: Iraqi possession of "massive stockpiles" of biological weapons, "thousands of tons" of chemical agents, ballistic missiles, unmanned drones, and mobile weapons facilities. The aluminum tubes, he alleged, proved Iraq's nuclear intentions. An early version of the speech mentioned the Niger yellowcake connection, but it was removed after Tenet cautioned against it. Even without it, Bush treated his nationwide audience to the recycled nuclear metaphor: "Facing clear evidence of peril, we cannot wait for the final proof—the smoking gun—that could come in the form of a mushroom cloud." Four days later the House and Senate overwhelmingly approved a war-enabling resolution.

The administration's warmongering continued at a reduced frequency right up the invasion on March 20, 2003. Cheney made repeated visits to the CIA that intelligence analysts interpreted as pressure to hew a more hawkish line in daily briefings. Tenet ultimately proved to be a compliant bureaucrat and essentially embraced the neocon perspective. In a crucial unclassified White Paper delivered to Capitol Hill on the eve of Congress' critical vote on the resolution to grant President Bush the power to use military force against Iraq, Tenet's CIA frequently slanted the report in the neocons' favor ignoring caveats conveyed in the classified national intelligence estimate (NIE) to which most members of Congress did not have access prior to the vote. For example, with regard to the most massive of the weapons of mass destruction, nuclear weapons, it is stated matter-of-factly in the NIE, "Saddam does not yet have nuclear weapons or sufficient material to make them." That line was perverted in the White Paper to say, "Although Saddam *probably* does not yet have nuclear weapons or sufficient material to make any, *he remains intent on acquiring them* (italics added)."[34] The italicized inserts make the Iraqi threat far more menacing. That Saddam "remains intent on acquiring them" was easy to believe, but also pure conjecture. The neocons, however, from Cheney on down, firmly believed it. The NIE itself was widely considered a flawed document, but at least it contained many of the caveats and alternate estimates not made public.

In his State of the Union speech on January 28, 2003, Bush, making an end run around the CIA, spoke sixteen words he later admitted were untrue: "The British government has learned that Saddam Hussein recently sought significant quantities of uranium from Africa." Then he repeated the neocon error that aluminum tubes were suitable only for nuclear weapons production. Unless he did not read the intelligence from the government agencies, in which case he would have been derelict in his duty, he could not have been unaware that he was misstating the facts.

On February 5, Powell indelibly sullied his distinguished career in making the administration's case for war before the United Nations Security Council. After carefully vetting the speech prepared for him at the CIA, his staff rejected twenty-eight of thirty-eight disputed claims that staffers from Cheney's office had inserted. Powell, to his ultimate embarrassment, accepted the existence of mobile biological labs and to bolster the claim, displayed dramatic, but unpersuasive pictures from space of parked vans that showed nothing of what was inside them. German intelligence had already told the CIA that it considered the source of that claim, Rafid Ahmed Alwan, codenamed "Curveball," to be a prevaricator and mentally unbalanced.[35] Powell alleged that Iraq possessed enough chemical stocks to cause mass casualties in an area twenty-five times greater than Manhattan Island where he was delivering his speech. He also spoke menacingly of the "sinister nexus" that did not actually exist between Iraq and al-Qaida.

CON JOBS AND CHICKEN HAWKS

Adding it all up, America waged the Iraq war on false pretenses that included the aluminum tubes, the discredited purchase of uranium oxide in Niger, an alleged buildup of chemical and biological weapons, mobile laboratories for the production of WMD, unmanned aerial vehicles for WMD delivery, Iraqi training of al-Qaida terrorists, and Iraqi support of 9/11. Bush and his highest ranking foreign policy officials continued to utter false and misleading statements after the invasion to justify their action.[36] Not one of these claims was true, said Joseph Cirincione in a 2005 review of John Prados' scholarly book,

Hoodwinked. Cirincione, then director for non-proliferation of the Carnegie Endowment for International Peace, homed in on the ugly truth: By winning a second four-year term in 2004, Bush and Cheney "got away with the greatest con job in the history of the American presidency."[37]

The Bush policymakers went to a great deal of trouble to start a war that disrupted an ancient, highly cultured society and put hundreds of thousands of young Americans in harm's way. When a fraction of the total returned from the war zone in flag-draped coffins, the President would pay tribute to their "ultimate sacrifice." How bitter sweet for the man and his aides who shunned the hazards of war for themselves. President Bush avoided combat in Vietnam by serving in the Texas air national guard. Vice President Cheney dodged the draft. "I had priorities in the sixties other than military service," Cheney declared. Wolfowitz, Feith, Perle, Libby, Bolton, and Karl Rove did not serve. For their non-service and war advocacy, they became famous in the blogosphere as "chicken hawks."[38] Rumsfeld, a junior naval officer from 1954 to 1957, stands out as an armchair hawk in a position of power who did serve in the regular armed forces. But the wrestling mat is the closest he came to combat between wars. He was a Navy wrestling champion. Wurmser had worked out of the Pentagon as an intelligence officer in the Navy Reserve. Stephen Hadley, also in the power loop, spent 1972 to 1975 in the Navy. Other neocons with less exposure, such as Michael Ledeen, Kenneth Adelman, and Elliot Abrams, also advocated war without paying their dues.

The contrast between words and actions is not the only incongruity of the neocon hawks. Several of them have lived in comfortable Washington suburbs far from the pain and dying in Iraq that they helped bring about. Some families are very close. They socialize; their children play at the same parks and attend the same schools. They are literate and very smart, graduates of America's finest universities. Feith is recognized as an intellectual giant. Perle is admired for his lemon and grapefruit soufflés, as well as his contempt for the CIA.[39] They are a prosperous, elite, ingrained circle of intrigue trying to remake the world and manipulating the levers of power to get others to do the heavy lifting.

Outside this inner circle the neocon network is strong, with a significant media outreach through the *Weekly Standard*, bankrolled by the Australian media magnate, Rupert Murdoch. The *Standard* did its share to stoke the fires of war in Iraq. William Kristol, the publisher, often appears as a commentator on the Murdoch-owned Fox network and spent a year writing a weekly column for the *New York Times* op-ed page. Another prominent neocon, Charles Krauthammer, is published regularly on the op-ed page of the *Washington Post*, as is Michael Gerson, former White House speechwriter who participated in the WHIG campaign to sell the Iraq war. The conservative think tank, American Enterprise Institute, boasts an impressive stable of scholars of far right to moderate views on foreign and domestic issues. Broadcast networks and cable news channels often turn to the AEI for experts who can articulate the "conservative" side of a story.

Of course, the neocons have a right to their opinion, a right to speak out, a right to build infrastructure for spreading their ideas, no matter how fanciful they may be. But do they have a right to distort the historical facts? Well, they try. Feith has argued that he never tinkered with intelligence. His office was only forging policy. [40] Perle denied the existence of a neocon ideology that drew America into the Iraq war. [41] While Bill Kristol was trumpeting a "tremendous victory in Iraq" based on the surge, the commander on the ground, Gen. David Petraeus, together with Ambassador Ryan Crocker, called its gains "fragile and reversible." [42] By the end of 2011, Americans troops had cleared out of Iraq under provisions of a treaty signed by George W. Bush before he left office. The claim that America won the Iraq war is the latest neo-"con job" to cover up the hawks' aggressive role in promoting it. In reality, by withdrawing from Iraq America was getting out of a mess under modestly favorable circumstances that it should never have got into. The Machiavellian Rove cannot be ignored either. He denied that

WHIG existed in 2002 so that he could avoid talking about its nefarious role in promoting the war with exaggerated intelligence and shifty rhetoric. For one who often astonishes interlocutors with his grasp of political details, his denial is not believable. After all, he chaired the WHIG meetings.

Based on their performance in the race to war in Iraq, the neocons have earned zero credibility. We should never forget that they twisted the truth as they herded the nation into an unnecessary conflict that caused death or catastrophic disability to thousands of young American troops, death to a hundred thousand Iraqis, and the displacement of millions. The Bush Administration drove the U.S. deeper into debt by borrowing to fund the war while cutting taxes that primarily benefited those who could afford to pay for it. The war's cost in lives, treasure, and lost credibility is appalling. The gains remain obscure.

In his memoir, *Decision Points*, President Bush persisted in defending his decision to invade Iraq by citing the supposed threat of Saddam Hussein to his Arab neighbors, Israel, and even the United States. That justification does not wash. Richard N. Haass, president of the Council on Foreign Relations, an independent foreign policy think tank, has written of the difference between a war of necessity and a war of choice. The Gulf War in 1990-91 to undo Iraq's occupation of Kuwait, he argued, was a war of necessity. The Iraq war beginning with an unprovoked U.S.-led invasion in 2003, he labeled a war of choice.[43] In making this important distinction, Haass was direct and thorough, but his language seemed somewhat tempered by diplomacy-speak. Based on the absence of America's national interest in the latter war and the Bush administration's confidently and even arrogantly given but utterly false claims that Iraq was behind 9/11 and possessed weapons of mass destruction, Iraq can more accurately be described, to borrow a term used by Trudy Rubin of the *Philadelphia Inquirer*, as a war of "willful blindness."[44] The Bush policymakers were cocksure of themselves in their rationale for war. They "knew" that an attack of 9/11's magnitude could only have been carried out with state sponsorship. They "knew" Iraq was the sponsor. They "knew" where the weapons of mass destruction were hidden. They "knew" that Iraq was currently building a nuclear weapons program because they had done so in the past. They "knew" that an Iraqi intelligence officer had met with one of the 9/11 terrorists. But they were dead wrong on all counts. That's no way to start a war.

Chapter 5

Torture from the Top Down

Abu Ghraib and other situations like that are non-biodegradable. They don't go away. The enemy continues to beat you with them [as with] a stick.

—Gen. David Petraeus

THE SCANDALOUS TREATMENT OF PRISONERS in cell block 1A at Abu Ghraib outside Baghdad burst on the world's consciousness in the spring of 2004 with the shock that one might experience at discovering the dark side of an idol. America's propaganda mills in Hollywood, New York, and Washington often depict the troops as humane, even heroic in the treatment of their enemies. There may well be some truth in that image—or was until the Bush Administration changed the rules. At Abu Ghraib the United States abandoned the humane approach and replaced it with an ugly display of American soldiers abusing Iraqi prisoners.

When the scandal broke, top administration officials all the way up to the president condemned those pictured abusing prisoners as a few low-level enlistees acting on their own. In his post–presidency memoir, Bush wrote of feeling "really sick" about the way American soldiers treated detainees "in defiance of their orders and military law."[1] On the contrary, the orders for torture, or whatever you want to call it, came from the top down. They were hatched in the Pentagon and the Central Intelligence Agency and nurtured in the White House with the approval of the President. The initiative, in fact, came from the office of the Vice President. They did not call it torture; they called it "robust" or "enhanced" interrogation, and they tried to keep it secret. They did not want the public to know what they knew, that they were the real culprits who devised the new interrogation strategy and let the low-level grunts take the fall when it was exposed. Defense Secretary Donald Rumsfeld offered to resign, but the president kept him on the job until the Republicans' election disaster in 2006.

Conservative officials in the Bush Administration had turned a sensible program into disgraceful policy. What started as a procedure to train American military personnel to withstand the pain and embarrassment they might experience if captured by terrorists, the administration changed into a formula for the harsh interrogation (i.e., torture) of terrorists in American custody. As might be expected, many innocents were caught in the round-up of suspects. The program, modeled on the inhumane Chinese torture of American prisoners to induce false confessions during the Korean War, went over from defense to offense. Barbaric Chinese torture of Americans became barbaric American torture of Islamists. Morally, America had retreated, in the words of Vice President Cheney, into the "dark side."

THE HARD EVIDENCE

The jailers of the 800th Military Police Brigade took at least 279 photographs and shot nineteen videos that provided ample evidence of their own witless cruelty.[2] The pictures showing the guards' efforts to humiliate and debase the Iraqis in their custody were described as measures to soften up prisoners for questioning by Military Intelligence or the CIA. Among the photos that so shocked the president is the by now familiar graphic image of a female soldier holding a dog leash looped at the other end around the neck of a naked Iraqi prisoner lying on a concrete floor. In another scandalous picture, a prisoner stands on a box, hooded and robed, arms outstretched, with wires attached to his hands. He was told that if he fell or stepped off the box he would be electrocuted. Other photos show prisoners cowered by attack dogs; naked prisoners piled up in a pyramid; prisoners handcuffed in stress positions to a bed frame, or a cell door, or a window bar, some naked, some with underwear pulled over head and face; one image has a naked prisoner hanging by his knees from a top bunk-frame, his head reaching almost to the floor; another has a prisoner lying face down on the concrete floor with a soldier's knee in his back.

All the above reflect techniques approved by the highest authority in the Bush Administration. Beatings and rapes fall into a different, unauthorized category. Soldiers who participated in such criminal activities exceeded their legal mandate. Some pictures show signs of beatings. One prisoner's face is smeared with blood. Another photo reveals a soldier kneeling amid four men lying on the floor with one arm around a prisoner's neck and the other cocked with clenched fist as if to strike him.

One incident depicted in a series of annotated photos taken by military jailers reflects directly on the CIA. Military guards did no softening up. On November 4, 2003, a team of SEALs arrested an Iraqi man, Manadel al-Jamadi, thought to have been involved in an attack on the Red Cross in Baghdad. According to Sgt. Walter A. Diaz, the duty officer, Jamadi walked handcuffed into the military intelligence wing at Abu Ghraib in the early morning before dawn under his own power and was turned over for interrogation to the CIA (OGA in military jargon, which stands for "other government agency"). An hour later he was dead. Diaz told investigators he was called in to reposition Jamadi's handcuffs and noticed that the prisoner's face was swollen and that he had no pulse. Later, the Armed Forces Institute of Pathology determined that Jamadi had died from "blunt force injuries to the torso complicated by compromised respiration." In short, the death was ruled a homicide. The corpse was packed in ice, placed in a body bag, and left overnight in the shower room where Cpl Charles A. Graner, Jr., and Spc. Sabrina Harman found the bag leaking fluid, opened it, and took pictures of the corpse. The dead man's most prominent feature was a bloodied black eye swollen shut that he reportedly suffered from a rifle butt to the head when the SEALs arrested him. For some of the pictures Graner and Harman posed over the corpse, smiling with thumbs up. The body was taken out on a stretcher the next morning with an I.V. stuck in his arm to make it appear to Iraqi guards that he was merely ailing, not dead.[3]

Two generals who investigated the incident, Lt. Gen. Anthony R. Jones and Maj. Gen. George R. Fay, tried to obscure the Pentagon's role in the scandal by suggesting that the working relationship with the CIA put military personnel at risk of non-compliance with the Geneva Conventions.[4] As Corporal Graner said seventeen months later in a statement to the Army Criminal Investigation Division, "You know these guys can kill people. The OGA guys do whatever they want."[5] However, while the CIA may have been out of control under its cloak of secrecy, military intelligence was also very forceful in its interrogation techniques—part of a broad atmosphere of fear and loathing created by the Bush Administration in reaction to 9/11.

Graner, who participated in a number of dehumanizing activities, was one of nine Abu Ghraib enlisted personnel court-martialed on charges of prisoner abuse. He received a ten-year sentence, a dishonorable discharge, and was reduced in rank to private. He was the most severely punished. Pfc. Lynndie England, the female soldier pictured holding the dog leash tied to a naked prisoner, was sentenced to three years imprisonment along with a dishonorable discharge. Six other enlisted men and women were given prison terms ranging from six months to eight years. All received dishonorable or bad-conduct discharges. One other was reduced in rank and docked half a month's pay.[6] Only one officer, Lt. Col Stephen Jordan, former deputy commander of the 205th Military Intelligence Brigade, faced a military tribunal. He was acquitted of all charges relating to torture, but was convicted of speaking out about the scandal.[7] The Army took non-judicial action against seven other enlisted men and eight other officers in the chain of command.

The highest ranking bestained officer was Brig. Gen. Janis Karpinski, commander of the 800th Military Police Brigade, who was reprimanded, relieved of command, and demoted to colonel.[8] She has since retired.

A federal prosecutor reviewed 101 cases of CIA enhanced interrogation. The reviewer absolved CIA personnel in ninety-nine of them. Two cases involving terrorist suspects who died in CIA custody were referred to the Obama Justice Department for possible criminal prosecution. Unofficially, one of these was the notorious case of Manadel al-Jamadi, the Iraqi mentioned above who died at Abu Ghraib. The other involved an Afghan, Gul Rahman, who was being held in 2002 at a secret prison in Afghanistan known as the "Salt Pit." The *Washington Post* reported that he froze to death after being stripped naked and chained to a concrete floor in subfreezing temperatures.

The abuses at Abu Ghraib represent the low hanging fruit of the torture scandal, easy to pick because of the photographic evidence. They do not tell the whole story there, nor do they show the prisoner abuses at other prisons in Iraq, Cuba, Afghanistan, or the scattered "black sites" (secret prisons) of the CIA's discredited and discontinued extraordinary rendition program. More secrets could emerge if the Rahman case goes to court. But even then, the revelations will not take us to the top of the Bush Administration where the events that led to torture originated.

Maj. Gen. Antonio Taguba, who wrote the report that first broke the story of Abu Ghraib, said after his retirement that all questions about the Abu Ghraib scandal have been addressed—except one. "After years of disclosures by government investigations, media accounts and reports from human rights organizations, there is no longer any doubt as to whether the [Bush] administration has committed war crimes," Taguba wrote. "The only question that remains to be answered is whether those who ordered the use of torture will be held to account."[9] Gen. Taguba's question is addressed at the end of the chapter.

POWER TO THE PRESIDENT

This story began on September 11, 2001 in a secure bunker beneath the White House. Vice President Dick Cheney and several White House aides watched television in silence as flames and black smoke poured out of the World Trade Center. When the south tower collapsed, the room filled with a collective groan. But no sound came from the vice president, according to eyewitnesses. He took charge immediately, declared an emergency, and barked out orders in rapid succession. The White House aides were seeing Cheney at his best—cool and collected, in total command of his faculties. He may even have assumed powers reserved for the president when he ordered, based on faulty information, that the last of the four hijacked planes be shot down (the plane had already crashed in a Pennsylvania field). He tried to call President Bush in Florida, but it took some time to get through. When finally connected, he warned the president to stay away while the emergency existed.

While Bush flew to bases in Louisiana and Nebraska, before deciding to return to Washington that evening to address the nation, Cheney's attention turned to the task of expanding the power of the presidency. It was his way of saving his country in its hour of peril. For that he needed his counsel, David Addington. Aides finally contacted Addington walking, as directed by White House security, from the Executive Office Building to his home in northern Virginia. They told him to turn around; the Vice President needed him. When he got back to the White House, Cheney asked him to start drafting extraordinary emergency powers for the executive—powers beyond those given the President in the Constitution and existing law. [10] It is obvious that the new executive powers would extend Cheney's own reach, because he was by far the president's most influential advisor and almost always the last to see the president before important decisions were made. But one would have to enter Cheney's mind to know if he was thinking of himself when he laid out his orders to his loyal advisor.

Addington called in Timothy E. Flanigan, deputy White House counsel, who together with John C. Yoo, deputy chief of the Office of Legal Counsel in the Justice Department, drafted a Congressional authorization for the President "to use all necessary and appropriate force against those nations, organizations, or persons that [the President] determines planned, authorized, committed, or aided" the terrorist attacks on September 11, 2001, and against those who harbored the terrorists.[11] The resolution was boosted with a statutory sleight of hand. Not only did it give the president a virtual carte blanche in the use of the armed forces for his "war on terror," it declared that the president's authority was within the War Powers Resolution passed in 1973 under the shadow of America's Vietnam debacle. That resolution placed strict limits on the executive power to temporarily wage war without Congressional authorization. The new resolution, broadly written, would give the President virtually unlimited power to wage war against enemies of his choosing. Nevertheless, Congress bought into it, passing it into law with near unanimity on September 18, one week after al-Qaida's attack on America.

Yoo—son of Korean immigrants, a once and future law professor at the University of California, Berkeley, and advocate of absolute presidential authority in wartime—then wrote a secret memo to Flanigan, dated September 25, which argued that the President's authority to wage war on terrorists was even broader than that implied in the new Congressional resolution that he had co-written several days earlier. Neither the 1973 War Powers Resolution nor the 2001 Joint Resolution, he declared, "can place any limits on the President's determinations as to any terrorist threat, the amount of military force to be used in response, or the method, timing, and nature of the response. These decisions, under the Constitution, are for the President alone to make," said Yoo.[12]

DESCENT INTO TORTURE

During the Korean War (1950-1953), the Chinese used coercive techniques on American prisoners to wring confessions out of them. The Americans called these practices torture in violation of the Geneva Conventions. But recognizing that enemies do not always play by Geneva rules, the Pentagon created a program immediately after the Korean War called Survival Evasion Resistance and Escape (SERE) to train American military personnel (especially airmen and Special Operations Forces most vulnerable to capture) in situations they might face as prisoners of war. SERE teaching tactics, some of which had been used by the Chinese to debase American prisoners, included nakedness, stress positioning, slapping, sleep disruption, extreme temperatures, loud music, flashing lights, hooding, and even waterboarding. By the time the conflicts in Iraq and Afghanistan rolled around, SERE was an ongoing program in the Joint Personnel Recovery Agency (JPRA), part of the U.S. Joint Forces Command.[13]

SERE was a positive program. It taught resistance to techniques designed to make prisoners talk or otherwise comply with their captors' demands. But when Islamists caught in Afghanistan defied American interrogators, some people in the Bush administration looked at SERE through a different lens. They wanted to know about SERE techniques, not to strengthen the resistance of American prisoners to terrorist torture, but to browbeat recalcitrant Islamist prisoners in American hands. As early as December 2001, the Defense Department's general counsel, William James "Jim" Haynes, II, a close friend and ally of Addington's, requested information about SERE. Presumably, as the Pentagon's top lawyer, he was assigned that task because he would have some sense of what was legal in the context of international and domestic laws against torture, or at least, would know how to find out. He was, in fact, a Cheney ally, in the same camp as neocons Wolfowitz and Feith, the numbers two and three officials respectively in the Pentagon.

The following February, the weak President Bush followed the advice of his strong vice president, Cheney, and made himself complicit in the torture scandal by signing a Presidential Order that set aside Common Article 3 of the Third Geneva Convention, which lays out minimal standards for humaneness toward captured non-combatants. The new presidential order declared that Common Article 3 was not applicable to al-Qaida or the Taliban, a position that Vice President Cheney had enunciated ten weeks earlier.[14] JPRA then turned its unbounded and seemingly enthusiastic attention to an examination of its teaching program as a template for questioning terrorist captives. During the first half of 2002, JPRA briefed Pentagon officials on the techniques, pressures, and physical/psychological effects of its interrogation procedures. In July it submitted a bundle of documents to the DOD general counsel's office that included a list of SERE techniques such as sensory deprivation, stress positioning, waterboarding, and "treating a person like an animal." Deputy General Counsel Richard Shiffrin told the Senate committee years later that the DOD intended to "reverse engineer" the SERE techniques.[15]

At this point the infamous "torture memos" from the Justice Department entered center stage. The legal opinions of the DOJ's Office of Legal Counsel (OLC) are fundamental to the functioning of the executive branch of government. The OLC interprets particular laws in particular circumstances, and these interpretations have the force of law for all federal agencies. In this instance, the OLC had been asked to determine whether the SERE techniques were lawful under domestic and international law. The key memo drafted by Yoo[16] and signed by Jay Bybee, then-chief of the OLC, was addressed to then-White House counsel Alberto Gonzales on August 1, 2002 at Gonzales' request. Would the language against the torture of the soldiers or agents of a state at war, Gonzales asked, apply equally to international stateless terrorists? In response, Bybee set a very high bar for torture.[17] For treatment of prisoners to rise to that level, Yoo/Bybee wrote, any pain inflicted must be akin to that accompanying "serious physical injury, such as organ failure, impairment of bodily function, or even death."

For mental pain or suffering to amount to torture, the memo went on to say, "it must result in significant psychological harm of significant duration, e.g., lasting for months, even years." And, said the memo, it might still be permissible against al-Qaida and its allies if applied to "interrogations undertaken pursuant to the President's Commander-in-Chief powers."[18] Jonathan Fredman, chief counsel to the CIA's Counter Terrorist Center, described the question of whether a particular act is torture as, "basically subject to perception. If the detainee dies you're doing it wrong."[19]

A second memo on August 1, 2002 listed the harsh techniques justified by the first memo that could be used by interrogators, including waterboarding (to instill fear of drowning), sleep deprivation, stress positioning, cramped confinement, and slapping, among others. Both memos submitted to Gonzales remained secret until April 2009 when President Barack Obama released them under the shadow of a lawsuit brought by the American Civil Liberties Union.

In September 2002, about a month and a half after the torture memos reached the White House, a team of interrogators and behavioral scientists from Guantanamo attended training sessions in SERE at JPRA's base camp at Fort Bragg, North Carolina. After they returned to Gitmo and received a visit from three high ranking administration lawyers—Addington, Haynes, and John Rizzo from the CIA, two of the behavioral scientists requested that they be granted permission to employ additional interrogation techniques, such as nakedness and the use of attack dogs, that were not specified in the OLC memos. Permission was granted.

Philippe Sands, a prominent news commentator on both sides of the Atlantic, began tracing the steps that led to Abu Ghraib with a memo from Haynes for Rumsfeld's signature under the heading, "Counter-Resistance Techniques."[20] By signing it on December 2, 2002, Rumsfeld cleared the way for the use of SERE and other aggressive techniques in the questioning of Islamist prisoners at Guantanamo. A high value detainee, Mohammed al-Qahtani, was already being questioned about his role in 9/11. From August through October 2002, he was held in "severe isolation" with constant bright lights and the use of dogs to intimidate him.[21] Gitmo authorities suspected at the time that he was the missing twentieth hijacker. By November, according to an FBI report, Qahtani was exhibiting symptoms of "extreme psychological trauma" (hearing voices, talking aloud to no one, and crouching under a sheet for hours at a time).[22] Still, it was not enough. With Rumsfeld's approval, he became the first suspected terrorist at Guantanamo to feel the pain and humiliation of the new SERE techniques that reportedly included (in addition to earlier techniques used on him) making him perform tricks as if he were a dog, twenty-hour interrogations, sleep deprivation, nakedness, beatings, stress positioning, threats against his family, religious and sexual humiliation, exposure to low temperatures, and loud music.[23] Qahtani's ordeal lasted about five weeks until mid-January 2003 while protests against the new interrogation techniques mounted within the uniformed services. Among the protesters, Navy General Counsel Alberto Mora told Haynes that some of the techniques "could rise to the level of torture." On January 15 he delivered a draft memo to Haynes outlining his concerns and promised to sign the memo the next day unless Rumsfeld rescinded his December 2 order. Rumsfeld rescinded it and Gitmo laid off Qahtani. Five years later, on May 13, 2008, charges against him were dismissed.[24]

Rumsfeld convened a working group to decide interrogation issues. Yoo wrote another memo at Haynes' request that repeated the assertions made in the first August 1, 2002 memo and countered efforts by the group's military and civilian lawyers to keep prisoner interrogations within the bounds of civility. Its business completed in early April as invading U.S. forces were closing in on Baghdad, the working group recommended several SERE techniques for approval without mentioning SERE by name. Rumsfeld ignored many of these recommendations while approving twenty-four aggressive interrogation techniques, but left room for appeal. In the enhanced vision of hindsight, that elaborate exercise had the appearance of being scripted for the purpose of undercutting the objections raised by the uniform services—a diversionary Kabuki dance while, behind the scenes, Rumsfeld's approved interrogation techniques of December 2, 2002 found their way to Afghanistan and remained standard operating procedure even after the defense secretary's rescission of January 16, 2003. That was just the kind of subterfuge at which the vice president and his aides excelled. After the conquest of Iraq, the interrogation procedures turned up at Abu Ghraib and other prisons where so-called enemy combatants were detained. By this time, Rumsfeld's new list of techniques became universally operational.

In the late summer of 2003, Maj. Gen. Geoffrey Miller, commander of the Guantanamo prison, led an inspection team on a visit to Abu Ghraib and found it wanting. Col. Thomas Pappas, commander of the 205th Military Intelligence Brigade, reported that Miller told them to get tougher with the detainees. Another source quoted Miller as saying the unit in Iraq was "running a country club" for detainees. After Miller's tour, Maj. Gen. Ricardo Sanchez authorized stress positions, environmental manipulation, sleep management, and the use of dogs in interrogations. Some of these were later rescinded, but confusion remained over what was or was not authorized. In any case, Abu Ghraib was no longer a country club, and the MP jailors took incriminating pictures to prove it.

Throughout this period, the new interrogation techniques never went unchallenged—to the credit of lawyers for the uniformed services. Finally, in the fall of 2003, months before the Abu Ghraib story broke in the spring of 2004, the foundation for the Bush torture policy came undone. Bybee and Yoo had departed the Office of Legal Counsel. Jack Goldsmith, Bybee's replacement as assistant attorney general, found time early in his tenure to read the torture memos, which even within the Justice Department were considered "problematic." Goldsmith rescinded the first Yoo memo signed by Bybee of August 1, 2002 and the Yoo memo of March 2003. Haynes could no longer rely on these memos to support his case, Goldsmith informed him. Unfortunately, that did not stop the torture from going forward until it was publicly exposed in the spring of 2004 with photographs that shocked the world.

THE CIA'S PARALLEL TRACK

The CIA jumped into the torture caldron several months before the Pentagon got involved. After Pakistani police with help from American operatives captured Zayn al-Abidin Mohamed Husayn, a.k.a., Abu Zubaydah, on March 22, 2002, the CIA prepared a program for the interrogation of high level Islamist prisoners based on SERE techniques. Meetings on the subject took place in the White House in the spring of 2002. National Security Advisor Condoleezza Rice asked DCI Tenet to brief the National Security Agency (for codebreaking and eavesdropping) on the CIA program. Rumsfeld attended those briefings. She also asked Attorney General John Ashcroft to "personally review and confirm" the OLC's legal advice on torture.[25]

The CIA interrogation program contained a few wrinkles that set it apart from the military's. Abu Zubaydah, who managed al-Qaida training camps, and other captives like him were taken to secret prisons in countries friendly to the United States ominously referred to as "black sites" where torture was allegedly performed. The program was known as "extraordinary rendition," which must be distinguished from the common legal practice of rendition. Under "rendition," a detainee is delivered from one legal jurisdiction to another to face due process. Under "extraordinary rendition," the suspect is transferred in secret to an undisclosed site to avoid due process. According to another definition used by the American Civil Liberties Union, torture would be expected at the secret prison.[26]

More captives followed Abu Zubaydah into the secret prisons. The Pakistani police rounded up Ramzi Binalshibh exactly one year after the 9/11/01 attack that he helped to coordinate after failing to gain entry into the United States because Yemenis were persona non grata after the USS *Cole* attack.[27] They also arrested Khalid Sheikh

Mohammed (KSM), the mastermind of 9/11 and grandiose planner of other terrorist and assassination plots, on March 1, 2003,[28] and Walid Muhammad bin Attash, who had a major role in the bombing of the USS *Cole* in Aden harbor, about two months later in May 2003.[29] In August that year, Thai police pitched in with the capture of Riduan bin Isomoddin, better known as Hambali, the Indonesian terrorist linked to the bombing of Bali resorts that killed and injured 411 people, mostly young Western revelers.[30] In prisons controlled by the CIA, interrogators were authorized to use the procedures formalized by the Bush Justice Department, including such practices as "waterboarding," sleep deprivation, dousing the prisoner with cold water, stripping him naked, making him stand for hours on end, or slamming him against a flexible wall to frighten, but not seriously hurt him. Eventually, the extraordinary rendition program was exposed, and captives kept in black sites were transferred to Guantanamo Bay, Cuba.[31]

Passive acquisition and imprisonment of captured terrorists was only part of the CIA's program. Sometimes CIA agents actually kidnapped suspects who were citizens or residents of friendly countries, and were not above brazenly grabbing their prey off a city street in broad daylight. CIA rendition groups dressed farcically in black and wore face masks as if going to a Halloween party. They often broke local laws as they followed a standard operating procedure for abductions. But they were not playing games. Whether carrying out their own snatch or taking a hand-off from local authorities, they would blindfold the prisoner and cut off his clothes, inject an enema to clean out his bowels, administer drugs to help him sleep, and outfit him with diapers and a jumpsuit for the long and often circuitous trip to the "black site."[32]

President Bush argued in his memoir that the harsh interrogation techniques yielded important information. In 2002, the CIA presented him with a list of new techniques it wanted to use on Abu Zubaydah. Bush said after a Justice Department review that he rejected two of the measures listed (without naming them), but approved waterboarding.[33] During World War II when the Japanese used waterboarding on American prisoners, the U.S. called it a war crime.³⁴ KSM, by far the CIA's biggest catch, was subjected to the heaviest torture. He was waterboarded 183 times, according to a 2009 report in the *New York Times* based on a Justice Department memo. Abu Zubaydah, a somewhat lower value detainee, was waterboarded 83 times.³⁵ Both men talked, but KSM said later that he did not always tell his interrogators the truth.

As might be imagined, the CIA net also caught innocent people. Maher Arar, for example, born in Syria, came to Canada as a teenager, studied in Canadian schools and graduated from the prestigious McGill University in Montreal. On September 26, 2002, American agents arrested him as he changed planes at Kennedy Airport in New York and took him to Syria where he spent a year in prison. Arar said he was beaten in Syria with two-inch thick cables and kept in a small windowless cell without light that was "like a grave." Eventually, he confessed to being trained by al-Qaida in Afghanistan because, he averred, that was what his jailers wanted him to say. After a year, the Canadian government got him released. Later, a Canadian board of inquiry found no evidence to link Arar with terrorism.³⁶

Khalid el-Masri was mistaken for Abu Ayyab al-Masri, erstwhile aide to the late Abu Musab al-Zarqawi, the leader of al-Qaida in Iraq. Khalid was Lebanese born in Kuwait in 1963. He moved to Germany in 1985, became a German citizen in 1995, married a year later, and fathered six children. In December 2003, he told police, he had a spat with his wife, and took off through the Balkans for a vacation. In Macedonia, authorities detained him and later turned him over to the CIA, which flew him to Afghanistan. According to Masri, agents beat him on his head, the soles of his feet, and the small of his back, and left him "in a small, dirty, cold concrete cell." Back at CIA headquarters in Langley, Virginia, they learned that they had picked up the wrong man. From that point on, the CIA engaged in damage control, trying to keep a lid on their mistake, but the *Washington Post* exposed it.³⁷

The CIA's extraordinary rendition program fell apart in the *Imam*

Rapito (Kidnapped Imam) affair in Italy where Hassan Mustafa Osama Nasr, the Imam of Milan, a.k.a., Abu Omar, was snatched off a Milan street on February 17, 2003 on the way to his mosque for noon prayers. This was not a case of mistaken identity. It was more like life imitating art, a CIA impersonation of the fictional French Inspector Clouseau. The CIA took him to Egypt, which he had fled in 2001. Before he left, Egyptian intelligence was investigating his radical group, al-Gamaa al-Islamiyya.Italy granted him political asylum. But by the spring of 2002, Italian and American intelligence agencies and local Italian police had him under surveillance for suspected links to al-Qaida and the recruitment of terrorists. There was the crux of the problem. The CIA snatch of February 2003 got in the way of Italian law enforcement, whose suspect had suddenly disappeared. But it did not take long for the Italian police to pick up the CIA trail. They traced cell phone calls in the vicinity of the disappearance and a few hours later at Aviano air base that went to the American consulate in Milan and to Northern Virginia where CIA headquarters is located. The CIA agents also used easily traceable credit cards in their own names that revealed their movements. At the very least, they should have encrypted their calls and paid the bills in cash, basic spy craft, but apparently did not because they thought they would be covered by their alliance with SISMI, the Italian Military Intelligence and Security Service.[38] In November 2009, an Italian court returned convictions for twenty-three CIA agents that carried sentences of five to eight years and two Italian agents who received three-year sentences.[39] The Americans will probably never serve a day in an Italian prison, but to avoid prison, neither will they ever again experience the joy of Italy's wonderful Mediterranean cuisine.

One other twist in the interrogation scandal that could be called "the privatization of torture" remained unresolved. The Center for Constitutional Rights (CCR) and four Iraqi men brought a civil suit against a U.S. civilian contractor, seeking compensatory and punitive damages for following the CIA's torture routine at Abu Ghraib. Al

Shimari v. CACI, et al, alleges that employees of CACI International, inc., and CACI Premier Technology, Inc., together with certain "government co-conspirators" tortured four Iraqi plaintiffs while questioning them at the Abu Ghraib "hard site" beginning in 2003. CACI, originally California Analysis Center, Inc., is a prime defense and intelligence contractor that uses information technology to guide its clients in solving problems. Usually, the company relies on advanced technology, but if the allegations in this case are true, CACI used old-fashioned strong-arm techniques to pry information out of the prisoners. The Shimari case cites electric shocks, beatings, sleep deprivation, forced nudity, hooding, stress positioning, sexual assault, and isolation, among other techniques. The four plaintiffs—Suhail Najim Abdullah al Shimari, Taha Yaseen Arraq Rashid, Sa'ad Hamza Hantoosh al Zuba'e, and Salah Hasan Nusaif Jasim al-Ejaili—were held for years but never charged with a crime. The alleged torture took place over briefer time periods. Allegedly, the plaintiffs continue to suffer from physical and mental injuries caused by abusive treatment. As of January 1, 2012, the case was still making its way through the U.S. federal court system.[40]

TAGUBA'S QUESTION

Major General Taguba's question remains unanswered. Will those high public officials who ordered enhanced interrogation—those who allegedly committed war crimes—be held to account? For the Bush administration to disparage the low-level personnel as a few bad apples not representative of the system was to scale the heights of hypocrisy. No higher army officers or civilian officials have faced justice for the misdeeds at Abu Ghraib (or Guantanamo, or Bagram, or the "black sites" of the CIA), despite the efforts of some victims and their supporters to put them in the dock. In 2004, the Center for Constitutional Rights (CCR), the human rights legal organization based in the U.S., and four Iraqis filed a criminal complaint in Germany against several top Bush Administration officials for war crimes—filed in Germany because German law provides "universal jurisdiction" for the prosecution of war crimes committed anywhere in the world. Topping the list of defendants were Secretary of Defense Rumsfeld, CID Tenet, and General Sanchez, the top commander in Iraq at the time. Seven other defendants were named: Stephen Cambone, undersecretary of defense for intelligence; Major General Miller, the Guantanamo commander who traveled to Iraq to urge implementation of Gitmo's intensive interrogation techniques; Maj. Gen. Walter Wojdakowski, Sanchez's deputy; Brigadier General Karpinski; Colonel Pappas, the head of military intelligence at Abu Ghraib; Lieutenant Colonel Jordan, Pappas' former deputy, and Lt. Col. Jerry L. Phillabaum, commander of the 320th military police battalion. Alberto Gonzales, then-White House counsel, was added later. But under pressure from the Bush administration, the German prosecutor refused to accept the case.[41]

In 2007, eleven former inmates at Abu Ghraib and one at Guantanamo Bay made another effort to get a German court to try many of the same defendants, excluding Wojdakowski, Karpinski and Phillabaum, while adding Bybee, Yoo, Haynes, and Addington. Again, Germany deferred to American pressure. The latter list of defendants amounted to a roundup of most of the virtual suspects, but it did not quite reach the top. Vice President Cheney and President Bush also deserved a judicial spotlight for allowing America's good name to be dragged through the muck.

In 2008, Democratic Congressman Dennis J. Kucinich of Ohio tried to remedy that deficiency by drawing up impeachment papers against Bush on multiple charges that included one article of torture in violation of the U.S. Constitution and the Geneva Conventions. But Speaker Nancy Pelosi refused to put impeachment on the House calendar, fearing a circus atmosphere that would hinder passage of important legislation. For the time being, at least, it appears that President Bush and his top aides will get away with torture.

The torture scandal originated in the panic that gripped the Bush administration in the wake of 9/11. Congress gave the president virtually absolute power in time of war, and the president's men reinterpreted national and international law to loosen the guidelines for torture. No one should cry for Khalid Sheikh Mohammed or his al-Qaida comrades who contributed to the murder of thousands of innocent people. They should stand trial for their ugly deeds, or if trial is considered too risky, they should remain behind bars in perpetuity. But they should not be tortured. The torture, which has roped in so many innocents, is not worthy of a great nation. It has blackened the American image as a land of justice and humanity. In this dangerous world, it matters what other people think. America needs their friendship. It needs all the friends it can get.

Chapter 6

Class Warfare

Experience declares that man is the only animal which devours its own kind, for I can apply no milder term ... to the general prey of the rich on the poor.

—Thomas Jefferson

In today's world, people tend to think of the class struggle as a thing of the past. They associate it with the industrial revolution of the nineteenth and early twentieth centuries that saw rioting in Europe and bloody factory strikes in the United States. But the class struggle still rages, with little or no violence, clothed in silkier euphemisms and altered by technological evolution. To speak of it is taboo in polite circles. Its cutting edge—the difference in remuneration between the highest income earners and the lowest paid workers—is expressed as the "income gap." According to economist Emmanuel Saez of the University of California, Berkeley, the ratio between them in 2005, the halcyon days of the G.W. Bush presidency, was 440:1, $440 received by the top 300,000 for every $1 scratched out by the bottom half of income earners, about double the 1980 gap when regulation began to loosen its grip on big business in America.[1] David Leonhardt of the *New York Times* reports that the wealthiest income earners have been losing ground since 2005,[2] so the gap has narrowed somewhat.

Nevertheless, the income gap is obscenely out of proportion, and the wealthy class uses its affluence for conspicuous consumption (mansions, penthouses, limousines, yachts. and private jets) and not-so-subtle control of the body politic. The amazing microchip, the tiny device that has revolutionized the production and delivery of goods and services, poses a structural threat to today's workers by energizing machinery that performs functions once dependant on humans—as well as functions never before conceived by humans. The microchip is embedded in the machinery that makes other machines, the robots that run the assembly lines, inventory and delivery systems, communications, transportation, entertainment, science, and just about everything that affects modern human activity, requiring less, if smarter human input.

Bush and other apologists for unregulated free enterprise blame the microchip for the widening income gap, and that is clearly part of it. But if he knew the problem, why didn't he do something about it? He did little or nothing; in fact, his policies made it worse. If the microchip interferes with social well being it must be regulated so that it does not take over Spaceship Earth the way the computer HAL tried to take over the spaceship in the movie "2001, A Space Odyssey." That is, if it causes a widening gap between rich and poor, or structural unemployment, those are problem that must be fixed. Bush failed to regulate them because he is wedded to an anti-regulation, free-market ideology.

It is hard to imagine governance more dedicated than Bush's to the interests of the moneyed class. Operating under the camouflage of another euphemism, supply side economics (really a contrivance for maintaining upper class power), he pushed major tax-cut legislation through Congress that gave the lion's share to the rich and a mere pittance to the poor. He gutted programs designed to help the poor, tried to privatize Social Security, and weakened the financial underpinning of Medicare with a program that lavished billions of taxpayer dollars on private pharmaceutical and insurance companies. He was fighting the class war for sure, on behalf of the upper class.

FOREVER UNEQUAL

Since the early twentieth century, 1 percent of the American population has owned an outsized share of the nation's wealth, ranging from
about 24 percent in 1929 before the stock market crashed to about 9
percent in 1976 in the headiest days of union power and back up to
23.5 percent in 2007 during the G.W. Bush Administration. During
the Great Depression in the 1930s, the Democratic Franklin Roosevelt
Administration introduced New Deal reforms that established Social
Security, instituted strong financial regulation, and enhanced the
power of organized labor while Republicans railed against them. But
from the 1950s on, it did not seem to make much difference in the
income gap whether the Democrats or Republicans were in power. The
wealthiest 1 per cent fared worst toward the end of the Republican
Nixon/Ford administrations in 1976 and best during the Democratic
administration of Bill Clinton in the 1990s and the Republican G.W.
Bush Administration in the 2000s. The dot-com bubble in the 1990s
pumped up elitist wealth, and when the bubble burst toward the end of
Clinton's time in the White House the wealth of the richest declined
somewhat. During the subsequent Bush Administration the top 1
percent's share of the nation's wealth jumped back up based on paper
transactions of no substantive value, known in Wall Street jargon as
"derivatives."

Inescapably and sadly, the figures tell us that income inequality
is here to stay. But it does not have to grow so large. Since 1980, or
about the time supply side economics became popular and deregulation "reforms" began dismantling New Deal financial safeguards, the
rich got richer while the poor remained poor. Most Americans did
not experience the dramatic income growth of the top income earners
during the Reagan, Clinton, and Bush boom times. But a growing body
of evidence shows that the nation would have been better off if they
had. Richard Wilkinson and Kate Pickett, two British epidemiologists, using such straightforward, neutral databanks as the U.S. Census,

United Nations, World Bank, and World Health Organization, argue that in advanced industrial societies greater income equality leads to greater social and physical well being.[3]

Epidemiologists study the incidence and distribution of disease in a population. The wide range of Wilkinson and Pickett's exploration took them beyond what we might normally think of as the field of epidemiology to include social pathologies such as murder, educational achievement or failure, and relationships. Wilkinson and Pickett concluded from their findings that poor nations benefit more from economic growth while rich nations prosper in health and happiness from relative income equality. They show that Japan and the Scandinavian countries, all industrially mature and more equal in the distribution of income, have longer life expectancies and lower infant mortality than the United States, United Kingdom, and Portugal, three nations burdened with higher income inequalities. The more equal countries also have fewer homicides, imprisonments, and teenage births; less mental illness, alcoholism, and drug addiction; even lower rates of female obesity and higher levels of trust. And if American parents want their children to catch up with Japanese children in math and science, Wilkinson and Pickett suggest that they should try making America a more income equal society, like Japan.[4] The findings are so consistent that the two scholars can deduce a country's performance on different social problems from knowledge of its performance on one. "If—for instance—a country does badly on health," they wrote, "you can predict with some confidence that it will also imprison a larger proportion of its population, have more teenage pregnancies, lower literacy scores, more obesity, worse mental health, and so on. Inequality seems to make countries socially dysfunctional across a wide range of outcomes."[5]

If Wilkinson and Pickett are right—and their research is highly credible, public policy should be directed toward shrinking the gap between rich and poor. One way of doing that was in place following the reforms of the Great Depression: progressive taxation (high earners pay a higher rate of taxes) and redistribution of the wealth through social programs. Another technique in the same time frame would empower unions to bargain collectively for wages, benefits and working conditions. Of course, these ideas go directly to the principal flashpoints of American politics. The highest income earners were once taxed at 90 percent during and after World War II. New Deal reforms created Social Security and cleared the way for collective bargaining. President Johnson established Medicare for the elderly and Medicaid for the poor. The "Reagan revolution" is all about reversing these redistribution policies, and has visited upon the nation the curse of greater inequality. Although Democratic President Kennedy started the tax-cut trend, reducing the top rate from 90 percent to 70 percent, Republicans Reagan and G.W. Bush pushed it down even further to where it is now at 35 percent, leaving top income earners with a Midas aura. The onrush of electronics and the corporate outsourcing of jobs for cheap labor abroad have weakened unions and undermined workers. Budget constraints have put Social Security, Medicare, and Medicaid under severe financial stress. Bush policies deepened income inequality. He sought big tax breaks for the rich, pursued an anti-regulation policy, and tried to privatize Social Security. He succeeded in pushing a Medicare prescription drug bill through Congress that diverted billions of taxpayer dollars to private pharmaceutical and insurance companies. Even a politically motivated attempt to increase home ownership for minorities, a wonderful idea, went disastrously bad.

TAX CUTS FOR THE RICH

Like the neocons' urge to wage war on Iraq, the idea of tax cuts was not new with Bush. Democratic President John F. Kennedy, acting on the advice of the economist John Maynard Keynes, first tried it out in the 1960s to grow the economy. Ironically, many Republicans opposed him at the time on grounds that tax cuts would grow the budget deficit. But their opposition was probably as much a knee-jerk reaction that put them in opposition to any new idea proposed by a Democrat. Once the Republicans found out that tax cuts were popular with the American people, however, they took tax cuts as their own.

Republican Ronald Reagan popularized them in the 1980s. Grover Norquist, born and raised in Weston, Massachusetts near Boston with a BA and MBA from Harvard, became in the mid-1980s, and remains more than a quarter century later the chief Knight Templar of the anti-tax crusade. At Reagan's request, he founded the Americans for Tax Reform in 1985. ATR is most notable for two things, first, weekly Wednesday meetings chaired by Norquist and attended by more than a hundred conservative activists and elected officials to discuss and strategize conservative projects, and, second, an anti-tax pledge that almost all Republican and a few Democratic federal officeholders or office seekers are asked, sometimes coaxed, sometimes hectored to sign. The "Taxpayer Protection Pledge" exacts two promises, to "ONE, oppose any and all efforts to increase the marginal income tax rates for individuals and/or businesses, and TWO, oppose any net reduction or elimination of deductions and credits, unless matched dollar for dollar by further reducing tax rates."

In the 1986 non-presidential campaign, the first year the pledge was offered, Norquist reveals in his 2008 book, *Leave Us Alone*, that it gained 120 signatures from House and Senate candidates for election or re-election. In 1988 every major Republican candidate for president, except Bob Dole, pledged not to raise taxes. Vice President George H.W. Bush did not actually sign "the pledge," but promised in a separate letter to honor it. As president, he broke the promise and agreed in a compromise with Democratic leaders to raise taxes. That cost him substantial support within his own party, and he lost his bid for reelection in 1992. In 2007 all Republican members of Congress had signed the pledge, except seven in the Senate and eight in the House. Five Democrats also signed it, one in the Senate and four in the House. Any Republican signer who goes back on the pledge, Norquist considers to be "a rat head in a coke bottle," his gross image to describe anyone who would besmirch the noble Republican brand name.[6]

The federal debt, growing at near warp speed—to put it facetiously, is a threat to the nation's financial well being. The growth in the debt is best constrained by economic development to create jobs and thus more taxpayers. Other options are raising taxes and/or cutting back on programs. Democrats usually prefer higher taxes; Republicans want smaller government. The pledge to hold the line on taxes counters the option to reduce the budget gap by increasing taxes. For a politician to sign and honor the pledge is to forfeit his/her ability to compromise. To go back on it is to incur the wrath of Grover Norquist and earn his nasty sobriquet of a rat head in a coke bottle. What really strikes fear in the hearts of Republicans who renege on the tax pledge is the prospect of defeat in the next election. The pledge gained a measure of prominence in a clash between the two parties when the federal debt approached its legal limit during the Obama administration. In the past, as the debt grew Congress had always routinely raised the limit to avoid default, but this time hard core Tea Party conservatives who had gained control of the House Republican caucus chose to hold the debt ceiling hostage to spending cuts. This interesting confrontation is covered in the final chapter.

Although Norquist wrote his screed, *Leave Us Alone*, before Wilkinson and Pickett published their findings in *The Spirit Level*, he is indisputably at odds with the notion of income equality. He is a flat-tax advocate, comfortable with wealth for the privileged few. His first step to tax reform is abolition of the inheritance tax (death tax, he calls it), which he condemns as "discrimination based on wealth." Those on the left who push the "death tax," he warns, are "playing on the politics of hate and envy and class division" and following "the morality that could justify the Holocaust."[7] (Now that's a stretch.) Anyone who wants to strive in the public arena for greater income equality as a social benefit will find Norquist blocking the way, armed with rhetorical thunderbolts and dangerous in political debate.

By the time Republican G.W. Bush arrived on the scene, tax cuts loomed large as a conservative article of faith. Bush vowed not to make his father's mistake of retreating on his "no new taxes" pledge. He would go, in fact, in the opposite direction, cutting taxes with a vengeance even as his expressed rationale kept shifting. As Democrat Bill Clinton prepared to vacate the White House, he proudly announced that he was leaving behind a budget surplus of $236 billion. During the campaign of 2000 Bush promised to cut taxes because, he said, the surplus was the people's money and if he did not give it back, the government would simply spend it on new programs. His conservative base loved the rhetoric. It fit their goal of limiting the power of government. But as Bush took office, the dot-com bubble was running out of air to keep it afloat. He turned on a dime to embrace a rationale more acceptable to the broader electorate. Now, he said, the tax cut would stimulate the economy. In other words, for any available reason there would be a tax cut. Within five months, he wiped out the Clinton surplus in a single stroke with a $1.35 trillion tax cut that heavily benefitted the richest 1 percent of the population.

One other thing Bush promised was a broad-based tax cut that would apply to everybody. That was true on the face of it, but conditions were somewhat like George Orwell's famous allegory, *Animal Farm*, after the animals drove Farmer Jones off his land for his drunken, dictatorial treatment of them. In the immediate aftermath of the rebellion, the animal leaders issued "commandments," one of which read, "All animals are equal." After the pigs took control of the farm—they are said to be the smartest of farm animals—they began to look and act human. They even walked around on two legs and engaged in conspicuous consumption. The commandment on equality was revised to read, "All animals are equal, but some animals are more equal than others." In the same way, the Bush tax cuts benefitted all taxpayers, but they benefitted a few wealthy taxpayers a lot more than most. A sign in Bush's Oval Office should have been put up to read, "All taxpayers are equal, but some taxpayers are more equal than others."

Supporters of the 2001 measure saw it as an economic elixir that would do all things for all people. It would create jobs, they claimed, while increasing, not lowering revenues pouring into federal coffers. The conservative Heritage Foundation, using what it called a "dynamic simulation" of the initial 2001 proposals, predicted that in ten years the bill would increase the annual disposable income of an average family of four by $4,544 and effectively pay off the national debt. It would allegedly save Social Security, and accumulate a surplus that could be used to reform Medicare, eventually reducing the payroll tax.[8] It was their vision of heaven on earth. Hallelujah! Within a few years, the vision had gone to hell.

Citizens for Tax Justice, a non-partisan group that conservatives denigrate as liberal, did a study of the Bush tax cuts showing that the wealthiest 1 percent of Americans received a total of $477 billion in income tax breaks, or on average, $347,000 each over the first decade of the twenty-first century. These cuts were phased in annually and did not take full effect until later in the decade. By the end of the decade, 52 percent of total tax reductions went to the top 1 percent of money-makers. Their average annual income was $1.5 million and their average annual tax break, $85,000, more than what the majority of families earned in a year. In stark contrast, the 80 percent who earn less than $73,000 a year gained an average tax break of only $350 in 2002. For many, if not most of them, what they received that year was their full tax reduction from the 2001 legislation.[9]

THE SLEAZY SALES PITCH

The lead-up to the 2001 bill's enactment entailed a garden variety of campaign tactics: exaggeration, subterfuge, half truths and lofty unful-filled promises. The president went on a five-state tour to promote his plan, similar to the campaign he had waged a year earlier in his bid for the presidency. He promoted the tax cut as all-inclusive, benefiting every taxpayer from poorest to wealthiest; he masked its heavy tilt to the rich; he said it would create jobs; he argued that lower taxes would increase revenues by creating jobs and close any feared budget deficit. He offered the best of all worlds, all things to all people—and he sold it.

The Bush team played fast and loose with the truth all through the tax debates in 2001 and 2003. They understated the benefits to the wealthiest by phasing in their huge tax breaks annually and inserting a "sunset" provision that would terminate the entire tax package after ten years. They also overstated the extent to which the tax cuts would cover the budget gap by assuming for the sake of expediency that the AMT (Alternative Minimum Tax) would cover tens of thousands more in the decade ahead, and thus provide revenues needed to cover any budget gaps. The AMT had been enacted in 1969 during the Nixon administration to make certain that the wealthiest taxpayers—the high rollers who knew how to beat the system with exemptions and write-offs— would pay at least some tax. In addition to individuals, it also covered corporations, estates, and trusts. Because the AMT was not adjusted for inflation, the law as it stood was expected to cover tens of thousands more individuals with growing incomes in the decade ahead. But after Congress approved the Bush tax cuts, it fixed the AMT to placate those tens of thousands of threatened taxpayers (who were also voters)—and left a gaping hole in the budget.[10] FactCheck.org, sponsored by the Annenberg Public Policy Center, took Bush to task for exaggerating the giveback of the 2003 tax cuts. The White House reported "average" tax cuts of $1,586. But the administration was far off the mark. FactCheck.org revealed that half of the taxpayers would receive less than $450, and half would receive more. "The 'average'," FactCheck.org pointed out, "is misleading because it is inflated by very large cuts given to a relative few at the top."[11]

In the lead-up to the 2003 tax bill, the sleazy campaign tactics seemed to intensify. Tax analyst Martin A. Sullivan decried the decline of "tax distribution analysis" (the breakdown of who benefitted by how much from the tax cuts), a highly technical but crucial line of inquiry.

Sullivan, writing in the blog, *Tax Notes*, in 2003, trained his rhetorical guns on the Treasury Department's Office of Tax Policy (OTP), which was politicized by Bush loyalists. By 2002, Pamela F. Olson, a financial expert who had worked on the Bush campaign, was running the OTP. (After her stint in government, she went back through the revolving door to head the Washington Office of the well connected firm, Skaddam, Arps, Slate, Meagher, & Flom, from which she had entered.) Tax bills are so complex that they can be distorted simply by an omitted word. In the text of case studies submitted to the news media and passed off as examples of fair and unbiased Bush tax legislation, OTP analyzed the "income tax" distribution contained in the bill without using the word "income," making the income tax appear to be the entire range of taxes. To put it that way made the analysis seem relatively fair to the working poor, but if one were to include the regressive payroll tax that funds Social Security and part of Medicare and is assessed on all working taxpayers, the analysis would show a heavy tax bias against low income earners. So subtle was the deception, said Sullivan, that the distinction was made clear in detailed charts that would be difficult for inexpert newsmen to pick up. Sullivan described this "income tax only" approach as "an egregious use of misinformation." He suggested that to reflect reality while keeping its OTP acronym "the Office of Tax Policy may have to change its name to the Office of Tax Propaganda."[12]

Economic Impact

Conservatives insist that tax cuts create jobs, although the real impact of tax cuts on the economy remains uncertain. The claim comes out of their mouths like a mantra from religious monks. (Tax cuts create jobs—mmmmmmmmmmmmmmmmm.) To speak facetiously, the idea probably started as a talking point created somewhere in the Republican hierarchy for party acolytes to recite in public statements, and repeated so often that they began believing their echo. Republican House Speaker John Boehner was careless about the facts when he said on the NBC "Today" program of May 10, 2011, that the Bush tax cuts created eight million jobs in ten years and that the nation lost five million jobs during the recession that began in 2008. By the time Boehner uttered that statement, Obama had been in power more than two years, so by implication Obama, not Bush, was responsible for the slump in jobs. ("Bush—go-o-o-o-d; Obama—no go-o-o-o-d.") This is a common example of fact-distortion practiced by accomplished politicians.

Confusion arises in the Boehner comment from the fact that the recession was in full swing during three-and-a-half of those ten years, including the final year of the Bush presidency. *PolitiFact.com* checked it out, giving Boehner every possible latitude, and found that in the six-and-a-half years between June 2001 when Bush signed his first tax bill and January 2008 when the recession officially began, the nation gained nearly six million jobs as measured by the Bureau of Labor Statistics under its most commonly used job survey, Current Employment Statistics. Under a different BLS yardstick, Current Population Survey, the gain was about 9.5 million jobs over the same time period. So it would seem that Boehner was close to the mark on one key job count. But considered in isolation, neither of these figures means anything because when compared to other two-term presidencies of recent history, they actually reflect negatively on Bush's accomplishments in job creation. Other two-term presidencies, including Clinton, Reagan, Nixon-Ford, and Kennedy-Johnson all had stronger job growth during their two terms.[13]

Comparing job growth in the G.W. Bush and Clinton presidencies is particularly striking. Ten months earlier, *PolitiFact.com* had done a check on a statement by Democratic Senator Sherrod Brown of Ohio that job growth was 22 million in the Clinton years and only 3 million in the Bush years. *PolitiFact.com* learned that the numbers were even worse for Bush. This time taking the full eight years of the two Bush terms (including that final year during the Great Recession) and using the same survey for both presidencies, it found that job growth was 22.7 million for Clinton and 1.1 million for Bush. Furthermore, *PolitiFact.com* confirmed Brown's claim that workers' incomes rose dramatically more during Clinton's time in office than in Bush's two terms—21 percent for Clinton and only 2 percent for Bush. What makes this comparison so interesting is Clinton's tax policy. In 1993 he actually raised taxes for 1.2 million of the wealthiest taxpayers while cutting taxes for small business and low income families. Clinton's eight years saw one of the longest periods of sustained economic growth in American history, and he produced the aforementioned budget surplus before he left office.

So what do tax cuts have to do with job growth? There is no clear answer. Sure, economic growth reached nearly 5 percent per year during the 1960s, but the growth had already started before the Kennedy tax cuts were enacted in 1964 after Kennedy's death. Sure, government revenues doubled in the 1980s after Reagan tax cuts in 1981, but they quintupled in the 1940s during and after World War II, more than doubled in the 1950s, 1960s, and 1970s, and nearly doubled in the 1990s after Clinton raised taxes.[14] One must take into account other economic factors, such as new technology, military procurement, construction activity, business cycles, etc., and that leaves tax cuts swirling in a slew of particulars. Clinton got a boost from the dot-com bubble. Bush was blown away by the Great Recession, which many would say was at least partly of his own making.

After Clinton raised taxes for the wealthiest, the economy took off. After Bush restored tax cuts for the highest taxpayer bracket, the economy slowed. Contrary to conservative predictions that the Bush tax cuts would launch new economic growth, income was lower at the peak of the next business cycle than at the peak of the previous one. "It is rare," said reporter Jonathan Chait writing in the *New Republic* in 2010, "that events so utterly repudiate an economic theory. None of this evidence has penetrated the conservative mind to the slightest degree."[15]

It can be logically argued that tax cuts stimulate economic growth and thereby increase government revenues, just as government programs do—the difference being that tax cuts produce the stimulation from the private sector, and the programs are stimulated by government. In either case, there is risk that the stimulation will not take hold. As noted, conservatives abhor big government, and love private business, big and small. They also love to run on the tax-cut issue. But in the absence of clear supporting evidence and in the presence of many conflicting factors, the tax-cut argument is speculative. It is equally uncertain what the optimal tax rates should be for particular income earners. If they are too high they might discourage growth; too low, and the government would be missing out on revenues needed to balance the budget. On that point, there is room for endless debate in Congress in the mode of the fraternity food fight depicted in National Lampoon's "Animal House."

In the case of Clinton's budget surplus, the fight has raged over whether credit should go to the Omnibus Budget Reconciliation Act of 1993 enacted by a Democratic Congress without a single Republican vote or the 1997 companion bills, the Tax Relief and Balanced Budget Acts, when Republicans controlled Congress. The Democratic 1993 bill included a tax hike for the richest 2 percent of taxpayers while the combined Republican 1997 bills contained tax cuts that primarily benefited families with children (and the super-rich, only modestly). According to the Congressional Budget Office, the 1997 tax cuts were about half the size of the 1993 tax increase. After passage of the 1993 bill, the budget deficit narrowed from $310 billion in 1993 to about $180 billion in 1997.[16] The surplus first appeared in 1998 and lasted until 2002 when Bush buried it in a tax cut binge that overwhelmed the budget. That left uncertainty about the effectiveness of tax cuts and plenty of pabulum on both sides for the political food fight.

CUTS AND CONSEQUENCE

The tax cuts were dearly bought with reductions in services as the Bush White House discovered that cutting back the federal budget is easier said than done. In 2004 the Bush White House projected a budget deficit of $521 billion for that fiscal year and $364 billion for the following year. After having achieved tax cuts of $1.35 trillion in 2001 and $350 billion in 2003, it was proposing a negligible saving of $4.9 billion by eliminating 65 government programs and cutting back on 63 others. The projected cuts were for education, the environment, poverty programs, and federal law enforcement services, all of them consistent with conservative goals to weaken the power of the federal government.[17]

Many of these programs had been on the Bush hit list from the day he entered office. One target touched a nerve with some Southern and Midwestern conservatives who worried about devastation in their districts from Mississippi River flooding. In the past, Congress had made sure that the Army Corps of Engineers got everything it needed for flood control, plus hoppers full of "perks" it did not need. But the Bush cuts in the Corps' budget that came to more than half a billion dollars penetrated so deep that they drew blood. Missouri Republican Congresswoman Jo Ann Emerson warned that "lives very likely would be lost."

On the day that Bush signed the 2001 tax bill, he appointed a solid conservative, former Republican Congressman and gubernatorial candidate from Mississippi Mike Parker to head the Corps. As Parker settled in, he was shocked at the extent to which the Corps' budget had been slashed. He asked that enough funding be restored to allow it to carry out its responsibilities. No dice! In testimony on Capitol Hill in February 2002, Parker was asked if the cuts would hinder the Corps in its work. His honest answer was yes. A few days later, the White House fired him. (How dare he tell the truth?)

The day of reckoning for the cuts in the Corps' budget came on August 29, 2005 when Hurricane Katrina struck the Gulf coast. The storm took more than a thousand lives in four states and inundated 80 percent of New Orleans with water as deep as fifteen feet in some areas of the city. The worst flooding occurred where the Corps' levees broke.

A number of experts, including Parker, said the city's flooding would not have been so bad if the funding had been available to strengthen the levees.[18] An independent report funded by the National Science Foundation cited flaws in design, construction, and maintenance. "People died because mistakes were made," said Albert Seed of the University of California, Berkeley, the chief author of the report, "and because safety was exchanged for efficiency and reduced cost."[19] Bush along with local Democratic officials took some well deserved heat over the failings of relief services. All but invisible in the flood's awful devastation, however, was the mindless penny-pinching that accompanied the Bush tax cuts.

Many voters remained unaware of or indifferent to the Bush deceptions and the damage done by the tax cuts. The safety net in the form of Social Security, Medicare, unemployment compensation, etc., that remained essentially intact, helped to calm the aggrieved masses. So did the distractions available from television and the internet—neither of which existed in the 1930s—that brought the arts, entertainment, hobbies, and the endless cycles of political and athletic competition into the living room. In a curious way, even war contributed to the social quietude. World War II, an all-out conflict that captured everybody's attention, pulled America out of the Great Depression. In the new century, two small wars in far-off Iraq and Afghanistan were fought by a relatively small military force while much of America, with due deference to the sacrifices of the troops, seemed to regard the wars as just another distraction. When war broke out after the 9/11/01 terrorist attack on America, the commander-in-chief of the armed forces, President Bush, advised Americans to go shopping. The damage Bush policies did to the middle class was buried in the deluge of issues, information, and trivia streaming from the media.

Thus, the struggle of working people was not nearly as raw in early twenty-first century America as it was in the chaotic worlds of the mid-nineteenth century and the Depression years of the 1930s. Workers who once stoked fires in the steel mills or fitted parts on the auto assembly line found in the new century that many of the jobs had disappeared, replaced to a substantial degree by robots that don't ask for high wages or health and retirement benefits. Their unions, weakened by technological change and foreign competition, have not saved the self-styled middle class from layoffs catastrophic to many families.

In the modern economy, decent factory jobs are hard to come by. Those available reflect the evolution of the microchip and require a higher educational background than previously needed. Nonmanufacturing jobs like flipping hamburgers or manning checkout counters are at the lower end of the pay scale and short on benefits. Families that once rode the wave of American prosperity struggle to put food on the table and keep up the mortgage payments. At the other end of the spectrum, the wealthiest families are doing just fine. The gap between rich and poor grows wider. Oh, and one other thing, people over sixty-five have done well, too. Most of them are on Social Security, which the conservatives want to privatize. The fat cats are fatter than ever, and many of them use their wealth to keep the gap from shrinking by lobbying the government, buying influence, and putting themselves up for elective office. The United States has made great strides in realizing racial and gender equality after years of enlightened leadership, bitter struggle, greater communication, soul-trying patience, and drawn-out conflict in a noble American context of simple fairness. The struggle for greater income equality, even just a better awareness of its benefits, will be much more difficult to achieve.

Chapter 7

Poison Politics, Poisoned Environment

The Fault is great in man or woman
Who steals a goose from off a common;
But what can plead that man's excuse
Who steals a common from a goose?

—Anonymous

WINSTON SMITH LIVED IN LONDON, the capital city of Oceania, and worked for the government in the Ministry of Truth. His job was to revise history by tying it to the philosophy of the party. To perform at a high level, he needed to practice *doublethink*, defined by George Orwell as "the power of holding two contradictory beliefs in one's mind simultaneously, and accepting both of them."[1] In Winston Smith's world, "truth" was reconciled with the party line by fixing history. It would be a stretch to link the presidency of George W. Bush with any characteristics of the regime created by Orwell in *Nineteen Eighty-Four*, his classic novel of a police state perpetuated by lies and foreign wars. Or would it?

Two decades later in real life, Philip A. Cooney held the position of chief of staff for the President's Council on Environmental Quality (CEQ). The name itself—Council on Environmental Quality—had a certain Orwellian ring. It sounded environmentally friendly, but it functioned to discredit climate science. A lawyer with a bachelor's degree in economics and no background in science, Cooney had come over to the Bush White House early in 2001 from the American Petroleum Institute (API), the oil industry's chief lobbying arm. In his last position at API he strove to bring about government actions on global warming consistent with oil industry objectives. He adhered to a 1998 API internal "Communications Action Plan," with a clearly defined mission that played out like a worm eating the apple from the inside. "Victory," the action plan declared, "will be achieved when ... average citizens understand uncertainties in climate science ... [and] recognition of uncertainties becomes part of the 'conventional wisdom.'"[2] The strategy worked particularly well on the right side of the political spectrum—especially when the propaganda came with campaign donations.

Scientific uncertainty is a familiar polluter's ploy. The tobacco industry used it successfully for sixty years to keep regulators at bay by citing a lack of conclusive proof that tobacco caused cancer while smokers— including David McLean, an actor who portrayed the iconic cowboy, Marlboro Man, in television commercials—continued to die painful deaths.[3] When Cooney went to work for the Bush Administration, he did the same job he had done at API in a new location, and according to the House Committee on Oversight and Government Reform (Rep. Henry A. Waxman, chairman), "The Bush Administration ... acted as if the oil industry's communications plan were [the CEQ's] mission statement."[4] So in a manner similar to that of Orwell's Winston Smith, Bush's Philip Cooney reconciled truth with the party line by fixing— or perhaps, unfixing—the science. (America, like Oceana, was even fighting wars in far-off lands.)

Mum's the Word on Global Warming

Cooney's job in the White House well served the petroleum industry whose product was a major polluter of carbon dioxide (CO_2).

Most climate scientists agree that CO_2 creates a canopy in the upper atmosphere that traps the sun's heat close to the earth, causing global warming, extreme weather, and rising ocean levels over time. His placement at CEQ repeated the old story of the fox guarding the hen house. What a cozy spot, mutually beneficial for the industry to achieve "victory" and for the White House to earn the industry's campaign contributions. According to the Center for Responsive Politics at OpenSecrets.org, the oil and gas industry contributed 238.7 million to candidates in the two decades from 1990 to 2010, 75 percent of which went to Republicans.[5]

For four years Cooney worked under the radar, directly accountable to Vice President Cheney, the former CEO of the oil services company, Halliburton. And while Cooney was a big-time player, he was not alone by any stretch of the imagination. Some edits by him and his staff were small, but they pointedly softened the impact of climate science reports and diminished the human role in global warming. For example, in drafts of a government document entitled, "A Strategic Plan for the Climate Change Science Program," he substituted "may" in place of "will," so that a sentence finally read "...may cause" warming in the Arctic; added "potentially" to a sentence that connected warming to certain biological degradations, and in a sentence linking global warming to human activity, changed "demonstrated" to "indicated," and inserted "likely" to modify "consistent with a significant contribution from human activity." Altogether, Cooney and his staff made nearly 300 edits in the "Strategic Plan."[6] But Cooney had a wider purview in Bush's quest for political correctness on global warming. The White House Office of Management and Budget (OMB) as well as the Commerce Department and party loyalists in other agencies also kept their eyes trained on suspect scientists to make sure they toed the line on climate issues. CEQ operated as a kind of clearing house, moving government documents and scientific testimony around the network to see that ideological purity softened climate science.

Media requests for interviews at environment-related agencies were routinely routed through the CEQ, which decided who could or could not speak for the administration. For example, CEQ blocked a request from National Public Radio for an interview with Dr. James Hansen, director of NASA's Goddard Institute for Space Studies.[7] Hansen was an established climatologist with a penchant for independent thinking. He frequently spoke out about global warming's dangers to the planet, always emphasizing that the views expressed contradicting Bush administration policy were his and not the agency's, a moderately damaging acknowledgement for the Bush hard liners.

On the other hand, Dr. James R. Mahoney, assistant Secretary of Commerce for Oceans and Atmosphere, was approved for media contact. Bush had appointed Mahoney as director of the Climate Change Science Program (CCSP), created in 2002. The term "climate change" was the administration's preferred euphemism for "global warming" (recommended by Republican pollster Frank Lutz[8]), and to study the phenomenon re-enforced uncertainty about its human connection, something the petroleum institute could accept as victory. Mahoney was fluent in the language of bureaucracy, a realm of fuzzy policy-related expressions. In testimony before a Senate subcommittee in July 2005, he spoke of "climate variations and change" without mentioning "global warming."[9] When the *New York Times,* requested an interview a month later, CEQ approved but asked the NOAA public information office for a written summary.[10]

When in October 2005, the CNBC program, "On the Money," requested an interview with Dr, Thomas R. Knutson, a top National Oceanic and Atmospheric Administration (NOAA) scientist, on the question of whether global warming was causing greater hurricane frequency and intensity, it provoked a lively exchange of memos within Bush's censorship network. Knutson, who had recently completed a study of that very problem, thought the impact was subtle and long term, not quite what the Bushies wanted to hear. Two other scientists who believed there was no such linkage would have been preferable, but they were tied up on other projects. So CEQ rebuffed CNBC with the excuse that Knutson was too busy in the aftermath of Hurricane Katrina.[11]

The Bush censors routinely altered testimony before Congress. Julie Gerberding, director of the Centers for Disease Control and Prevention, said she was "absolutely happy" to deliver her edited statements.[12] They also revised the testimony of Dr. Thomas Karl, director of NOAA's National Climatic Data Center before the Waxman Committee. In a sentence that read, "...modern climate change is dominated by human influences," the word "dominated" was softened with "affected." Another sentence, "...[W]e are venturing into the unknown territory with changes in climate, and its associated effects," was deleted because it begged hard questioning.[13] On and on it went. Big Brother kept a sharp eye on its non-conforming scientists. In the first three years of the George W. Bush Administration, the White House "altered, suppressed, or attempted to discredit close to a dozen major reports" on global warming.[14] The Union of Concerned Scientists reported at least 435 incidents of political interference with the work of 150 government climate scientists over a five-year period from 2002 to 2007.[15]

Cooney met his waterloo in 2005. Rick S. Piltz, a scientist who had resigned from his job studying climate change for the Environmental Protection Agency (EPA), got fed up with Cooney's political censorship and blew the whistle on him. Piltz expressed his frustration with having an industry lobbyist with White House authority "intervening in scientifically based communication." Cooney's editing, wrote Piltz in 2008, "had the effect of introducing an exaggerated sense of fundamental scientific uncertainty about human-driven climate change, about which there was no fundamental uncertainty in the science community."[16] Piltz reached out to the *New York Times* through the Government Accountability Project, which provides legal assistance for government whistle blowers. He delivered testimony and documentation of Cooney's handiwork, which the *Times* published on June 8, 2005 in an article by Andrew C. Revkin. Cooney resigned from the CEQ a few days later. But it was not a personal tragedy for Cooney and his family. ExxonMobil, the prodigious oil industry enabler of CO_2 emissions, soon hired him.

ENVIRONMENTAL DECEPTION MINISTRY

The "Environmental Protection Agency" in the Bush presidency was perfect Orwellspeak. It belied Bush's performance that imperiled, not protected the environment. Of all the government agencies in Washington, this is where liberal and conservative hot wires most often touch and sparks fly. Liberal Democrats see it as nature's caretaker against man-made pollution. Conservative Republicans argue that narrow minded EPA bureaucrats make "job-killing" regulations that stifle economic growth. It appears that the twain shall never meet without flying sparks. So it remains no small irony that a Republican president, Richard Nixon, joined in creating the EPA in 1970.

Bush appointed Christine Todd Whitman, a former governor of New Jersey, considered a center-right politician, as his first EPA secretary. No one could reasonably call her a liberal, but her pro-choice position on abortion and support of gay rights set her apart on social issues from the Republican radical right. When governor of New Jersey she had also enhanced her soft image by joining other northeastern states in a lawsuit against American Electric Power of Ohio to retrofit its old coal-burning plants with pollution-control technology. But generally, on matters related to the environment and economy, as a privileged daughter of the conservative gentry she was decidedly pro-business. Her record as governor of New Jersey was far from environment friendly. She created a conflicts resolution agency to help businesses get around state regulations. She weakened enforcement by cutting thirty percent out of the environmental budget. As a result, 738 employees of the state Department of Environmental Protection (DEP) lost their jobs, while the rest were cut back to a four-day week.[17] Laura Flanders, author of *Bushwomen*, called Whitman "an attractive shill, a lure for liberals and moderates."[18] A 1997 survey of DEP employees testified to a long list of complaints about lax enforcement, excessive corporate influence, and manipulation of scientific findings when Whitman ran the state bureaucracy. "Cozy accommodation of corporate violators appears to be her regulatory style," said Jeff Ruch, executive director of the watchdog group, Public Employees for Environmental Responsibility (PEER), which conducted the survey.[19]

So Whitman appeared to be a perfect fit as Bush's first administrator of the EPA—tough on environmentalists, easy on corporate polluters. But within two months Bush undercut her authority in what seemed to be a clash between her and the party's far right over America's participation in the Kyoto Protocol, an international agreement to control global warming. During the 2000 campaign, Bush had singled out global warming as a serious problem and promised to cap CO_2 emissions. One of his first acts as President was to renege on his promise. He did so in a way that humiliated Whitman. Taking Bush at his pre-election word, she had started her stewardship of the EPA advocating the regulation of CO_2 emissions. This set off alarm bells on the far right, which wanted to avoid control measures that would eat into corporate profits. Four Senators with strong ties to major industrial polluters sent a letter to the president complaining about Whitman's public statements and demanding clarification of the President's policy on climate change. Whitman suspected that Vice President Cheney instigated the letter, if he did not actually write it. She asked to see the President and was granted an audience, but before she could speak her piece, Bush told her he had already made his decision and read her parts of a letter in response to the senators, saying that the U.S. would oppose Kyoto as unfair and ineffective, in large part because it exempted China and India.[20]

Without the President's backing, Whitman had lost the effectiveness she should have possessed as EPA administrator. In the twenty-eight tumultuous months of her tenure, she encountered one crisis after another trying to align environmental science with the politics of the Bush White House. She was okay with the White House policy of protecting the interests of industry polluters, but at odds with the career government employees who worked under her. She began by suspending a tough Clinton Administration rule that limited arsenic in water, put there largely by mining operations. A pair of granny characters had given arsenic a comical edge in the hit play, "Arsenic and Old Lace." But arsenic in public drinking water is no joke. A national uproar followed Whitman's decision. That, together with confirmation from further scientific inquiries, persuaded her to quietly reinstate the Clinton rule while the nation's attention was focused on the 9/11 terrorist attack. She acknowledged that she had made a political mistake. "I should have just let it go and allowed the courts to decide," she said.[21]

The cloud of toxic air at ground zero where the World Trade Center once stood obscured more than the arsenic controversy. Whitman and the White House managed to obfuscate the facts about the toxicity of the air. Two days after the terrorist attack, Whitman, prodded by the White House, declared the air safe. Two years later, the EPA inspector general, putting it gently, concluded that data and analyses were not sufficient at the time to support Whitman's statement. The inspector general reported that CEQ had edited EPA press releases in a three- to four-week period after 9/11 by adding words of reassurance and removing cautionary statements that might be considered alarming. The report was signed by Nikki L. Tinsley, but that was two years after the fact. In a September 13, 2001 press release the White House censors put words in Whitman's mouth, "EPA," she was quoted as saying, "is greatly relieved to have learned that there appears to be no significant levels of asbestos in the air in New York City." The edited EPA draft had not quoted Whitman directly and had cautioned, "... even at low levels, EPA considers asbestos hazardous..." CEQ deleted the warning.[22] Considering the inherent dangers to public health, the CEQ's actions seem criminal, but while the spread of toxic air generated protests, investigations, and civil lawsuits, there was no criminal investigation.

Big Brother's fingerprints also showed up on a September 16 EPA press release. The original EPA draft reported, "Recent samples of dust gathered by OSHA [the Labor Department's Occupational Safety and Health Agency] on Water Street show higher levels of asbestos in EPA tests." When CEQ was done with it, the statement came out grossly distorted, "The new samples confirm previous reports that ambient air quality meets OSHA standards and consequently is not a cause for public concern.... EPA continue [sic] to believe that there is not significant health risk to the general public in the coming days."[23] That suggested safety in the near term, and ignored the danger of ongoing, long-term exposure, of which there was much. In February 2006, Federal Judge Deborah A. Batts found Whitman guilty of making "conscience-shocking," post-9/11 statements that may have put the public in danger. The finding allowed a class action lawsuit that had been filed in 2004 on behalf of residents and school children in Lower Manhattan and Brooklyn to go forward against Whitman and the EPA.[24]

Whitman family ties to Citigroup, the parent company of Travelers Insurance Group, and the family's possession of Port Authority of New York and New Jersey bonds gave an appearance of conflict of interest in her post-9/11 role. Whitman had declared in disclosure documents filed when she took office that she and her husband, John, owned $100,000 to $250,000 worth of stock in Citigroup and $15,000 to $50,000 in Port Authority bonds. Travelers was liable for medical insurance claims of 9/11 victims and the Port Authority owned the World Trade Center. Her husband had worked for the bank from 1972 to 1987 and later formed a venture capital firm, Sycamore Ventures, spun out of Citicorp Ventures, Ltd. Citigroup was a major investor in Sycamore and paid a six-figure bonus to John Whitman as recently as 2000.[25] To avoid the suspicion of conflict of interest given her family's financial investments, she should have abstained from official involvement in the 9/11 tragedy.

Asbestos, a well known carcinogen, was not the only toxic material to hover over lower Manhattan after 9/11. The air also contained a witches brew of lead, cadmium, glass fibers, concrete dust, PCBs (polychlorinated biphenyls), and dioxin, among many other poisons—some of them from the collapse of the twin towers and some from the smoldering ruins that burned for months afterward. The toxins penetrated inside nearby offices, schools and residences.[26] A screening program conducted by New York's Mount Sinai Medical Center found that nearly 70 percent of 10,000 ground zero rescue and demolition workers treated at Mount Sinai suffered symptoms of respiratory illness. Those who arrived at ground zero within a day or two of the attack were most severely affected. "Our patients are sick," said Robin Herbert, a co-director of the screening program, "and they will need ongoing care for the rest of their lives."[27] As of June 2010, the New York State Department of Health had confirmed 836 deaths from all causes of individual rescue and recovery workers at ground zero, and was conducting further studies to determine specific causes of death.[28] After an exhaustive study using a variety of complex data, the state agency issued a final report on September 19. 2011 that could not shed further light on the extent to which conditions at ground zero contributed to responder fatalities.[29]

The perils of Christine continued as Whitman seemed to fall tightly in line with the thinking of the White House ideologues. For one thing, she compromised the cleanup of highly toxic superfund sites, a move that benefitted the administration's corporate friends. At a nuclear waste dump in a Denver working class neighborhood early in 2002, she limited Citigroup's liability in the cleanup to $7.2 million, a fraction of its cost variously estimated at $22 million (EPA's lowest estimate) to $100 million (an independent outside estimate). Taxpayers would make up the difference, whatever it turned out to be.

EPA ombudsman Robert J. Martin, a thorn in the side of the EPA for nearly a decade, challenged the Citigroup settlement, whereupon Whitman ordered that his independent ombudsman's office and investigative files be transferred to the inspector general's jurisdiction, thus emasculating the ombudsman's independent authority. Martin resigned, and together with his chief investigator, Hugh Kaufman, filed suit in federal court to block Whitman's order, charging conflict of interest involving her family ties to Citigroup.[30] Kaufman had been making waves at EPA twice as long as Martin. They were engaged at the time reviewing EPA performance at about two dozen superfund sites around the country—among them a chemical dump at Anniston, Alabama where findings against the giant chemical company Monsanto were altered in Monsanto's favor days after Whitman received a forty-five minute briefing in the case. Whitman's action saved Monsanto millions of dollars.[31]

The Clear Skies Initiative was another Orwellian invention of the Bush Administration meant to undermine environmental regulation. The stronger Clean Air Act already existed, so the real purpose of "Clear Skies" was to besmog "Clean Air." Clear Skies was a market-based, cap-and-trade, voluntary program; Clean Air was direct government regulation. Significantly, CEQ, not the EPA, drew up Clear Skies. CEQ Chairman James L. Connaughton, its chief author and Cooney's boss, formerly worked as a lobbyist for the asbestos industry. His preparations for Clear Skies were cloaked in a veil of secrecy and deceit that hung over the Bush White House on many policy matters, including energy and environmentalism.

President Bush announced the initiative in February 2002 as a method for controlling power plant emissions such as sulfur dioxide, nitric oxides, mercury, and particulate matter, but not carbon dioxide, the major cause of global warming. The sulfur and nitrous oxides from Midwest power plants combine with water vapor in the atmosphere to form acids, and drop as acid rain in the northeast. High levels of mercury emitted in coal vapors induce brain disorders in fetuses. Particulates cause asthma in children and chronic bronchitis in adults. The cap-and-trade feature would set emission goals and require permits for each ton of pollution emitted that could be traded, creating, according to its supporters, financial incentives to cut back on pollutants without the need for expensive lawsuits to enforce regulations. Critics opposed it precisely because it weakened hard and fast anti-pollution standards that were never adequately enforced.

As Whitman neared the end of her time in office, she dutifully followed the lead from CEQ. She testified on Capitol Hill in February 2003 that Clear Skies would substantially reduce emissions of the three most powerful pollutants from power generation faster and more efficiently than the Clean Air regulations. That could not have been true because new emission standards—the quantity of pollution allowed— had not yet been established. In any case, her testimony did not have a decisive impact. The bill lingered in Congress for two years of bitter debate and then died in the Senate. Two New England Senators, Lincoln Chaffee, Republican of Rhode Island, and James Jeffords, an Independent and former Republican from Vermont, joined seven Democrats to block passage out of committee.[32]

Nothing more clearly exemplifies the purpose of the Clear Skies Initiative to erode the Clean Air Act than the fate of one particularly contentious provision known as New Source Review (NSR). Congress passed the Clean Air Act in 1970 during President Nixon's time in office. Utilities that built new plants would have to meet pollution standards by switching to cleaner burning natural gas. In the main, the companies opted to simply upgrade their old coal-burning plants without installing the latest pollution-control technology, so Congress added NSR to the Clean Air Act in 1977 during the Carter Administration. It required that utilities making significant improvements to older coal-burning plants must install the new scrubber technology, which is ninety-five percent effective. At first, the companies haggled over where to draw the line on plant repairs that would trigger installation of new technology. They did not really want to do it because it was expensive. Eventually, when the EPA rules became abundantly clear, the utilities mostly ignored the NSR until the Clinton Administration started preparing lawsuits against the worst polluters. That scared them enough that some companies agreed to install pollution controls, while others went political and contributed large sums of money to Bush's 2000 campaign for President. When Bush took power, he filled mid-level positions in energy and environmental agencies with industry lobbyists like James Connaughton and Phil Cooney.[33]

Whitman should be remembered as a center right Republican who might have compromised with environmentalists if she had not been hogtied by Bush's radical conservatives and industry lobbyists. After she was gone, the political appointees at EPA simply rewrote the NSR rules. In an act of arrant cynicism, they set the emission standards ridiculously high—ruling that a utility could spend up to 20 percent of a generating unit's replacement cost in equipment upgrades before it would have to install scrubbers. Career employees at EPA had suggested a limit of 0.75 percent. The new limit allowed far more pollution than the old coal-burning plants were already pumping into the air, making enforcement meaningless and undercutting lawsuits that the Justice Department was preparing to bring against the worst polluters.[34] NSR was dead, at least for the time being. Toxic plumes of sulfur dioxide, nitrous oxides, and mercury continued to pour out of the tall power plant smokestacks and dispersed downwind to take their toll of public health while corporate polluters added up their profits. Whitman left the EPA in May that year and went into the perennially lucrative business of retired office holders, lobbying—often expressed euphemistically as consulting. Conventional wisdom had it that she was worn out from crossing swords with the ideologues in the White House. But she denied it. She said she had no conflict with President Bush. In this case her word should probably be taken at face value. If she was frayed from the constant struggle, it was more likely from hassling with the career bureaucrats at the EPA who took the regulations seriously. One of her main post-EPA lobbying pursuits was nuclear energy, which comes with its own perils stemming from radioactivity but does not emit CO_2 and certain other oxides and dangerous pollutants.

Michael O. Leavitt, a three-term governor of Utah, took Whitman's place at EPA on November 6, 2003. By turning to Leavitt, Bush dropped any pretense that his administration believed in environmental protection. While governor, Leavitt's state ranked at or near the bottom in air quality and environmental enforcement, and several green groups opposed his nomination for the EPA job. The Sierra Club gave him thumbs down for secretly negotiating with Interior Secretary Gale Norton to open millions of acres of Utah wilderness for road-building that would facilitate logging and private development.[35] Leavitt stayed only fifteen months at the EPA, and then moved over to head the Department of Health and Human Services in Bush's second term.

Stephen L. Johnson, a career government scientist who had been Leavitt's deputy, inherited the top job at EPA. He passed muster with the White House because he harbored disaffection for regulation, but he forged an uneasy relationship with liberals in Congress where the hot wires cross. At his Senate confirmation hearing in April 2005, he firmly promised to follow White House guidelines, which pleased committee Republicans, but he ran into trouble with Democratic Senator Barbara Boxer of California over a small experiment in Florida using infant children as guinea pigs. The agency was offering $970 over two years to low-income families in Duval County near Jacksonville to test the effects on their babies of routine household pesticide use. Johnson devised the program while serving as EPA's number two. Boxer vowed to hold up Johnson's confirmation until the program was scrapped,[36] and, in fact, his approval came through only after he halted the experiment a few weeks later.

Johnson administered the EPA with a built-in conflict. He studied biology at an evangelical Christian school, Taylor University of rural Upland, Indiana, which also teaches creationism. His early grounding in Christian doctrine, he told reporters John Shiffman and John Sullivan of the *Philadelphia Inquirer*, gave him a moral compass that influenced his leadership of the EPA.[37] He was at least as controvesial as Whitman, if not more so. After the President signed a Democratic energy bill in 2007, the EPA tried to override the CO_2 auto emission standards of seventeen states led by California. Johnson refused to sign a rider to the energy bill that would allow California to set stricter standards that could be followed by the other states. He said the uniform limits in the new federal law, although weaker, pre-empted the patchwork of state controls.[38] The House Oversight and Government Reform

Committee hauled Johnson onto the carpet for a three-hour grilling, but in December 2008 the EPA's inspector general upheld the legality of Johnson's decision.

Although his background in science often gave him pause, Johnson doggedly adhered to the White House pro-business agenda. In December 2007, EPA scientists prepared a document that sharply contradicted the White House position on global warming. It declared that climate change imperiled public welfare, citing strong evidence of melting glaciers, destructive weather from extreme hot and cold temperatures, floods, draughts, rising sea levels, etc. America's culpability stood out. "The U.S. emits more greenhouse gases from cars," the document said, "than most countries do from all pollution sources." Johnson strongly believed in the science, but realized that the report would be resisted by the White House ideologues. The draft document went to the White House as an email attachment. Staffers there knew what was in it and decided not to downloaded it and thereby make it a public record too controversial to resist. Instead, they asked Johnson to take it back. After resisting them at first, he meekly obliged. Seven months later, EPA released a weakened version of the report that removed the muscular language on U.S. tailpipe emissions and any suggestion that global warming was a threat to public welfare.[39]

From start to finish, from Whitman to Leavitt to Johnson the George W. Bush Administration was the public enemy of environmental protection.

CHENEY'S EXCLUSIVE ENERGY CLUB

While the Bush White House was ignoring the greenhouse effect of carbon dioxide emissions and other environmental hazards it was showering special attention on the hugely profitable industry that processes the dangerous carbon-based compounds. Both Bush and Cheney had past ties to energy business. Bush had ventured unsuccessfully in small oil companies as a young man in West Texas. Cheney had been CEO of

Halliburton, the oil services and construction giant. They saw energy as the lynchpin of economic progress—and environmental regulations as an obstacle. Early in his administration, Bush created the National Energy Policy Development Group and appointed Cheney as chairman. Its stated mission was to develop policy recommendations to meet America's energy needs. Cheney packed it with agency heads and other Bush-appointed government officials and White House aides with a strong industry bias. None of the members came from industry, but some possessed substantial energy investments. Had Cheney appointed industry lobbyists or outside experts, he would have been required under law, the Federal Advisory Committee Act (FACA), to fully disclose the group's activities. As it was, he managed for a time to keep a tight lid on who appeared at task force meetings and what was discussed. The group, presumably wearing earplugs, did host one brief cover-your-ass session with environmentalists.

Inevitably, watchdog groups tried to expose the secrets. The Sierra Club, an environmental watchdog, and Judicial Watch, a citizens' rights organization, brought suit in federal court charging that Cheney's task force was in violation of FACA, but the suit was dismissed. Separately, the NRDC sued the Department of Energy under the Freedom of Information Act and obtained about 20,000 heavily redacted documents that yielded some information. In an unusual move for a government agency, the General Accounting Office sued to gain access to the Cheney group's files, but the effort was blocked in federal court. Despite these setbacks, the details eventually seeped out from inside the hunkered down confines of the White House. Enron, one of many energy biggies in the loop and a major contributor to Republican political coffers, often called on Cheney. After one of the meetings, Cheney turned down a plea from California Governor Gray Davis to cap outrageous energy prices that Enron and Reliant Energy Services were then charging the state.[40]

The group's report surfaced in May 2001. As might have been expected, it gave short shrift to reducing fossil fuel use. Rather, it cited the need for thirty-two percent more energy capacity by 2020 that would require the construction of 1300 to 1900 new power plants. It anticipated, however, that these goals were not achievable and foresaw more oil and gas imports to make up the difference between wish and reality. As an offset to this deficit, the task force made a worthy pitch for more energy efficiency through advances in technology and put some old conservative standbys on the table, such as coal, nuclear energy, and drilling in the Arctic National Wildlife Refuge (ANWR) on Alaska's North Slope. (Remember the rallying cry, "Drill baby, drill!") It larded tax incentives and subsidies into the recommendations. On the whole, the report stressed America's continued dependence on imports of oil and natural gas without conceding the environmental drawbacks. Robert F. Kennedy, Jr., serving as an attorney for the NRDC, described the report as "an orgy of industry plunder, transferring billions of dollars of public wealth to the oil, coal, and nuclear industries" while "paying lip service to conservation and environmental concerns."[41]

The task force sent its recommendations to the President in May and the White House passed them on to Congress. A powerful industry lobbying group, the Alliance for Energy and Economic Growth, came together. It consisted of oil, mining, and nuclear groups that paid $5,000 each to join. Industry lobbyists quietly slipped in and out of Cheney's task force meetings to lay out their needs. Their visits were "off the record," and they heeded advice not to submit documents, although it turned out that many task force recommendations read like the industry lobby's position papers.[42] Despite the heavy industry effort to sway Congress, the energy bill proposed by the White House, the National Energy Policy Development Act had a rough go on Capitol Hill, partly because environmental groups united in an all-out effort to defeat it. The Bush energy bill cleared the House then controlled by the Republicans pretty much intact, but made no headway in the Senate as long as the Democrats maintained their slim majority with the help of Senator Jim Jeffords of Vermont who had switched from Republican to Independent.

In 2003, however, the Republicans took back the Senate and renewed their effort to satisfy the industry's wish list of expensive giveaways by turning them into law. The environmentalists' only hope was a Democratic filibuster, which requires a supermajority of sixty votes to overcome. Things looked dark when several trusted Democrats from the Corn Belt announced their support for the bill because the Republicans tacked on a provision boosting ethanol production. But six Republicans, horrified by the environmental and fiscal insults, five of them from New England (plus John McCain of Arizona), joined the Democrats, and the effort to cut off the filibuster failed. The Cheney energy plan died for the moment, but was resurrected after Bush's stunning second-term victory delivered the political capital to pursue his policy agenda. Congress sent the President a compromise bill in August 2005 that gave the energy industry most of what it had lobbied for—tax breaks for producers of oil, natural gas, coal, and nuclear energy. Anna Aurilio, chief lobbyist for U.S. Public Interest Research group (U.S. PIRG), found it sufficiently objectionable to describe it as, "Christmas in August for big energy, and consumers get lumps of coal."[43] But it did ban drilling in the ANWR. Congress also added tax credits for purchase of hybrid cars in 2005, and a meaningful energy conservation bill two years later set new vehicle fuel economy standards, quadrupled the use of biofuels, phased out incandescent light bulbs, and limited water usage in dishwashers and washing machines.[44] In 2006 mid-term elections, the Democrats regained control of Congress and Cheney's influence on the President waned. So Bush signed the 2007 bill and praised it as, "a major step toward reducing our dependence on oil, confronting global climate change, expanding production of renewable fuels, and giving future generations a nation that is stronger, cleaner, and more secure."[45] He also fought to weaken auto standards that California and other states wanted to impose on carmakers and to skirt regulations that required old power plants to install pollution-control technology when upgrading production capacity.

Americans consume twenty-five percent of all energy produced in the world. Most of it comes from burning fossil fuels, which spew pollutants into the atmosphere and mutates the earth's ecology. Energy and pollution from fossil fuels come together as polar opposites. One is good, the other bad. But you can't have energy from fossil fuels without pollution unless you spend the money to clean up the process. The Bush Administration addressed this conundrum by growing the production of fossil fuels to satisfy the demands of America's voracious energy consumers while largely downplaying the effects of pollution. That is one approach; another is to mitigate and curtail the use of fossil fuels. But mitigation is not cheap, and primarily for that reason, Bush gave lip service to cleaning up the environment, but put it at the bottom of his priority list. For Bush and his mentor Cheney, business always came first. They empathized with the oil and car industries that would have to bear an added cost for pollution control, and tried to lay the damage from toxic emissions on the general public until Democrats gained the upper hand in Congress in the 2006 election. In the final analysis, environmental protection offers another glaring example of the subterfuge and deceit that the Bush Administration routinely practiced in pursuit of its conservative agenda.

If the consensus of environmental science is correct, the outlook for the future of mankind is unremittingly grim. When drought turns the fertile soil of the Great Plains to dust, tornadoes rip apart cities like Joplin, Missouri and Tuscaloosa, Alabama, and heavy rains from Atlantic storms flood homes in the Northeast, it is already too late. The damage from global warming has arrived. It could get worse, and probably will. Planet earth is in trouble. The big blue marble is turning brown. Mother Nature is not likely to forgive the insults, and we are powerless to resist her fury. We cannot go back to live in caves—unless that proves to be the only way to protect ourselves as we compete for shrinking resources. The best we can do, perhaps, while we indulge our addiction to fossil fuels and wait for the icecaps to melt, the oceans to rise, and the deserts to expand is to appreciate the good times we have had and adapt to our new environment.

Chapter 8

Imperiled Safety Net

Should any political party attempt to abolish social security, unemployment insurance and eliminate labor laws and farm programs, you would not hear of that party again in our political history. There is a tiny splinter group, of course, that believes you can do these things....
Their number is negligible and they are stupid.

—Dwight David Eisenhower

SIX DECADES AFTER THE HERO OF WORLD WAR II served as President of the United States the "tiny splinter group" that would abolish Social Security has become the predominant force in Eisenhower's own Republican Party. In 2001, one of the group's contemporary leaders, George W. Bush, took over the presidency, and tried his best to derail the program that provides benefits for the elderly. He failed, but the once tiny splinter, now a giant tree that needs to be chopped down, continues the right wing assault on the social safety net. As for Bush, before he became President he peddled his product—Social Security "reform," he called it—by deflecting his intent and obscuring its cost.

In the first place, the term "reform" implies improvement. Bush's stand begged the question, improvement for whom? Not the beneficiaries. He wanted to privatize the system, but did not want to say so. He used the term "personalize" instead. Despite his protestations to the contrary, his goal was to destroy, not "reform" Social Security, by turning it over to Wall Street. He painted a grim picture of Social Security's future without "reform," which was disingenuous at best. He tried to cover up a trillion dollar dodge that would partially disembowel the Social Security trust fund.

At the third 2000 presidential debate in the campus Field House at Washington University in St. Louis, the most contentious of three debates, Vice President Al Gore and Bush faced one of those ticklish children's questions posed by sixth-grade pupils through their teacher, Thomas Fischer. How, Fischer asked in a question slathered with skepticism, would the candidates keep all the promises they had made. Gore, after vowing to keep his promises, turned the question on his Republican opponent. "...He has promised "a trillion dollars out of the Social Security trust fund for young working adults to invest and save on their own," said Gore. "But he's promised seniors that their Social Security benefits will not be cut, and he's promised the same trillion dollars to them. Which one of those promises will he keep?" he asked. Then he put the question directly to Bush, "and which will you break, governor?"

It was an effective question that laid bare the facile contradiction in Bush's promise to "fix" Social Security by destroying it. Bush seemed not the least embarrassed at being caught in his own trillion dollar trap. He, too, pledged to keep his promises and accused Gore of using high school debating techniques by changing the subject to avoid answering the question. He punctuated his denouncement with a wimpish laugh. "...One of my promises is going to be Social Security reform," he declared, "and you bet, we need to take a trillion dollars out of that $2.4 trillion surplus. Now remember Social Security revenue exceeds expenses up until 2015." With that $1 trillion, younger workers would be able to invest it "under safe guidelines so [they] get a better rate of return ... than the paltry 2 percent that the federal government gets ... today."[1]

What Bush said was true up to that point. But he made it sound as if Social Security would run at a deficit in 2015. Far from it! According to the 2000 report of the Social Security and Disability Insurance Board of Trustees, 2015 would be the last year that tax revenues alone would exceed expenditures. After that, total revenues, including interest on earnings, would exceed outlay until 2025. And then the government could support all Social Security obligations by dipping into trust fund assets until the fund would be exhausted in 2037. At that point payroll tax revenues would still cover 72 percent of annual Social Security costs.[2] To be sure, a fix was needed, but the situation was not dire by any stretch of the imagination. Bush made it sound dire so Republicans could push their agenda to privatize the safety net. What he left unsaid was an estimate by the Center on Budget and Policy Priorities that if Bush actually withdrew the $1 trillion for partial privatization, the trust fund would run short of money fourteen years earlier—in 2023, not 2037.[3] But a problem lurked beneath the foreseeable horizon. If the Bush plan had been in effect in 2008, much of the $1 trillion would have vanished in the stock market crash and the young workers would have seen much of their retirement savings evaporate. In the larger conservative scheme of things, however, it is more important to remove the money from government control and put it in private hands, even if it should disappear into the yawning trap of Wall Street greed.

In the final analysis, the concern over Bush going back on his campaign promises was misplaced. It would have been wiser to worry that Bush would actually keep his promises (and in fact, he tried very hard to keep this one). Voters must not have understood what he meant by "reform" of Social Security. They woke up in his second term when he went on a campaign swing to persuade the American people of his plan's merit. The more he explained it, the more he slipped in public opinion polls. His party actually lost control of Congress in 2006 and control of the Executive Branch in 2008, and it's fairly certain that the Republican stance on Social Security played a part (as did the war in Iraq, which America was losing in 2006). If the voters had realized in 2000 that Bush and his conservative allies were out to scuttle Social Security they might not have elected him in the first place. In this chapter, we will come around to Bush's campaign to sell privatization after his reelection in 2004. But first, we will cover a dangerous "reform" in his first term, a partial privatization that weakened the financial under-pinning of Medicare.

STEALTH ASSAULT ON MEDICARE

The United States spends more on health care than any other nation on earth, yet it ranks well below other advanced industrial societies in efficient delivery. President Bush kept that dubious distinction alive— made it worse, in fact—with policies to turn Medicare into a cash cow for the health insurance and pharmaceutical industries. Medicare for seniors, one of President Johnson's Great Society programs, became law in 1965. It had two parts—Part A (hospitalization) was financed, like Social Security, with a payroll tax. The money for Part B (doctors) came from general revenues. Congress paid little attention to prescription drugs in those days because the drugs were not yet an important part of medical therapy. But pharmaceutical research flowered and demand grew, especially among older people, in the years that followed. Prescription drugs for seniors became an issue in the 2000 election. Both candidates offered a plan, with government control vs. privatization the major difference between them.

So when Bush won, his presidency came with a privatized drug plan as one of his priorities. Once tax cuts were out of the way, his proposal arrived on Capitol Hill as the Medicare Prescription Drug Improvement and Modernization Act of 2003 (Medicare Modernization Act, or MMA), and would channel taxpayer money through Medicare to enrich private health insurers and pharmaceutical companies. Behind the façade of reform (or in this case a new euphemism, "modernization"), the new law would add a heavy financial burden on Medicare and bring it a step closer to insolvency. Conservatives had used the specter of bankruptcy that they now fortified to validate their call for "reform." They did it as they put part of the Medicare program in private hands.

The legislation barely passed the House where Republicans held a thin majority and several party members, who balked at the whopping cost and did not share the growing conservative bent for total reliance on market forces, opposed the bill. At one point, the measure seemed headed for defeat, with most Democrats and substantial numbers of rebellious Republicans arrayed against it. The Republican leadership held the electronic voting open for several hours while, with help from the White House, they tried to woo wayward colleagues back into the fold. The mutineers made themselves scarce. Some turned off their cell phones or mingled in crowded throngs where they could not be easily singled out. One hid behind a banister on the Democratic side. Eventually, the majority party had its way, and at nine minutes short of 6 a.m., the bill passed, 220 to 215. Twenty-five Republicans voted no, and sixteen Democrats voted yes.[4]

The new Medicare law provided prescription drug coverage for the first time—Medicare Part D. That was the good news. Beginning in 2006, the MMA permitted elderly people on Medicare to sign up for a so-called "stand-alone" (Part D without Part A or B) prescription drug plan or enroll in a Medicare Advantage program that included almost the entire gamut of Medicare services. Medicare Advantage revised Medicare+Choice—Medicare Part C, which in 1997 created private HMOs as an alternative to traditional Medicare. Under the 2003 law, any MA plan must cover all traditional medical (Part B) and hospital (Part A) Medicare services except hospice care, and may offer additional services for vision, hearing, dental, and health/wellness programs.

The Medicare Modernization Act was not cheap and it came with the same kind of deceit that characterized the sales pitch for the war in Iraq, the cover-up of torture, and the tax giveaway to the rich. To begin with, much of the MMA's lengthy, complicated text was not available for legislators to read and understand until less than a month before they had to vote on it.[5] Prior to the bill's enactment in December 2003, Bush and his budget advisors estimated the cost to be $400 billion over ten years. Several conservative Republican legislators had vowed to oppose the program if the cost exceeded that figure. They put their trust in the White House estimate and voted for the bill, only to see their trust violated. In September 2004, nearly a year after passage, the administration raised the cost estimate to $534 billion. In February 2005, Medicare Director Mark B. McClellan acknowledged that the cumulative cost of the program would be $1.2 trillion with savings and offsets that would pare the net cost down to $720 billion, 80 percent higher than the original estimate.

The pre-enactment deceit in 2003 was buried in a false ten-year period, 2004 to 2013, chosen for the budget estimate. It was false because the program was not fully implemented until 2006. In those two years from '04 to '06, Medicare participants could apply for discount drug cards for $30 per year that would allow them to buy drugs at 10 to 25 percent off. Beginning in '06, the new program kicked into high gear. If the projection is based on a true ten-year period, e.g., '06 to '15 with the program in full swing, you get the higher figure.[6] That figure would grow as more seniors signed up for Medicare Advantage, which turned out to be the preferred way to get drug coverage. The Bush administration hid the truth until after the bill was enacted.

Neither was the new drug bill cheap for beneficiaries. One commentator suggested that Medicare Advantage enrollees were being charged double, once as taxpayers and again as consumers.[7] Income earners pay for Social Security and Medicare Part A through the payroll tax during their entire working lives. Beginning in 2006, under the stand-alone plan beneficiaries paid premiums averaging $418 annually in the first year, a $250 annual deductible, plus copayments for each drug. Medicare Advantage paid 75 percent of drug costs up to $2,250. The famous doughnut hole followed. The MA member, who could hardly be called a beneficiary at this stage, paid the entire cost of drugs when the annual tab ran between $2,250 and $5,100; the plan paid nothing. Beyond the $5,100 threshold of what was considered catastrophic illness, the insurance company would pay 95 percent of all drug costs annually.[8] These prices shifted upward as the years wore on. All these plans were subsidized by Medicare, so it was really the taxpayers, not private insurers footing the bill. In other words, the privatization did not stand on the supply-demand basis of pure capitalism, but on the government subsidies (together with beneficiaries' contributions) that covered both the cost of the drugs and industry profits.

Although the new Medicare law was supposed to promote competition, the power to regulate was turned over to private insurance and pharmaceutical companies, leaving the private sector to perform a government function. The insurance companies would determine the list of drugs to be covered, and would set prices in negotiations with the drug companies. The government was expressly prohibited from being involved, even though the private parties were playing with the taxpayers' money. Prices set in this manner amount to additional taxes, as far as the consumer is concerned—taxation without representation, the same issue that helped to trigger the Revolutionary War and the birth of the nation. Where was Grover Norquist when this cockamamie idea was hatched?

One key reason for the drug industry's huge profits is the exclusion of the Medicare agency in negotiations over drug prices. In stark contrast, the Veterans Administration does negotiate on drug prices at less than half of Medicare's costs. "If Medicare had been allowed to negotiate in the same way as the Veterans Administration," said Dean Reynolds of the Center for Economic Policy Research, "the savings would have been more than enough to eliminate the doughnut-hole gap in coverage." Reynolds estimated that excessive profits for the drug industry as a whole, measured as the gap between VA and Medicare drug prices, would come to about $50 billion in the first full year of operations under the MMA, more than twice the size of the large doughnut hole that consumers must fill.[9]

If taxpayers and Medicare beneficiaries are losers in the Medicare Modernization Act of 2003, Insurance and drug companies are runaway winners. MA Plans receive an average of 12 percent more in taxpayer subsidies over traditional Medicare fee-for-service. These overpayments are expected to add $160 billion of taxpayer money to MA revenues over ten years.[10] In dollars the monthly premiums that the government paid to private insurers under MA averaged about $800 a month per enrollee and could go as high as $2000 depending on the health of the enrollee. The Government Accounting Office (GAO) reported In 2008 that the payments of taxpayer money to private health insurers under Medicare Advantage rose substantially from 2006, the first year of full implementation of the MA program, to 2008, the last year of the Bush presidency—$60 billion in 2006, $77 billion in 2007, and $91 billion in 2008—as enrollment in MA programs increased.[11] In the words of Democratic Congressman Pete Stark of California, "The overpayments are going to profits."[12]

They were going to profits, plus advertizing, lobbying, high executive salaries, and company outings, according to a report by the Democratic staff of the House Energy and Commerce Committee in December 2009. The committee, chaired by Democratic Representative Henry Waxman of California, found that from 2005 to 2008 two-thirds of thirty-four MA insurers surveyed spent more than 15 percent of premium money—$1,450 per beneficiary in 2008—on "profits, marketing, and other corporate expenses." The report did not name the companies surveyed. Six of the insurers spent less than 75 percent for medical care in at least one of the years. By contrast, the more efficient traditional Medicare spent more than 98 percent of its funding on medical care and only about 1.5 percent on administrative costs. The private companies spent ten times as much on profits and corporate expenses than did traditional Medicare on administrative expenses. The thirty-four companies surveyed paid more than 1.2 billion in executive compensation in '07 and '08. One company paid its top executive more than $35 million and sixteen other company officers more than $1 million each in '07. Another company paid $210 million to 260 executives. It needs stating that Medicare Advantage was only part of their business, ranging from less than 5 percent to more than 45 percent. In the two years '07 and '08, some companies enjoyed expensive retreats in Hawaii; San Jose del Cabo and Cancun, Mexico; Rome, Italy, and Edinburgh, Scotland.[13] Clearly, Medicare Advantage companies were living high on the hog—the hog being the taxpayers' money.

Drug companies also fared well under Medicare Advantage. Pfizer profited from the soaring sales of Lipitor, the cholesterol-clearing statin for the prevention of cardiovascular disease that helps older people live longer. Lipitor became the best selling drug in history, but it thrived for a relatively short time. Even before Lipitor went off patent in November 2011 its sales were slipping worldwide from the growth of competing statins. But thanks to the regulations that prevent Medicare from negotiating for lower prices (as the VA does), Pfizer and other drug companies make billions from Bush's privatization of Medicare. Drug consumers can buy the same drugs substantially cheaper in Canada, but the MMA even tried to prevent beneficiaries from taking advantage of the Canadian prices.

Bush's Medicare Advantage is not free enterprise, but rather a waste of taxpayers' money to subsidize the profits of private companies. Under Medicare as originally conceived, money from the payroll tax or from general revenues is used by the government to pay medical providers (doctors, nurses, hospitals, etc.) for services rendered. Under Medicare Advantage as conceived by the Bush Administration, the taxpayers' money is paid to private insurers who pay the providers. Insurers are an unnecessary middle man taking the taxpayers' money for profits. (Conservatives argue that the consumer gets better care from the MA system.) Then the insurers negotiate with the drug companies to determine the price of drugs. Because the prices are not influenced by competition, they come out excessively high. The government and Medicare consumers foot the bill, which amounts to an added drain on the Medicare fund and a second tax on Medicare consumers. In short, Medicare Advantage is a prime example of reckless Bush policy. (Under Obama, government payments to insurers would be frozen at 2010 levels and then gradually reduced to bring them in line with payments under traditional Medicare, not a perfect solution, but an improvement.)

HUGGING THE THIRD RAIL

Social Security was more than a good idea. It was superbly structured for long-term solvency. Workers would pay into a trust fund during their working days through a payroll tax taken out of their paychecks. At the age of sixty-five they would be entitled to full benefits. It was not intended that Social Security should provide all of the workers' compensation in retirement, but only that it serve as an income supplement. The payroll tax went into effect in 1937, and retirees first began drawing on the fund in 1940.[14] Disability insurance was added in 1956, and Medicare and Medicaid were separately financed in 1965. The Social Security and Disability fund remained apart from the overall federal budget supported by general tax revenues. The Social Security/ Disability revenues so outpaced expenditures that by 1968 the fund had built a surplus of more than $25 billion.[15] That year, President Johnson created a "unified" budget, meaning that the safety net trust funds were thrown in with general revenues.[16] That made it possible for Johnson to use the Social Security/Disability surplus to help pay for the Vietnam War. From then on, the trust funds were never safe from the sticky hands of Washington politicians, despite feckless Congressional efforts in the 1980s to separate the funds from the federal budget. In 2001 when Bush entered the presidency, what would have been the retirement surplus if not combined with general funds stood at $1 trillion, according to the Social Security Administration. In 2008, his last full year, it was $2.2 trillion.[17] Bush and his conservative supporters argued that the surplus was not real money. Sadly, in a unified budget where revenue from payroll and income taxes is pooled this was, and still is true. The surplus is merely an entry in the ledger that tells you how much money would be on hand if the Social Security trust fund stood separately. It is an accounting gimmick recording IOUs that symbolize what the government owes itself. Whatever surplus the Social Security trust fund may show has already been spent on government programs and can only be redeemed by overburdened taxpayers.[18]

Instead of stimulating a movement to restore the stand-alone trust fund, Bush and his followers used this accounting trick to free their conservative minds from accepting the "myth" of a surplus and rationalized their demand for what they called reform. President Johnson—and all subsequent presidents who dipped into the Social Security/Disability fund to help pay for profligate government spending—did the elderly a disservice, or to put it in plain English, cheated the payroll taxpayers by using the Social Security surplus for general purposes. Had it not been for their high powered embezzlement, Social Security/Disability would have been solvent for many more decades to come. The same goes for Medicare, although to a lesser degree.

Bush had long been an advocate of reforming Social Security by setting up personal accounts. After his reelection in 2004, he wasted no time embarking on the costly plan that Gore had picked apart in their third 2000 campaign debate. "I earned capital in the [2004] campaign, political capital," Bush told reporters, "and now I intend to spend it."[19] He would spend it all on Social Security reform, knowing full well the risks involved. "For as long as I can remember, Social Security has been the third rail of American politics," he wrote in his memoir. "Grab ahold of it and you're toast. In 2005, I did more than touch the third rail. I hugged it.... It is unfair to make a generation of young people pay into a system that is going broke."[20] He had learned, to borrow from "Dr. Strangelove," to stop worrying and love the third rail just as Strangelove loved the A-bomb.

In essence, the Bush plan would allow young workers to invest about one-third of their 6.2 percent payroll tax in personal accounts that would offer a variety of options and, he said, would yield a higher return than government bonds. For those already on Social Security or near retirement, benefits would not change. He shrank from calling it privatization, but it was obvious that the financial services industry on Wall Street would benefit from all the new accounts that would be opened. It sounded good, as long as the market kept going up, but it was not so good when it declined. Social Security investors with personal accounts would have lost their shirts in the market free-fall of 2008.

Bush told Congress in his State of the Union Address on February 2, 2005 that Social Security must be saved, and the next day he flew out to Great Falls, Montana to test his stump speech for Social Security reform. Right off the bat, he squandered some of his capital by not informing the senior senator from Montana, Democrat Max Baucus, of his plan to visit Baucus' state. After reading about the President's visit in a dispatch from the Associated Press, Baucus hurried out to Great Falls in the performance of normal political duties to greet the President, and then suffered the humiliation of being placed well back among the dignitaries on stage behind Bush. It was a costly slight to a senator who had earlier told Bush that he wanted to work with him on Social Security reform, even if he could not sway the vast majority of the Democratic caucus. The enraged Baucus went back to Washington and told Minority Leader Harry Reid that he was willing to lead the fight against Bush's Social Security plan.

A month later Bush embarked on a tour of "60 cities in 60 days" to sell his plan to the American people, while Republican Members of Congress were encouraged to hold pro-reform rallies in their districts. The president was generally received with quiet dignity and polite reserve. He had no reason to suspect from their reaction that the people were not swallowing his ideas. But organized labor and liberal groups such as MoveOn.org and the Campaign for America's Future and the seniors' lobby, AARP, greeted the Republican Congressmen and women who staged rallies in their districts with advertizing campaigns and sidewalk rallies against privatization. An ad hoc group called Americans United to Protect Social Security took shape with satellite offices in twenty-nine states. Jim Messina, the chief of staff for Senator Baucus, ran it out of Harry Reid's office. The more Bush explained his plan for Social Security, the more he lost ground. Public opinion polls showed that popular support for privatization steadily declined, and Bush's personal popularity declined with it. By early summer the president's political capital had vanished, and Social Security "reform" reappeared in 2006 as a Democratic issue in the mid-term elections, which the Republicans lost.[21] Thus, President Bush frittered away his cherished plan to save Social Security. The failure is interesting in that he had laid it all out on the line. Without too much flimflam, except possibly a little fudging on the cost, he let the people know exactly what he had in mind, and they rejected it.

The basic problem for Social Security now is demographic. The baby boomers born in prolific numbers after World War II have begun to reach the Social Security full retirement age. That makes them eligible to cash in on the money they contributed during their working years. At the same time the work force has shrunk, so there are fewer people paying into the trust fund and more people taking money out. It does not help that President Obama keeps raiding the trust to give working families a tax break and extend unemployment compensation—a wonderful short-term measure that threatens to further weaken the long-term financial stability of Social Security. Rep. Paul Ryan of Wisconsin, the Republican chairman of the House Budget Committee, has proposed to fix Social Security by gradually raising the retirement age and cutting back on benefits for 70 percent of recipients. The plan comes with a means test so that the greater the individual's income, the lower his/her monthly payments, to the point where the disbursement to the highest income earners is virtually worthless and they are encouraged to opt for a private retirement plan.[22]

There are ways to fix Social Security other than privatization, such as nudging up the retirement age and extending the 6.2 percent payroll tax to income earners beyond the current $106,800 upper limit. When Social Security was enacted in 1935, life expectancy at birth in the United States was 61.7 years, well below age 65 when the full Social Security benefits would kick in. By 2007, life expectancy had risen by more than sixteen years to 77.9. So it is past time for the retirement age to creep up. As for extending the payroll tax to high income earners, a 6.2 percent tax on a billion dollars earned by Warren Buffett would net the Social Security/Disability fund $62 million, which would buy a lot of apples to keep the elderly and disabled healthy—and indications are that Buffett would approve the idea, but Grover Norquist would not. These measures could go a long way toward saving the system with a minimum of pain. Unfortunately a hard-line faction on the political right, instead of cooperating on a solution, has kept the Social Security issue alive after Bush's time in office. They want privatization or they will call down the fires of damnation. The issue became part of a self-inflicted crisis in 2011 over raising the debt ceiling, a crisis which we shall take up in the final chapter.

Chapter 9

Crash!

Finance is... the stomach of the country, from which all the other organs take their tone.

—W. E. Gladstone

THE WORST ECONOMIC CRISIS since the Great Depression highlights the Bush domestic legacy. So deep was the slump that many observers in mock deference to those who shrink from the "D" word have called it the Great Recession. As everyone not living on Mars knows, the housing bubble burst during the end stage of the Bush presidency and the international market in the bundled mortgages of overleveraged homeowners who could not afford their monthly payments fell off a cliff. While the blame is big enough to go around, the George W. Bush administration has much to answer for in the meltdown, primarily a dogged adherence to the ideology of the free market that kept the financial regulators at bay. Bush responded to the crisis by creating a program called TARP (Troubled Asset Relief Program) that allocated $700 billion for the federal government to buy up so-called toxic assets.

Whether he acted out of courage, cowardice, or fear, Bush earned credit for rising above principle by compromising his free market values to support the government bailout of the banks (although many believe that the banks did not deserve to be bailed out). But it can also be argued that his misapplied free market values played a part in the onset of the emergency. The Nobel laureate Paul Krugman warns against attributing cause for such large failures to any one factor, so complex is the financial system in this fast-moving electronic age. But what stands out above all else in the two major financial crises of the past three decades is the absence of regulation, either from the deregulation of Depression-era finance laws or from the genius of market manipulators who found loopholes that kept them a step ahead of the regulators. Bush, like his predecessors going back to Ronald Reagan, was an enthusiastic believer in leaving the private sector to self-regulate. For nearly three decades, successive Democratic and Republican administrations had steadily dismantled New Deal regulations, culminating with repeal in 1999 of the Glass-Steagall Act that had separated commercial banking, investment banking, and insurance. During the three decades, the nation experienced successive financial crises: Savings and Loans in the 1980s and '90s, and the near financial meltdown of America's biggest banks in the 2000s.

Regulations are a necessary nuisance because they help to rein in greed. Regulations are also consistent with the principle of checks and balances embedded in the Constitution. No one need complain about corporations doing business. Where they go wrong is in trying to dominate the business of government in their misconstrued interests. What's best for the public should come first. Business grown large into monopoly or oligopoly is a powerful political entity. It makes just as much sense to check its power with regulations as it did for the founding fathers to balance the powers of the federal government among competing executive, legislative, and judicial branches. To sweep these business constraints aside in an intemperate outburst of deregulation is to give a free hand to a force that could upset the balance. In other words, if we get the government off the backs of business, who is going to get business off the backs of people? Who is going to keep the corporate bureaucrats from gouging consumers in the pursuit of profit? How else can a people prevent the accumulation of power that could throttle democracy? Most Americans consider it radical to put too much economic power in the hands of government. That's socialism, they say.

It is equally radical—as many far-right-wing conservatives advocate—
to over empower big business.

Notwithstanding the ranting of free market zealots, regulation
does not mean socialism, which is defined as government ownership
of the means of production. Krugman refers to what one might call
"free-market Keynesianism" as "a belief that markets are fine things, but
they work best if the government stands ready to limit their excesses."[1]
Regulation, done right, actually preserves the free market system. "Done
right" is the key; the regulation must be relevant to the problem it is
supposed to fix. Outdated regulations must be revised, not necessarily
discarded. Who in his/her right mind would deny that the free market
system works? Just ask the communist rulers in China, where capitalism has advanced by leaps and bounds since the failure of its Cultural
Revolution. In China, the communist government allows the capitalist captains of industry to hold down wages and working conditions.
In America, the capitalists would love to do the same, but regulations
and laws protecting workers keep them at bay in an on-going struggle. Constraining the human greed seemingly inherent in capitalism
makes it work better, as demonstrated more than once in the American
experience.

Historically, panics occurred when financial institutions got
ahead of the regulators. Early in the twentieth century, trusts originally formed simply to manage inheritances and estates for wealthy
clients (and therefore not regulated the same as ordinary banks) began
making risky investments in a booming economy. To grow their speculation, they offered depositors higher interest rates, which siphoned
deposits from moderately regulated banks. When the bubble burst
in 1907, financial panic gripped the nation's banking center in New
York. Depositors lined up in the streets outside the banks to withdraw
their money, but the banks and trusts did not have enough reserves
to cover the overwhelming demand. J.P. Morgan and other wealthy
citizens stepped in to shore up the weak reserves and allay depositors'
fears. Financial reform followed. In 1913 Congress created the Federal

Reserve to compel deposit-taking institutions to hold adequate reserves and open their books to inspection. But it was not enough. The boom of the 1920s was followed by the Great Depression. Serious bank runs occurred in 1930, 1931, and 1933, after which the Franklin Roosevelt administration put regulations in place that stabilized the banking system through three-and-a-half decades of widespread prosperity after World War II.[2]

Then the anti-regulation forces regained the upper hand and the great ogre Greed broke free from its chains to disrupt relative economic balance. If the government fails to properly regulate the economy, especially the financial sector, greedy con artists and hyperventilating capitalists will rush in like colonies of termites and eat up the social contract. This review of G.W. Bush's financial policies starts with the reforms enacted during the Great Depression and traces their unraveling on the way to the Great Recession of 2008, and shows how deregulation together with conservative anti-regulation dogma helped plunge the nation into successive financial crises.

DEREGULATION: REDUCTIO AD ABSURDUM

The Roosevelt administration put financial regulations in place during the 1930s to repair the banking failures of the Great Depression. A key measure, the Glass-Steagall Act, prohibited lending and investment by the same financial institution, prevented banks from engaging in the insurance business, established federal deposit insurance, and, to limit out-of-control bank competition, placed a ceiling on interest rates for depositors. Congress also passed transparency laws for the securities industry, requiring that stock exchanges and public companies submit quarterly and annual reports. (Insurance regulation and usury laws were left to the states.) Though not perfect, these regulations survived for nearly half a century. Beginning even before the Reagan years of the 1980s, banking lobbyists and free market ideologues stripped the regulatory system bare, one law after another, until the regulators could only stand helplessly by as the Wall Street predators ate up the profits and left the crumbs on Main Street.

Deregulation was a bi-partisan error committed over three decades in Republican and Democratic administrations.[3] The nation would have been better served with re-regulation to adapt the system to financial innovation and technological change, but policymakers forgot the lessons of the Great Depression and fell for the siren song of the free market. Shrewd businessmen that included grifters and con artists moved in to fill the voids created in the financial system. Deregulation began with a 1978 Supreme Court decision, *Marquette National Bank vs. First of Omaha Service Corp.*, in which the court ruled that the usury laws in a nationally chartered bank's home state applied nationwide. In one dazzling day of legislative activity, South Dakota eliminated its usury law to attract Citibank's credit card business to South Dakota. The relocation allowed Citibank to charge usurious credit card interest rates nationwide, and provided a model for other banks to follow.

New Deal regulation of the financial system unraveled over the next two decades. Thrift banking came first. In the late 1970s, inflation running at 10 percent or higher was reducing the market share of banks. The interest rate they could offer depositors under New Deal banking law was capped at 5.25 percent in ordinary savings accounts and up to 7.75 percent in time deposits. Thrift banks (savings and loan associations) that specialized in home loans could offer a quarter percent higher rate to encourage housing growth. But brokerage firms not subject to banking regulations were creating money market funds that offered higher rates and drew depositors away from the banks. A law passed in 1980 and signed by President Jimmy Carter created a commission to phase out interest rate ceilings over six years. But the new law still left the thrift banks tightly squeezed between income and expenditure. They held long-term mortgages at low interest rates and under the new law succumbed to competitive market pressures to lure depositors with higher rates. The "reform" also wiped out the small advantage in interest rates that the thrifts held over ordinary banks. So the difference between banks and savings and loans was obscured, if not erased entirely.

The thrift banks had already started on a downward slide when the administration of Ronald Reagan took matters a step further. Reagan had campaigned in 1980 with the promise to get the government off the backs of business. "Deregulation" became the buzz word of the 1980s and the banking industry devolved into a Darwinian mode, survival of the fittest. To help thrifts compete with money market funds Congress enacted legislation in 1982 that allowed them to engage in higher yielding but riskier commercial loans with up to 10 percent of assets. That created a boom, and then a bust. S&L investments shifted partially from single family homes to riskier condominiums and commercial real estate. But that market lost its glamour after Reagan tax cuts in 1986 eliminated many real estate tax shelters. Investors fled from the thrift banks. With the S&L industry losing money, its federal deposit insurance funded with industry contributions was overwhelmed and a government bailout with taxpayers' money failed to stop the bleeding until about half the thrifts nationwide went broke.

Repeal of the Glass-Steagall Act of 1933 was the final nail in the coffin. It stood in the mid- to late-twentieth century as the great wall that separated the activities of commercial and investment banks and insurance companies. Glass-Steagall, including deposit insurance, kept bank failures to a minimum. The first cracks in the wall beginning in the 1960s were money market mutual funds issued by investment firms that offered higher yields than banks. In other words the investment firms were performing a banking service outside of the regulations imposed on banks. Depositors switched to money markets in droves. Banks began to lobby intensively for the government to loosen the restrictions of Glass-Steagall. A better solution would have been to put the investment firms under the same regulations as the banks—re-regulation instead of deregulation.

Change arrived in the 1980s. America's central bank, the Federal Reserve, became the primary agent of deregulation while the executive and legislative branches also contributed. The Reagan administration set the tone with pressure on the regulators to lay off carrying out their regulatory duties long before Congress got around to erasing Glass-Steagall in 1999. In December 1986, the "Fed" board of directors thumbed its nose at Glass-Steagall by ruling that banks could derive up to 5 percent of revenues from the investment business beyond commercial real estate. Shortly thereafter, it overruled Chairman Paul Volker and voted to allow banks to deal in specific investment activities such as commercial paper, municipal bonds, and subprime mortgage-backed securities that almost wrecked the world economy two decades later.

In August 1987 President Reagan appointed Alan Greenspan to replace Volker as chairman of the Federal Reserve. Greenspan, an Ayn Rand disciple, was a free market greyhound and champion of deregulation. He cut to the chase almost immediately: the Fed stretched the banks' commercial investment limit to 10 percent. In 1996 during the Clinton administration, the limit went to 25 percent, and for all practical purposes, the wall between pure banking and investment collapsed because banks had no need or desire to exceed that limit. Bank mergers picked up, thanks in part to a law enacted in 1994 that removed restrictions on interstate banking and bank branches. The granddaddy of all financial mergers united CitiCorp and Travelers Insurance Group. The progeny of that marriage, CitiGroup, became the largest financial services company in history at the time. Technically, the merger was still barred under what was left of Glass-Steagall, but the executives of the two companies proceeded with guidance from the Fed and the Clinton Administration and full confidence that Congress was about to wipe it out permanently—and did so. Finally, years of lobbying on which the banks spent millions of dollars paid off, and the nation was left without the protection of Glass-Steagall.

CRISIS: SAVINGS & LOANS

The great fervor of anti-regulation that afflicted America for the better part of three decades featured the savings and loan debacle of the 1980s and 1990s and the disaster that came with the collapse of the housing bubble. An absence of regulation contributed to these emergencies. Greed blanketed the system in the earlier years, according to reporters Stephen Pizzo, Mary Fricker, and Paul Muolo, who did an exhaustive study of criminality during the S&L crisis.[4] However, professor Lawrence J. White of New York University, a member of the Federal Home Loan Bank Board from 1986 to 1989, offers a different perspective. He argues that the S&L crisis reached such huge proportions, not from the criminal activities of a few bad guys, but from imprudent investments on a grand scale rooted in the toxic soil of deregulation. "These thrifts largely failed," he wrote, "because of an amalgam of deliberately high-risk strategies, poor business judgments, ... excessive optimism, and sloppy and careless underwriting, compounded by deteriorating real estate markets...and the excessively lenient and ill-equipped regulatory environment that tolerated these business practices for far too long."[5] So, did the S&L crisis derive from "deliberately high-risk" lending or manifestly low-down behavior? It was probably a mixture of both to a degree that is hard to pinpoint.

President Reagan signed the Garn-St. Germain Depository Institutions Act on October 15, 1982 with the air of a God-fearing man whose prayers had been answered. As indicated above, his road to the White House had been paved with a promise to get the government off the backs of business. Now he was putting his name on the first major financial deregulation law of his presidency. At the time, thrifts were beginning to fall like autumn leaves due to an imbalance between assets (low interest from home loans) and liabilities (high interest paid to depositors). Instead of holding investment banks offering depositors high-interest mutual funds to the same regulations as the thrift banks, the new law would allow the thrifts to make shorter-term, adjustable loans, and, additionally, would permit limited investments beyond single-family homes, such as shopping centers, condominium housing, or other commercial real estate. Garn-St.-Germain also accelerated the phase-out of interest-rate ceilings and extended deposit insurance to $100,000 per account—deregulation, not re-regulation. The acolytes of the free market could not have been more pleased to watch New Deal regulations falling by the wayside. They looked forward to an era of unfettered prosperity.

Alas, it did not turn out as they hoped. Many economists considered the new law to be sensible and relevant to the then-existing circumstances. It might have worked if the regulators had seen to its enforcement. Regulation, however, was not a priority in the conservative administration of Ronald Reagan. Quite the opposite! From the White House down, the Republican political leadership encouraged the regulators to back off.[6] Let the invisible hand of competition regulate the market. Even prosecutors sworn to uphold the law needed an extra measure of dedication and energy to make their cases against wrongdoers. Sometimes deregulation created the conditions for fraud; sometimes it just made existing fraud easier.

Brokered deposits became popular. Pension funds, insurance companies, oil rich sheikhs, mobsters, and other large investors would look for S&Ls with the highest interest rates to park up to $100,000 (the deposit insurance ceiling) short term. The S&Ls paid for brokered deposits with higher interest rates, and would then invest the funds in shopping centers, condos, and the like, hoping to turn a fast buck, but often losing it just as fast.[7] Deposit insurance indemnified the depositors, but failures grew to an avalanche that swamped the insurance fund. By 1986 the pot was empty. Then the taxpayers had to pick up the tab.

The Renda case offers one example of how financial wheeler-dealers gorged themselves on shady business facilitated by deregulation. From 1980 until he was arrested in 1987, Mario Renda of Garden City, New York ran a company called First United Fund that brokered $6 billion in certificates of deposit for 6,500 investors in 3,500 banks and S&Ls.[8] His clients were looking for the highest possible return on investment under the 1980 law that removed ceilings on interest rates offered to depositors. The deposits up to the insurance ceiling of $100,000 were risk free. Two of Renda's early clients were Teamsters Local 810 and Sheet-metal Workers Local 38, steered to him by a friend, Martin Schwimmer, who managed their pension funds. From 1982 through 1984 Renda placed about $100 million in portions up to $100,000 of the union money in selected S&Ls from which he collected a commission. Renda skimmed off about $16 million in fees, part of which he kicked back to union officials, according to federal authorities.[9] Schwimmer was also in hot water for double dipping in a classic case of conflict of interest. Paid by the unions to manage their pension funds, he also collected about $3.4 million over three years as part of his kickback from First United.[10]

From brokered deposits, Renda expanded into a scam known as "linked financing." He would promise deposits to an S&L or bank in exchange for a return promise of loans to specified borrowers. The prospect of assured deposits and quick loans was sufficient to induce a bank to nudge up the interest rate on the deposits slightly above the going rate. Renda went partners with Franklin Winkler and Sam Daily who would hire "straw man" borrowers to take out the loans ostensibly for real estate ventures. The borrowers would take off a fee of 2.5- to 6 percent and turn the rest of the borrowed money over to Renda, Winkler, and Daily. The loans, of course, were not repaid; deposit insurance made up the losses so the depositors would not be financially harmed. The scam had its first trial run at tiny Indian Springs State Bank in Kansas City, and spread out, east and west, from Florida to Hawaii. Renda advertized the deals in major newspapers as "Money for Rent."[11]

Charles Keating, Jr., another high stakes player in the S&L scandal, gained fame for buying influence on Capitol Hill. He and his associates made political contributions through much of the 1980s to Senators Dennis DeConcini, Democrat, ($55,000) and John McCain, Republican, ($112,000), both from Arizona; and Democrats John Glenn of Ohio ($200,000), Alan Cranston of California ($889,000), and Don Riegle of Michigan who was next in line for chairmanship of the Senate

Banking Committee ($76,100). They were the famous (or infamous) "Keating Five." In April 1987 Keating asked them to intervene on his behalf with the Federal Home Loan Bank Board, which was reviewing the financial transactions of Keating-owned Lincoln Savings and Loan, a California thrift, and American Continental Corporation of Arizona (CCA, incorporated in Ohio and headquartered in Arizona), Lincoln's parent company that Keating ran. DeConcini convened a meeting one evening in his Senate office in Washington that included the other four senators and regulators from the San Francisco home loan bank. One of the regulators took notes, which later leaked out to the press and brought political hellfire down on the senators.

The meeting perfectly illustrates the atmosphere of deregulation in those days and the pressures brought to bear on regulators. It also serves as an object civics lesson on the American political system. DeConcini set the tone by letting the regulators know that the senators had "determined that potential action of yours could injure a constituent [Lincoln and CCA]." Glenn said, "...You should charge them [with a crime] or get off their backs." In response, the senators got an earful: A 1984 examination of Lincoln Savings had shown significant loan deficiencies; by 1986, the deficiencies had not been corrected. Between '84 and '86, Lincoln had made fifty-two loans worth $47 million of federally insured deposits with no credit reports on file. Lincoln was "flying blind" with federally insured money. One loan was entered in the books as a $12 million profit. The buyer backed out (as he had a right to do), yet the $12 million profit remained in the books. The regulators revealed that they would refer the matter to the Justice Department for possible criminal prosecution. The senators backed down. When the story leaked out nine months later, Riegle returned Keating's $76,100 donation. The Senate Ethics Committee officially reprimanded Cranston, declared that Riegle and DeConcini had given the appearance of acting improperly, and accused McCain and Glenn of using poor judgment (although the last two were otherwise exonerated).[12]

Reporters Pizzo, Fricker, and Muolo added up the penalties paid by Renda and more than twenty other shady characters involved in defrauding the thrifts and found for the most part that they got off easy. Renda, for example, received two five-year prison sentences on separate convictions and one two-year sentence on a plea bargain in three different jurisdictions. The sentences ran concurrently.[13] Keating was convicted in California state court in 1992 of fraud, racketeering, and conspiracy, and served four-and-a-half years of a ten-year sentence before an appeals court dismissed the case and commuted his sentence on a technicality.[14]

Nineteen eighty-six was a watershed year. Officials realized then that the FSLIC (Federal Savings and Loan Insurance Corporation) could no longer cover the failures out of the insurance premiums paid by the thrifts. The burden was shifted to the taxpayers. That year, too, Congress enacted tax cuts prescribed by the conservative ideologues of the Reagan administration. The legislation worsened the problem by eliminating certain tax shelters on commercial real estate in which the thrifts were heavily invested. Investors looked for shelter elsewhere, and the thrifts fell on even harder times. By 1995, only 1,645 thrift banks out of 3,234 remained standing, a decline of about 50 percent.[15] Up to then, it was "the greatest collapse of U.S. financial institutions since the Great Depression." By 1999 the cost to the taxpayers came to $124 billion.[16]

CRISIS: HOUSING BUBBLE

By the turn of the century the S&L crisis had passed, but the dangerous elements that made it happen—anti-regulation philosophy, corporate greed, and ambitious housing policy—still hovered over the economy. Before the next decade came to an end a new financial debacle, generally identified as the subprime mortgage crisis, would hit with cataclysmic force. The S&L crisis transpired largely during the Republican administrations of Ronald Reagan and George H.W. Bush. The Great Recession struck on the watch of Republican George

W. Bush, the Ivy League Texan and scion of a great political family. All the predecessors of the younger Bush over three decades, beginning with Democratic President Jimmy Carter, helped set the stage.

From the end of World War II to about 1980 while the housing market was securely regulated, a family would typically take out a thirty-year fixed mortgage to make what for most of them was the biggest wealth-building purchase of their lives. The loan made the house more expensive than the stated cost, but also more manageable over the thirty-year term. Besides, in an enlightened policy to encourage home ownership, the home-owning family could deduct about one-third of the mortgage interest on its federal income tax. The local S&L would be at risk for the money it lent out, so it would carefully check the borrower's ability to pay the loan back. The lender did not want foreclosure any more than the borrower.

The setting substantially changed when anti-regulation ideas took hold. The securitization of home mortgages at subprime interest rates was the centerpiece of the financial crisis of 2008. "Securitization" refers to pooling the mortgages and other assets and slicing them up for sale as bonds. The first securitization occurred in 1970 after the Government National Mortgage Association (Ginnie Mae) guaranteed mortgage-backed bonds to spread the risk of default. Since then, the government guaranteed $2.6 trillion in mortgage-backed securities, up to and including fiscal year 2007.[17] Investors found the bonds attractive for their steady income from the interest underlying the pooled securities—as long as the homebuyers generally met their monthly mortgage payments. At this stage before deregulation kicked in, it was a relatively safe innovation because standard mortgage practices, i.e., fifteen- or thirty-year fixed mortgages for credit-worthy borrowers inspired confidence in the bonds.

The variable subprime rates legalized in the deregulation laws of the 1980s made the securitized mortgages more dangerous investments, although still profitable. A prime mortgage in housing finance jargon is based on the conventional thirty-year fixed mortgage. Prime is reserved for low-risk borrowers with few or no credit-rating blights. Subprime rates apply to homebuyers at higher risk of default, those who in the recent past missed monthly payments or experienced foreclosure. Typically, the variable subprime rate is about two percent over prime. The 1980 law made it possible to charge higher interest rates. In 1982 Congress permitted variable interest rates and balloon payments. Repeal of Glass-Steagall in 1999 permitted one company to accept deposits, invest the money, and write insurance on the investments. The Tax Reform Act of 1986 prohibited tax deductions for consumer loans while permitting deductions on first- and second-home mortgages, thus increasing the demand for mortgages over other kinds of borrowing.[18] Early in his first term, President George W. Bush launched a campaign to increase homeownership, setting a goal of 5.5 million new minority homeowners by the end of the decade. His predecessor, Bill Clinton, in pursuit of a similar policy of poor and minority homeownership, had pressured Freddie Mac to underwrite subprime mortgages. The Clinton and G.W. Bush initiatives had obvious political overtones: Bush had won only 9 percent of the black vote and 35 percent of the Hispanic vote in the 2000 election.[19] Pushing poor and minority homeownership lent an aura of legitimacy to the epithet "compassionate conservative" in which Bush had wrapped himself in 2000. The essential difference between the two approaches was ideological. Clinton moved through the government-sponsored entities, Fannie and Freddy; Bush relied more on the private sector. Either way, it facilitated low-credit, high-risk borrowing both for home buying and investing in securitized mortgage-backed bonds.

Declaring homeownership to be part of the American dream, Bush proposed a package of tax credits and vouchers to help defray the high costs of down payments and monthly mortgages. In a speech delivered in October 2002, the president put his stamp of approval on the growth of subprime lending and the securitization of mortgages. "Partners in the mortgage finance industry," he said, "are encouraging homeownership by purchasing more loans made by banks to African Americans,

Hispanics, and other minorities."[20] Later, in his memoir, he sheepishly admitted that he was not thinking of the consequences. "I was pleased the see the ownership society grow," he wrote. "But the exuberance of the moment masked the underlying risk. [The housing boom created a house of cards] fated to collapse as soon as the underlying card—the nonstop growth of housing prices—was pulled out. That was clear in retrospect. Very few saw it at the time, including me."[21] By the time he left office in 2009, homeownership was back to about where it was when he entered the White House in 2001,[22] and home foreclosures were running wild.[23]

The conservative ideological outlook presented a serious impediment to Bush's homeownership policy. In 2002, a few of Bush's federal banking officials put their own and their president's feelings about regulation on public display. They piled up 9,000 pages of financial regulations and, using a chain saw, giddily cut them up into flying scraps of paper.[24] Bush and his policy aides paid little or no attention to the essentially unregulated shadow banking system (i.e., non-banks doing banking business) growing exponentially before their eyes. Nobel economist Paul Krugman pointed to the risks taken by the unregulated financial sector as the "the core" of the crisis. He argued that any company performing banking functions should be regulated just like a bank.[25] Author Kevin Phillips, former Republican strategist turned critic, called the non-bank banking system the "Wild West" of the financial industry. It included institutions such as "mutual funds, non-bank lenders, hedge funds, federally related mortgage entities, issuers of asset-backed securities, security brokers and dealers, and others." In 1976, banks, S&Ls, and insurance companies accounted for 67.6 percent of financial business and the non-bank companies that did banking business, 13.1 percent. In 2006, the proportions were reversed, 30.1 percent for the old guard of finance, 50.1 percent for new shadow bankers.[26] That turn-around could not have made Bush unhappy. In fact, he embraced it, as did many of his predecessors. Non-regulation was, and still is a conservative article of faith, and it led subprime lending into a swamp populated with aggressive, predatory creatures.

Bush's often-expressed desire to boost minority homeownership had the unintended consequence of contributing to the acceleration of the cost of housing and putting the homes out of the reach of the people he wanted to help. So he pushed for government subsidies to make down payments and closing costs affordable to first-time homebuyers and asked the home finance industry to come up with creative lending. Companies in that sector were creative, all right—in finding ways to sucker needy families with subprime loans. They would offer teaser opening mortgages below prime usually for two years that would then transition to floating above-prime rates that would make the monthly payments as much as 30 percent higher and beyond the means of the homebuyer.[27] As long as the value of the house kept rising, a family could refinance and use money drawn from the new mortgage to pay the higher rate. But when the market started to fall, that option was closed, and the low-income family might find that the loan was more than the house was worth. Then as a practical matter the only sensible choice would be to turn the house keys over to the lender and walk away.

Securitization took the housing crisis to another level. Despite the risks, the subprime bond market was so good as long as the market value of housing kept rising that the banking institutions kept huge numbers for their own portfolios. Before long, the housing market began to decline. The bonds became toxic assets and the number of home foreclosures grew to avalanche proportions. Financial institutions from gold-plated Wall Street investment firms to major international banks to shadow banks to insurance companies to government-supported entities like Fannie and Freddy were heavily swaddled in guarantees for subprime bonds as the market significantly weakened in 2006. The government had created Fannie and Freddy to lower lenders' risk by purchasing mortgages and making certain other types of loans and to increase the capital available for more housing purchases.

A subprime mortgage-backed bond is known in Wall Street-speak as a "collateralized debt obligation" (CDO). It is a form of "derivative," a security that derives its value from an underlying asset. The investment genius, Warren Buffett, warned in the 2002 Berkshire Hathaway annual report that derivatives were "time bombs, both for the parties that deal in them and the economic system." He called them "financial weapons of mass destruction, carrying dangers that, while now [in 2002] latent, are potentially lethal." Buffett was in position to know what he was talking about because he engaged in large-scale derivative transactions "to facilitate certain investment strategies" of his own company, Berkshire Hathaway.[28]

The CDO was the product of many mortgages, some of high credit and some of low credit, mixed together and sliced up into subprime bonds. Rating agencies like Moody's or Standard & Poor's would follow normal practice and rate the subprime bonds from AAA (excellent) to BBB (risky). But subprime bonds were not the same as corporate or government bonds. An investor might buy subprime bonds rated AAA and not know the extent to which truly risky mortgages were included in the mix. Picture meat from many cows piled on a chopping block in the back room of your local supermarket being ground up into hamburger and sliced into patties. Customers could not know which, from where, or how many bovines were in the patties or whether the government had actually inspected them. Subprime mortgage-backed bonds were something like that. The jargon identifying them was very impressive, "collateralized debt obligations," but they were nothing more than financial hamburgers dressed up in AAA ratings and sold as prime beef—and buyers could be certain if they took the trouble to investigate that the government had not inspected them. Smart Wall Street traders made fabulous profits on CDOs, but most outsiders, including most investors, were clueless about them. Even Alan Greenspan, former chairman of the Federal Reserve Board and once the lion king of free market advocates, admitted that he did not understand the mathematics of the CDO.[29] What chance would an unsophisticated investor have? And here's the essence of the subprime outrage: the market was unregulated; no laws were broken; no one on Wall Street went to jail, or was prosecuted, or even did the "perp walk" for fast and loose dealing in subprime bonds.

Investment firms hedged their bets on CDOs with "credit default swaps" (CDSs), another form of derivative that insured the CDOs. The swaps predate the arrival of CDO hamburgers. JPMorgan began using swaps in the mid-1990s to free up loan reserves required by federal regulation. The swaps were unregulated private transactions. When the market in subprime bonds shot up in the early 2000s, the swaps market shot up with it—to a value of $62 trillion (trillion with a "t") at its peak, nearly four times the value of all stocks traded on the New York Stock Exchange, according to *Newsweek*.[30] Swaps did nothing to diminish the risk from the falling housing market; they merely spread the risk to insurance companies.

Credit default swaps hit the financial system with a double whammy. Banks bought them with a false sense of security, and then, using them as collateral, invested in more CDOs on credit. Leveraging by major investment banks roughly doubled in the early to mid decade after 2000. In one sense, that closed the circle after eight decades, because leveraging, or buying securities on credit, rampant in the manic 1920s, was a major cause of the 1929 stock market crash. That was one of the whammies in 2006-2008; the other involved traders betting that the bonds would crash when subprime teaser rates ended and homeowners could no longer afford the steeply higher monthly payments. So they bought swaps against bond losses, and then sold the bonds short, which spurred the bonds' decline. Trading in swaps and bonds amounted to reckless speculation in ersatz instruments that enriched traders, but offered no positive benefit to the world beyond finance. When the crash arrived, however, the entire world economy staggered from the impact.

Bear Sterns was the first great Wall Street firm to fall. Losses from the declining value of subprime bonds and other asset-backed securities (toxic assets, for short) piled up through 2006 and 2007. The company doubled its leverage in five years—from $20 to $40 in credit for every dollar of its own spent on subprime bonds.[31] The reckoning came in March 2008 when JPMorgan Chase offered to buy Bear Sterns at the distress price of $2 per share (down from a fifty-two week high of $133.20) and two months later, after the Fed agreed to buy $29 billion in Bear Sterns' toxic assets, settled for $10 per share.

Throughout the summer of 2008, the Wall Street wolves circled Lehman Brothers on a death watch. Two other heavies in the real estate bond market were also in serious trouble, the insurance company, AIG, and the government-created entities, Fannie and Freddy (counting them as one). The latter went first in a carefully planned, swiftly executed federal takeover consummated after the markets closed on Friday, September 5. At both places, heads rolled at the top. Ten days later, Lehman filed for Chapter 11 bankruptcy after trying and failing to reach a merger agreement with major banks. The Bush administration let it die, bowing to bipartisan political pressure against spending Main Street money to bail out Wall Street. That same day in something of a miracle considering the circumstances, Merrill Lynch sold out to Bank of America for $50 billion. The Lehman bankruptcy hit Wall Street like a bolt of lightning, and added an air of near panic to negotiations involving Wall Street firms, international banks, and the U.S. government for ending the crisis. AIG had already defaulted on $14 billion in swaps, and to save it from Lehman's fate, the federal government lent it $85 billion. Subsequently, some notable banks went on sale. The Federal Deposit Insurance Corporation seized Washington Mutual with its $300 billion in assets, the largest S&L in American history, and auctioned it off to JPMorgan Chase for $1.9 billion. And Wells Fargo, outbidding CitiGroup, acquired Wachovia for $7 per share.

On October 3, Congress approved the Troubled Asset Relief Program (TARP) after rejecting it a few days earlier and adding more than 450 pages of legal mumbo-jumbo to the three-page law originally submitted by Treasury Secretary Henry Paulson. The bill provided for Congressional oversight, rejecting Paulson's demand for total control over TARP money. It did give Paulson the $700 billion he had asked for to buy the banks' toxic assets. Paulson went beyond toxic assets to actually buy common shares, giving the government a stake in several Wall Street firms, so that as the shares appreciated, the government would recover the TARP money. Not only did TARP save Wall Street from total financial collapse, it turned out to be a successful investment insofar as the banks were concerned. In 2010 the Congressional Budget Office projected a net profit of $14 billion from bank loans—although the CBO said that TARP would still lose money overall from bailouts in the auto and insurance industries.[32]

Wall Street could always justify its existence as an efficient distributer of capital to keep the world's economy running smoothly. Paulson put it well when he explained his proposed TARP legislation on September 19. "When the financial system works as it should, money and capital flow to and from households and businesses to pay for home loans, school loans, and investments that create jobs." The underlying weakness of the financial system, he concluded, "is the illiquid mortgage assets that have lost value as the housing correction has proceeded. These illiquid assets are choking off the flow of credit that is so vitally important to our economy."[33]

Credit rating agencies like Moody's and Standard and Poor's that gave their highest AAA ratings to bonds in which high-risk subprime mortgages were included, have taken some of the blame for the crash. The deceptive ratings effectively masked the risk, and aggrieved investors fighting an uphill struggle, have challenged the agencies in court. In one of several cases, the Wyoming Retirement System and the Detroit Police and Fire Retirement System argued that agencies including S&P and Moody's were involved in underwriting mortgage pools as well as rating them at arm's length. But a federal appeals court ruled that the defendants were only expressing an opinion protected by the free speech clause in the First Amendment.[34] (The free speech clause, it seems, has latitude beyond speech.)

Bush claimed that he never saw the crisis coming, but in fact, he wasn't looking. One of his housing experts, Armando Falcon, Jr., warned the president and his advisors in advance that Fannie and Freddie, the non-government entities that he oversaw, were overloaded with precarious subprime bonds and at risk to go under.[35] The Bushies ignored the warning, consistent with the administration's pattern of inaction in the face of looming crises. When the financial crisis did arrive, Bush called for Congress to bail out the financial firms stuck with worthless subprime bonds. He did little or nothing for homeowners who could no longer afford to pay for their homes. His shattered dream of minority home ownership lay amid the wreckage of a weakly regulated banking system.

A few perceptive market players foresaw the risk in subprime bonds and bet on them to fail. When the crisis hit, they became multimillionaires. John Paulson became a billionaire while managing a hedge fund that raked in $15 billion in 2007. His personal take was nearly $4 billion.[36] Steve Eisman, a former research analyst for Oppenheimer, bought tons of swaps and cashed in for nearly half a billion dollars. Michael Burry, one of the first to seize the opportunity, made $750 million in 2007 shorting subprime bonds for investors in Scion Capital.[37] They and others were winners against some big Wall Street losers, but something was missing in their triumph. Hugo Lindgren observes in a review for *New York Magazine* of Michael Lewis's book, *The Big Short*, the winners "engaged in activities that were fundamentally the same as the rest of Wall Street's, which [Lewis] describes as 'getting rich shuffling bits of paper around to no obvious social purpose.'"[38] Amen!

Historically, Wall Street investment firms were private partnerships until Salomon Brothers went public in 1978. Other investment banks followed the leader. That changed the dynamic on Wall Street, according to a pet theory of Michael Lewis.[39] Partnerships invest with their own money, so they more carefully weigh the risks of their actions.

Public companies use shareholders' money, so shareholders assume the risks. Not that the traders are willy-nilly careless, but investing someone else's money is not the same as investing one's own. The difference can have an imperceptibly large effect. The bank changeovers coincided with the rush to deregulate, which created more opportunities for profit and more danger of failure. Greed took hold, virtually unchecked by lax or non-existent government regulation. Wall Street went into a feeding frenzy of self-enrichment at the expense of society as a whole. The efficient distribution of capital degenerated into a free-for-all grab for profits. How can Wall Street now justify its existence without protection for investors? And how can conservatives justify the absence of regulation?

Chapter 10

After Bush

Democracy means government by discussion, but it is only effective if you can stop people talking.

—Clement Attlee

Events since Bush's exit have raised the possibility that things could get worse. America remained stuck in bad economic times that started with the crash of 2008. Officially, new President Barack Obama declared the recession over on June 9, 2009.[1] Unofficially, the facts belied his words. Household income fell about twice as fast in the two years since Obama spoke than in the previous two years of official recession.[2] Unemployment since Obama took office hovered stubbornly above 9 percent through 2011—and twice that high if you count part-time workers looking for full-time jobs and people so discouraged that they stopped looking altogether. Home ownership was spiraling downward as banks foreclosed on homes for which the mortgage rose higher than the declining market value of the property.

The political outlook was no less discouraging. Leaders of the Republican Party declared it their priority to make Barack Obama a one-term President, seemingly setting aside their primary responsibility to work with the President to further the national interest. Frustrated by the big spending in Washington, angry citizens gave birth to the Tea Party, which started from the conservative grass roots but soon became a loosely organized rant from the right, and its adherents, too, made the defeat of Obama in 2012 their overriding objective. From the left, the Occupy Wall Street movement made their voices heard without any gesture of support for their president or the Democratic Party. Obama tried to compromise with the uncompromising right, and his popularity measured by public opinion polls plummeted. After the Republicans regained control of the House in the 2010 midterm elections and created gridlock in the legislative process, he suffered their insolence as they branded him a weak-kneed leader who could not get things done. When he began to fight back in the late summer of 2011 with a $447 billion jobs proposal to be paid for with a surtax on the rich, he knew that Republicans would not accept it—and they did not. But his pushback had put the issue on the docket for the 2012 presidential election. The campaign was well underway.

BARACK OBAMA

In the early jockeying for president in the 2008 election, New York Senator and former first lady Hillary Rodham Clinton was the odds-on favorite to win the Democratic nomination. But Obama, a political neophyte with a compelling biography and a gift for oratory, upset her apple cart. In a creative campaign that featured internet solicitation for small donations and strong opposition to the war in Iraq, Obama took an early lead in the race for the nomination that Clinton could not overcome. Obama went on to defeat Republican Senator John McCain in the general election. Expectations were high as Obama took the Oath of Office on January 20, 2009.

Born on August 4, 1961 in Hawaii during the presidency of John F. Kennedy, Barack Obama was the offspring of a white American woman, Ann Dunham, and a black man from Kenya, Barack Obama Sr. They met at the University of Hawaii. When the child was two, he left the family behind to pursue graduate study at Harvard, and from there returned to Kenya. That left the mother to raise the child as a single parent. She was a devoted mother and he was an exceptionally bright child. After she divorced Barack, Sr., she married another former college classmate, an Indonesian named Lolo Soetoro. Mother and child moved to Jakarta when he was six. She found a job teaching English to Indonesian businessmen at the American embassy. But she could not afford to send Barack to the elite International School, so she would rise at 4 a.m. five days a week to teach him the finer points of English. To his frequent complaints about this demanding regimen, she would reply, "This is no picnic for me either, Buster."[3] When "Buster" turned ten, his mother decided that he should return to Hawaii where his maternal grandparents would see to his upbringing. His mother followed a few years later after her second marriage disintegrated.

Barack excelled at a succession of first–rate schools, Punahou Academy in Hawaii, Occidental College in Los Angeles, and Columbia University in New York. After receiving his BA at Columbia, he took a job on Wall Street, but the luster of high finance did not satisfy his yearning for a meaningful life. Two years later, he packed his bags and moved west for a job as a community organizer on Chicago's South Side. There, he found a calling worthy of his ambition. He plunged into the hard existence of the ghetto as a kind of secular priest advising community groups in their struggle to lift the neighborhood up from poverty. Meantime, his father had died while he was still at Columbia. Even though Barack, Sr., often wrote him and once visited him in Hawaii, the youngster had felt a sense of abandonment growing up. After three years in Chicago he traveled to Kenya to connect with that side of his family. It helped him fill a void in his life. Upon his return to the States, he entered Harvard Law School where he became the first black editor of the Harvard Law Review and graduated summa cum laude in 1991. Back in Chicago, he practiced civil rights law, taught at the University of Chicago Law School, organized voter registration drives during Bill Clinton's campaign for president in 1992, and married Michelle Robinson whom he had met as a summer intern at a Chicago law firm. He also took time to write an autobiography of his early years, *Dreams from My Father: A Story of Race and Inheritance,* which received critical acclaim and was translated into ten languages.

Obama entered politics as a Democrat in 1996, winning a seat in the Illinois State Senate. He worked with both Democratic and Republican colleagues especially on poverty, crime, and health issues. In 2000 he ran unsuccessfully for Congress. Four years later, he entered the race for the U.S. Senate. He gained national prominence when he delivered the keynote address at the Democratic national convention, and it helped him overwhelm Republican Alan Keyes in the general election with 70 percent of the vote. On Capitol Hill in Washington he was a solid Democratic vote, but he also worked across the aisle with two Republicans of high integrity, Richard Lugar of Indiana on limiting nuclear proliferation and archconservative Tom Coburn of Oklahoma on keeping track of federal spending. When he ran for President in 2008, he became the darling of the party's liberal base for his strong opposition to the war in Iraq. But he really traveled down the middle of the road, seeking accommodation between left and right, and this moderate approach to governing while in the White House caused him no end of grief dealing with the radical right of the Republican Party.

THE OBAMA PRESIDENCY

A mere twelve years after winning his first election race in Illinois Obama had ascended to the pinnacle of political success. When he entered the White House the financial crisis demanded his immediate attention. Bush had already taken care of much of the top half of the problem. In October 2008, he had signed the $700 billion Troubled Asset Relief Program (TARP) put together by a team under Treasury Secretary Henry Paulson. They used about a third of the money to bail out large and small banks throughout the country, plus the automakers General Motors and Chrysler and the large insurance company, American International Group (AIG), which was bludgeoned in the 2008 financial crisis for insuring toxic bonds. TARP was a bailout, but not a giveaway. The Treasury Department invested in the troubled corporations to replace money lost in the recession so that the affected companies could survive. It worked. TARP stabilized the banking system, and it was the genius of the plan that the government would get most, if not all of its money back once stocks recovered. The jury was still out in March 2011 when the Congressional Budget Office estimated that of the $700 billion originally authorized by Congress, only $432 billion had been or would be actually disbursed, and the ultimate cost of the program might be as low as $19 billion.[4] Most of the TARP loss up to that time stemmed from disbursements to small banks, AIG, and the automakers. The overall bank investments yielded a net gain of about $25 billion, especially from dividends and other returns of the big Wall Street firms.[5] The government cashed in on Wall Street profits.

With the banking industry well on its way to recovery when he took office, Obama focused on reviving AIG and the automakers. The transition from Bush's team to Obama's was smooth. The new Treasury secretary, former chief of the New York Fed Timothy Geithner, had worked with Paulson on TARP, so he could hit the ground running. The government poured $180 billion into AIG, $69 billion of that from TARP. It still was not enough to save AIG. So Geithner pressured the insurer to raise more money from private sources. AIG eventually pulled itself up by government and industry bootstraps and, barring a double-dip recession, will probably survive.[6] AIG reported a profit in the second quarter of 2011,[7] but showed a haughty indifference to the political sensitivities surrounding its bailout by paying huge bonuses to its top executives who participated in the reckless investing that brought the financial industry to its knees.

The government became more deeply involved in the bailout of the automakers. Ford never asked for outside help to survive the recession, but GM and Chrysler did. Conservative hardliners cautioned Bush to keep the government's hands off private industry. Let the market take its course, they advised. The course was certain failure for both companies and the possible dissolution of GM, the erstwhile world leader of the automotive industry. Bush reluctantly gave them $17.5 billion basically to tide them over until the new president came on board. Obama took a firm hand with the two supplicants. He steered them both into bankruptcy so they could rid themselves of serious debt obligations. Then he insisted that Chrysler negotiate to put itself under control of the Italian automaker, Fiat. As for GM, he demanded that CEO Rick Wagoner step aside and encouraged the company's initiative already under way to build hybrid and other battery-operated cars. When GM emerged from bankruptcy court, Obama dipped into TARP for money to aid their recovery. Before long, both GM and Chrysler became profitable, and Obama, ignoring the criticism of free market ideologues, had played a central role in their comeback.

But millions of homeowners who had taken out mortgages at subprime adjustable rates to buy their homes—the bottom half of the problem—would see their jobs disappear in the recession and their property go "underwater," that is, they would owe more on the mortgage than the house was worth. Unemployed and in over their heads, their monthly payments delinquent, they faced personal disaster. Bush had no remedy for them. He turned the problem over to Obama, who has tried to help them with little to show for his efforts. In April 2009 he dipped into TARP to pay for the Home Affordable Modification Program to refinance homes at a lower interest rate. The program has been less than a smashing success. Meant to help three- to four-million homeowners keep their property, it actually benefitted only 587,000 as of May 2011, according to a report by the Republican controlled House of Representatives.[8] In March 2010, the administration rolled out a plan to help unemployed homeowners facing foreclosure with Federal Housing Administration payouts to banks that reduced principal on the mortgage. Again, the funds to pay for it would come from TARP.[9] In October 2011, the White House bypassed Congress to help homeowners refinance their homes to take advantage of the lowest mortgage interest rates in several decades. Experts and politicians, including some from his own party, have argued that Obama's piecemeal approach would not solve the problem. Rep. Dennis Cardoza, a Merced, California Democrat, urged a large-scale program, such as the reduction of principal on underwater mortgages.[10] It is easy to propose, but not so easy to accomplish, especially in today's inhospitable political environment.

Obama prepared a Keynesian stimulus package unrelated to TARP even before he took office, so he began putting it into the legislative mill on day one. Within a month Congress, under total Democratic control, passed and Obama signed the American Recovery and Reinvestment Act of 2009 priced at about $800 billion of borrowed money. It comprised three broad components: tax relief, extended unemployment compensation to mitigate job losses, and the repair and replacement of infrastructure (in part by going green). Missing were Bunyanesque projects of the New Deal, like the Lincoln Tunnel connecting New York City with New Jersey, the Golden Gate Bridge in California, the Grand Coulee Dam in Washington state and government-run job-creating programs like the WPA (originally the Works Progress Administration and later renamed the Work Projects Administration) and the CCC (Civilian Conservation Corps). The WPA provided jobs for millions of unskilled workers at a time of massive unemployment. The workers built parks, roads, bridges, schools, libraries, and other public buildings; laid water pipes and public sewers; ran arts and literacy programs, and distributed food and clothing to children. The CCC, perhaps the most popular New Deal program, employed up to 300.000 young men, eighteen to twenty-five, to improve public lands by planting trees, upgrading parks, and building roads and service buildings. Most of the young workers became more physically fit, improved their work skills, and enjoyed a better outlook on life. Both programs were terminated during World War II. Were they socialistic? Certainly, they were government programs, but more important, they served a public need at a desperate time in American history. The Roosevelt Administration, not locked into a narrow free market ideology, went for practical solutions—and with that "liberal" attitude, saved the free enterprise system.

Nothing quite like the WPA or CCC existed in the Obama stimulus plan, although a "socialistic" program of that nature would certainly have eased the huge unemployment problem. More than eight million Americans lost their jobs in 2008 and 2009, and the subsequent recovery has been slow. The jobs picture remained bleak through 2011, and it promises to be the major issue in the 2012 presidential election. Republicans voted unanimously against the stimulus in 2009, even though it gave them the tax cuts they favored. With unemployment remaining above 9 percent, Republicans persist in smearing the stimulus as an expensive failure. But economists Mark Zandi of Moody's and Alan Blinder of Princeton, taking a less partisan view, argued more than a year after the measure was adopted that without the stimulus unemployment would have gone higher than 11 percent. The Congressional Budget Office had a similar assessment, estimating that the unemployment rate was 0.8 to 1.7 percent lower than it would have been without the stimulus.[11]

So the reality of the stimulus is not that it failed, but that it succeeded insufficiently, judged from the standpoint of job creation. That vindicated many Keynesian economists who said the stimulus package was not big enough. The stimulus cut taxes for most families and helped to tide them over with relief payouts like unemployment compensation. It also created jobs by funding "shovel-ready" local projects like the repair of roads, bridges, schools, and libraries and by grants to state and local governments to pay salaries for police, firemen, teachers, and other public employees who otherwise would have been laid off. Of course, it also widened the federal budget gap.

Someday, history may rate the stimulus a grand success, measured by how it will change society—and that could ultimately have a more dramatic impact on jobs. Money is in the Recovery Act to revolutionize the power grid and make it more efficient, develop more renewable energy, build more battery operated and hybrid cars, and fund other projects that relieve America of its dependence on fossil fuels. Beyond energy, there is money in the package to expand broadband for telecommunications, sponsor genome research for medical cures, build a high speed rail system, digitize health records, promote accountability in education, and a myriad of smaller programs.

The Recovery Act does not boast an unbroken record of success. A Silicon Valley solar panel company, Solyndra, received a $500 million grant from the Department of Energy, and then went bankrupt. House Republicans, needing fodder for the next election, are looking into it—as they should. If they wanted to be even handed, they could also explore the success of a Massachusetts lithium ion battery company, A123 Systems. With the help of heavy federal subsidies, A123 has grown into a global player in the new-age battery market in just one decade.

The stimulus money for these subsidies, successful or failed, comes from an office established in the Department of Energy called Advanced Research Projects Agency-Energy (ARPA-E), modeled after the Defense Advanced Research Projects Agency (DARPA) in the Pentagon. Both agencies act as government versions of venture capitalists. DARPA, which dates back more than half a century, is a smashing success. It ventured the seed money for the amazing Internet and the Global Positioning System that makes precision guidance and navigation possible. ARPA-E subsidizes start-ups too risky for private venture capitalists. Without it, A123 Systems could not have made the leap to a top-tier battery company.[12]

Health care has been a hot political issue for more than a century. Democrats, having made a clean sweep in 2008, took control of both Congress and the White House, and passed a far-reaching health care reform bill in March 2010 that comes close to achieving the long-held Democratic goal of universal coverage. Among other provisions, children can be covered in a family insurance policy up to the age of twenty-six; insurers cannot deny coverage based on a pre-existing condition, and the "doughnut hole" in prescription drug coverage for seniors will be phased out. One controversial feature is a mandate for individuals to buy health insurance, the way states require car owners to buy auto insurance. It was modeled after a mandate adopted by Mitt Romney when he was governor of Massachusetts. Now that Romney is running for president amid universal Republican loathing for "Obamacare," he says it was good for his state, but is not good for the federal government. Several states have challenged the constitutionality of the individual mandate and the issue has wound up in the Supreme Court. Provisions of the new law are being phased in, and while most of it will be in place by 2014, it will not be fully implemented until 2018. Therefore, it will be a few years before a comprehensive evaluation of its impact can be made. However, if far-right Republicans have their way, it will never be fully and fairly judged because candidates on the warpath vying for the 2012 Republican nomination for president vow as their first order of business to kill "Obamacare."

Despite the Obama Administration's new health care legislation, the system is such an expensive mess that it will still need a complete overhaul to fix, starting from scratch. All health care, including care for the elderly, disabled and poor (Medicare and Medicaid), should be brought under a single system with a single federal government payer funded with taxpayer dollars. It would cover everybody without need for individual mandates and would be cheaper if Bush's exorbitant Medicare Advantage program is eliminated. The political obstacles to such a system are so great that its achievement is dismissed as totally unrealistic. If the hyperinflation in the current quasi-private system fed by the huge profits of health insurers and drug companies is taken into account, a public single-payer system becomes more palatable because it is more affordable.

Here is a thought for attaining financial viability while assuring 100 percent coverage. A substantial part of the money that now flows from taxpayers into health care is siphoned off as profit. Reverse the flow. Turn the profits into contributions. Create tax brackets for health care only. The highest income earners would comprise the highest bracket and the rest would pay tax on a graduated scale depending on income. The money would go into a special fund for health care—comparable to Social Security as originally conceived. This arrangement offers a double reward to the super-rich. A share of their vast fortunes would fill a humanitarian need while simultaneously helping to narrow the income gap. They could still opt for private insurance in seeking the best available care, but they could not escape the tax. Some form of capitation, possibly real competition, would have to be imposed on the drug companies and medical providers to control the runaway inflation that plagues the system now. An added benefit at a higher rate of taxation could solve another problem by providing free education and training for doctors in exchange for a pledge to work for a specified number of years in public health. That would obviate the terrible debt that doctors assume before they even start their medical careers. These measures represent freedom—freedom from the fear of unavailable health care, freedom from the perpetually rising "tax" of medical inflation, and freedom from the bondage of debt. Politically, this is an improbable, if not impossible dream because Republicans are sure to resist it. But it offers a practical solution to a chronic problem. The principle is unassailable; health care is a fundamental right and the profit motive should never get in the way. That said, it would take a crisis of colossal proportions to put the idea in motion.

In their next breath, Republican candidates promise to eliminate the Dodd-Frank Act, financial regulation crafted by former Senator Chris Dodd of Connecticut and Representative Barney Frank of Massachusetts when Democrats controlled Congress. Dodd-Frank provides for regulation of Wall Street banks, other derivative inves-tors, and sub-prime lenders, regulation that did not exist when the market collapsed in 2008. The new law, which covers just about every facet of finance in 2,300 pages, seeks to restore public confidence in the market by preventing another crisis. Purportedly, it ends too-big-to-fail and taxpayer bailouts, and affords transparency with respect to exotic instruments and executive compensation. It even contains an "early warning system" to alert regulators of dangerous trends that might lead to another crash. If it is flawed, as Republican opponents contend, it is better than no regulation at all.

By far the most controversial section provides for a Consumer Financial Protection Bureau (CFPB). Voters who wonder why repealing Dodd-Frank is so high on the hit list of Republican candidates for president they need look no further than the CFPB. They don't speak of it in public because they don't want the electorate to know the real reason for their opposition to the new law. After all, its purpose is consumer protection, and no candidate for president would openly admit that he/she is against consumer protection. The Democratic Congress placed it within the Federal Reserve System to examine consumer complaints and help people read the fine print in contracts for bank deposits, mortgages, credit cards, etc. Harvard law professor Elizabeth Warren, a hard working consumer advocate, spent about eight months of her life drawing up plans for the agency and putting it together and organizing a staff of about five hundred. She expected to head it once it emerged, but industry lobbyists and their Republican allies in the Senate fought tooth and nail against, first the enactment of the law, and then her appointment to run the agency. Ultimately, the White House and Capitol Hill Democratic leaders persuaded her to give up on the new consumer agency and, instead, run in Massachusetts in 2012 for the Senate against Scott Brown, the surprise Republican winner of the interim election to serve out the unexpired term of the late Ted Kennedy, the liberal Democratic lion who died of brain cancer in 2009.

Blocking Warren may have been personal and mean spirited, but it was undoubtedly ideological. The Republicans also blocked the man Obama nominated next to head the CFPB, Richard Cordray, former Ohio attorney general, who had the bipartisan support of thirty-nine state attorneys general. The Senate vote on Cordray in December 2011 was 53-45 in favor, but it failed because it did not pass the sixty-vote threshold to break a filibuster. Scott Brown was the only Republican to support Cordray. Republican Olympia Snowe of Maine, who is retiring from the Senate, voted present. Republicans had notified Obama eight months earlier that they did not want any director of the new agency. They wanted to weaken it with a bi-partisan five-person directorate and greater Congressional oversight. The Republican blockage of Warren and Cordray against the interest of middle-class Americans fit perfectly with the GOP vow to work for Obama's defeat in 2012. Obama, however, put Cordray in place at the head of the agency with a recess appointment.

While Obama has experienced an up-and-down three years carrying out his domestic agenda, especially in dealing with the stubbornly high unemployment rate, he has posted an impressive record in foreign affairs. A large share of the credit goes to his rival for the presidency in 2008, the indefatigable Secretary of State Hillary Clinton. At the top of the list of achievements, Obama succeeded where Bush failed to get Osama bin Laden. Bush said America would bring bin Laden back dead or alive, but it did not happen while he was commander-in-chief. Obama asked the CIA to track him down and then after the many months it took for the spy agency to confirm his location to a high degree of certainty, ordered the superbly trained and motivated Special Ops Navy SEALs to raid his compound in Pakistan. They did not bring him back either dead or alive, but executed him on the spot, took photographs for evidence, and then stuffed the body in a weighted, tightly sealed bag and dropped it far out in the Indian Ocean where it could not be enshrined as a symbol of martyrdom for radical Islam. Obama withheld the photographs that confirmed bin Laden's death from public view.

Overall, judging from a military standpoint, the fight against al-Qaida seems to have gone extremely well. Pilotless drones, controlled from secure bases in South Asia, the Middle East, and the United States thousands of miles away, fly surveillance over terrorist territory. An operator in a control room can see activity and hear conversations in the mountains of Pakistan and Afghanistan from instrumentation in the aircraft and overhead satellites. If a worthy target presents itself, the operator, acting on higher authority, can launch a precision missile from the drone. The success rate has been nothing short of phenomenal. But using remote-controlled drones has yielded mixed results when you consider the humanitarian, political and diplomatic fallout. Although effective in killing al-Qaida terrorists, the drones have also caused civilian deaths, which traumatize innocent loved ones and create sensitivities for friendly governments. Drones have also been deployed to cover other terrorist encampments in places like Yemen and Somalia.

The American withdrawal from Iraq heals the wound inflicted by the needless U.S. intervention, but the war leaves an ugly scar. A substantial force meant to forestall wanton aggression (especially from Iran) has been left behind in Kuwait. Without an American presence, oil-rich Kuwait probably could not exist for long and the oil-rich kingdoms of the Persian Gulf could be severely threatened. It raises the incentive for America to develop more of its own energy resources—especially the green variety together with natural gas—to eliminate its dependence on foreign oil. Then America would no longer need to defend the Persian Gulf. Gradual withdrawal from Afghanistan has begun. The draw-downs can have multiple benefits: keeping the peace in South Asia and the Middle East, enhancing America's global image, and easing the budget crunch at home. Nuclear-armed Pakistan remains a powder keg. It harbors deep hostility toward India and nurtures the seeds of terrorism in its mountains. Yet, it tries to keep up its ties to and aid from America. Israel and Palestine remain at an impasse, but given the underlying realities, anyone who expects progress on that front in the near future is deluded, and it appears that the Obama Administration is no longer trying. George Mitchell, former Democratic majority leader in the Senate and one of America's most skillful diplomats, has resigned from his position as America's chief troubleshooter in the area.

America has kept faith with the NATO alliance by participating in the defeat of Libyan dictator Moammar Qaddafi without risking American lives on the ground. It stood by in passive support of the "Arab Spring," which brought down Qaddafi and other dictatorships in North Africa. From the standpoint of realpolitik, however, America lost a staunch ally in Egypt with the ouster of President Hosni Mubarak. Not everybody was sorry to see him go because his army used American weapons obtained in the multi-billion dollar U.S. aid program to suppress his own people. But Mubarak had been a crucial ally because he supported the treaty with Israel. His downfall is vaguely similar to that of the Shah of Iran in 1979, which brought Islamist clerics to power and destroyed the U.S.-Iranian strategic alliance. It hasn't gone nearly that far in Egypt. But Islamist parties, which deplore secular society and believe in divine sovereignty over earthly peoples, can be counted on to pursue policies that do not necessarily coincide with American and Israeli interests. Specifically, they will most likely try to undermine the Egyptian peace treaty with Israel. In fact, it was an Islamist group that assassinated Anwar al-Sadat, Mubarak's predecessor who negotiated the agreement with Israel. The Muslim Brotherhood, parent group of the well organized Freedom and Justice Party, has much to gain from the new Egyptian democracy. Although often brutally suppressed, the Brotherhood had remained in Egypt to work non-violently within the pluralist system when the most radical Islamist elements followed Ayman al-Zawahiri to the mountain retreats of South Asia to eventually join al-Qaida. Now Freedom and Justice holds a strong political position from which to influence Egyptian policy.

The Obama Administration has maintained correct relations with the other great powers, Russia and China. The misguided Bush initiative to place elements of a defensive missile shield on the soil of Russia's western neighbors, Poland and the Czech Republic, is on hold. In the Pacific, Obama has worked overtime to open up Asian markets to American goods—the better to grow jobs in the United States. In a bold new deployment, Obama announced during a trip to friendly Australia in November 2011 that a small tripwire force of U.S. troops will be stationed at Darwin on that country's northern coast across the Timor and Arafura Seas from Indonesia as a counterbalance to China's growing presence in the South China Sea and beyond. The deployment will begin with 250 Marines, and could go up as high as 2,500 troops, according to initial reports. It was a heady move in the dangerous game of global chess, seen with some trepidation by other powers in the region such as China and Indonesia.

All told, however, Obama and Hillary Clinton have attended carefully and competently to America's interests abroad. But beware the long-term effects of the Arab Spring. The promise of democracy will most likely benefit anti-democracy Islamist forces that believe in divine sovereignty.

Chapter 11

Believers and Clowns

There's none so blind as those who will not see... [and]
none so deaf as those who will not hear.

—Proverbs

A great empire and little minds go ill together

—Edmund Burke

The Tea Party may have sprouted randomly from the grass roots of American soil, but the far right has always cultivated it for its own purpose: to devour, like the meat-eating plant from outer space in the movie "Little Shop of Horrors," the presidential flesh of Barack Obama. That was clear even before the Tea Party propelled the Republican Party to a takeover of the House of Representatives in the 2010 election. Senate Republican leader Mitch McConnell declared in an October 2010 interview with Major Garrett of the *National Journal*, "The single most important thing we want to achieve is for President Obama to be a one-term President."[1] By and large, McConnell was enunciating a policy of non-cooperation with Obama, even though in the same interview he promised that he would meet the President halfway in a crisis. He and House Speaker John Boehner proved it by making a deal as the debt ceiling confrontation in the summer of 2011 was gaining the nation international contempt and drawing the world economy into financial chaos.[2]

As the 2012 election year approached, McConnell's wish fulfillment that Obama lose in his bid for a second term remained open to doubt. The Republican nominee for president was still to be decided in caucuses and primary elections. But whoever won the nomination, the slate of candidates was so weak that it shifted the odds more in Obama's favor. Obama had the advantage of incumbency, but that would not help him if unemployment did not improve. The Tea Party instilled conservative energy into the race, but it might not be there for the leading Republican candidate, Mitt Romney, whom conservatives do not wholly embrace. The stage was set for an interesting race that would likely have a profound effect on the fate of the nation.

THE TEA PARTY

Early local protests staged by conservative activists seemed spontaneous enough. Keli Carender organized a rally in Seattle on February 16, 2009 against the then-pending stimulus bill, and eleven days later she staged another protest, also in Seattle.[3] Michelle Malkin, a Fox News contributor, plugged both Carender events as well as a rally in Denver on February 17 put on by the Americans for Prosperity Foundation (APF), the right wing activist group funded by the billionaire Koch brothers. Two days later, Rick Santelli, a business news editor at CNBC, went on a rant at the Chicago Mercantile Exchange over an Obama plan to help desperate homeowners refinance their homes. To Santelli, such mortgage assistance would be equivalent to subsidizing losers. He called for a "tea party," like that in Boston harbor in 1774, to dump mortgage derivatives in Lake Michigan. Before long, fervor in conservative circles for Tea Party protests had spread across the nation.

Local Tea Party chapters popped up like mushrooms in a rain forest. There was no national organization or overall governing body, but FreedomWorks, a professional group in Washington headed by Dick

Armey, former House of Representatives Republican leader, exercised in the manner of a friendly uncle a certain influence over Tea Party activities and logistics. For example, as the movement snowballed in the late winter and spring of 2009, FreedomWorks brought Keli Carender and maybe two dozen other local Tea Party leaders from around the country to Washington to be trained in staging protests. The APF also casts a long shadow over the movement. It is a virtually unlimited source of funds, but because the Koch brothers operate covertly on the right, it is impossible to know the extent of their funding. Tea Party followers look for inspiration to certain heroes like Rep. Ron Paul, the libertarian from Texas; Sarah Palin, the former governor of Alaska and 2008 Republican vice presidential candidate, and Senator Jim DeMint of South Carolina. Republican Rep. Michele Bachman of Minnesota formed a Tea Party caucus in the House of Representatives, and Ron Paul's son, newly elected Republican Senator Rand Paul of Kentucky, organized one in the Senate.

Rand Paul came to Washington in the Tea Party tidal wave that swept the nation in the 2010 election. Other notable Republican victors that year included Marco Rubio of Florida who claimed erroneously that his parents fled Castro's Cuba, and Scott Brown of Massachusetts, who won a special election in the bluest of blue states to fill out the term of the late Ted Kennedy, the Democratic icon who had died of brain cancer. Altogether, the Republicans gained six seats in the Senate, not quite enough to take control from the Democrats. In the House, Republicans gained sixty-three seats and actually did win control, setting up divided government. Nothing could pass out of Congress without bipartisan support, and because many new members sprang from the bosom of the Tea Party enraged by heavy federal spending and budget deficits they drew the Republican leadership to more hardened positions on the right and would brook no compromise.

Even before the new Congress was sworn in, the weakened president negotiated an agreement with congressional Republicans in December 2010 that did not sit well with members of his own party. Obama wanted to end the Bush income tax cuts for the wealthiest 2 percent of income earners, but wound up allowing those cuts to stay in place for two more years in exchange for extending unemployment insurance for thirteen months. In the process, Obama bowed to Republican demands by agreeing to $39 billion in spending cuts. A reduction in payroll taxes, which satisfied both sides even though it cut into the Social Security fund, was also part of the deal. Democrats on Capitol Hill thought Obama had given up too much too easily on taxing the rich. Howard Dean, former presidential candidate and chairman of the Democratic National Committee who had guided the Democratic sweep in 2008, called it "a failure of leadership." [4]

POLITICAL COMBAT

The 2010 year-end clash over tax policy, however, paled in comparison to the coming battle over the debt ceiling. That the accumulated federal deficit is a serious problem cannot be denied. Consisting of borrowed money that the government has spent or designated for spending, it stood at more than $14 trillion as of mid-November 2011. In the past, periodically raising the debt ceiling to pay for programs already approved by Congress had always been a bi-partisan, pro-forma exercise condemned by deficit-hawks. But in 2011 the Republican House, fortified by its Tea Party members and the nearly unanimous (among Republicans) no-tax-increase pledge secured by Grover Norquist, served notice that it would not approve a higher debt ceiling without commensurate cuts in government services, especially in the so-called entitlement programs that conservatives have long targeted for liquidation: Social Security, Medicare, and Medicaid. Democrats who still held a thin majority in the Senate insisted on higher taxes for the rich. They considered it a matter of fairness that the burden of paying down the nation's debt should not be borne entirely by those who could least afford to pay. Conservatives argued that to single out the rich for higher taxes is to penalize those in the best position to create jobs.

In other words, the two sides were engaged in the same old class argument in a slightly different framework. The threat to freeze the debt ceiling put the nation at risk of defaulting with terrible consequences on a global scale. Many third-world dictatorships had crashed for spending lavishly beyond their nation's means. For the United States to crash—this beacon of freedom and democracy, this behemoth of economic and military power—would arguably have an impact without equal in history. Could the nation's elected leaders allow that to happen? Republicans thought they held the high cards. When it came down to hard bargaining, they believed, Obama would be a pussy cat; he would give in. Obama is a brilliant man. His academic achievements and political triumphs speak loud. He won a Nobel peace prize and liquidated Osama bin Laden. Yet something was missing in his leadership skills. He seemed to lack a killer instinct. He kept reaching out to compromise with no-compromise Republicans who wanted his scalp. He had them in a corner now and failed to deliver the knockout blow. It was fairly obvious that Tea Party activists had overreached their mandate. It was time for Obama to smack them down, but he kept trying to compromise.

Treasury Secretary Timothy Geithner, Democratic lawmakers on Capitol Hill, and constitutional scholars urged an alternative along the following lines: Relying on Section Four of the Fourteenth Amendment to the Constitution, which states that the validity of the debt shall not be questioned, he could declare the debt ceiling unconstitutional and direct Geithner to ignore it and borrow money beyond the ceiling. That argument was highly dubious because the Constitution assigns Congress the power of the purse. Yet, if Obama had acted on it, it would have immediately lifted the threat of default while the debate over the Constitutional issue could rage for months on its way to the Supreme Court. But the law professor in Obama moved him, in effect, to rule on the issue before it even got started. He ignored Geithner's advice and continued to negotiate with the adamant Republicans. His judgment about the constitutionality of the debt ceiling maneuver was probably correct, especially with a conservative court ruling on the issue. A more pertinent consideration, though, would be the political fallout, and Obama was unwilling to take the risk of being overruled.

Yet, this time Obama was no pussy cat. Without running the uncharted waters of constitutional law, he plunged full speed ahead. He held firm to the Democratic position that the rich should pay more in taxes if the poor and elderly must take cuts in services. Deep down, Republican leaders were as anxious as the President to make a deal. McConnell gave repeated assurances that there would be no default. There would be no compromise either; in the words of the tired old cliché, they would merely "kick the can down the road." On August 1 they agreed to create a twelve-member Congressional super committee of three Democrats and three Republicans from each house with extraordinary power to decide the issue. The Debt Ceiling Joint Committee, as it was named, would report back by November 23, giving it three months and three weeks to recommend a package of spending cuts and revenue reforms to reduce the deficit over a ten-year period to be presented to each full house for an up-or-down vote without amendment. If the committee failed to agree, or if the package was voted down by either chamber, government agencies would be subjected to draconian cuts in funding adding up to at least $1.2 trillion (about 50 percent of which would be absorbed by the Pentagon) starting in 2013 after the next presidential election. The creation of the super committee shrank the arena of conflict, but the issues still boiled down to a need for compromise. Again, there was no compromise; November 23 came and went without an agreement. Immediately, Congressional hawks began to draw up legislation to soften the blow on the Defense Department. But Obama drew a line in the sand. He would not back down, he said, on the $1.2 trillion fallback budget reductions without a tax increase on the wealthiest taxpayers. The president was now playing hardball.

If Obama regretted not accepting the deficit reduction proposal of the bipartisan National Commission on Fiscal Responsibility and Reform (NCFRR) that he created, he gave no indication of it.

Commonly known as the Simpson-Bowles Commission after its co-chairmen, former Republican Senator Alan Simpson of Wyoming and former Clinton chief-of-staff Erskine Bowles, the NCRFF offered a package that would have bruised just about every sacred cow in Washington by closing about a third of the Pentagon's military bases around the globe, eliminating earmarks, cutting the federal work force by 10 percent, reducing farm subsidies, federal pensions, and student loans, and clamping controls on health care costs. On the revenue side it would have charged an additional 15 cents per gallon gasoline tax, cut back the home mortgage interest deduction, and increased the payroll tax for Social Security while lowering corporate taxes from 35 percent to 26 percent. Finally, it would have upped the retirement age for Social Security.[5] The package would have shaved nearly $4 trillion from the $14 trillion deficit over nine years. Fifty-eight percent of the reduction would have come from cuts in spending, 25 percent from new revenues, and 17 percent from interest savings. A super majority of fourteen of the eighteen members was needed for passage, but only eleven voted for it.[6] So the proposal was hung out to twist in the wind, and Obama left it there. If he had adopted it, he might have averted the deficit ceiling crisis the following July and probably would have been a one-term president.

Obama's performance in the deficit ceiling imbroglio helped to bring down his poll numbers, so he turned to the single most important issue in his bid for a second term, jobs. If unemployment should get significantly below 9 percent by Election Day, he might prevail. So the White House rolled out a $447 billion jobs bill in the late summer of 2011 to be financed by a surtax of 5.6 percent on people earning more than a million dollars. It marked the beginning of his bid for reelection in 2012. He knew the Republicans in Congress would reject it, and so they did, twice. They argued that it was just another stimulus package, like the one in 2009, which they claimed was a failure, but which, more accurately, was an inadequate success. So the Senate Democrats broke the overall jobs bill into separate parts and offered the parts one at a time and the Republicans rejected each one as it came up for a vote—except, finally, one that provided incentives for businesses that hired veterans of the wars in Iraq and Afghanistan.

After the super-committee failed to agree on a debt reduction plan before Thanksgiving, another showdown came at the end of 2011. This time, Obama came out slightly ahead. He wanted to extend a 2 percent cut in the payroll tax of for another full year, to be paid for with a tax surcharge on millionaires. The deal would include extended insurance for the long-term unemployed. At first House Republicans said no, especially to the tax surcharge on the wealthy. In effect, they were condemning middle class working people to a tax increase while holding the line for millionaires whom they consider to be "job creators"—a losing argument with a majority of Americans, according to public opinion polls.

So the Republicans came around on the tax-cut extension, but continued to argue on how to pay for it. In addition to their intransigence on the millionaire surcharge, they demanded that Obama approve a new oil pipeline from Canada to Texas. They offered a variety of payment options that included a five-year freeze on salaries for government workers and a forty-week extension of unemployment compensation, reduced from a full year. The standoff continued as the time approached for members of Congress to go off on their Christmas vacations. As a last resort, Senate leaders agreed to a two-month extension of the tax cut to allow the fight to continue until the end of February. But House Republicans balked; they now wanted a full year extension or nothing; "No more kicking the can down the road," they said. That brought a chorus of criticism from conservative opinion makers, including the *Wall Street Journal*, who cried out, "Take the compromise." Speaker John Boehner caved in. It left Democrats rejoicing and House Republicans bitterly divided. Obama, the fighter and not the compromiser, had boosted his stock with his Democratic base. What made things even sweeter for the Democrats, before the February deadline arrived Republicans bowed meekly to the Democrats' terms.

2011: THE YEAR OF THE CLOWNS

"Send in the Clowns," a soft, plaintive song from the Broadway musical *A Little Night Music*, contemplates lost love as farce amid the realization that playing the field had been playing the fool. For that to be farce, it is suggested, the act needs clowns, and the song poses the obvious question, "Where are the clowns?" and when none appears, it concludes with heavy heart, "Well, maybe next year." If anything, the self-deception of politics is at least as farcical as that of lost love. To the surprise and discomfort of the American people who witnessed the full media panoply of the 2011 preseason Republican race for the party's nomination for president, the clowns showed up in abundance whether needed or not.

Twenty-eleven was the year of the clowns in American politics—not that serious candidates did not address serious problems, but some came off as ill-equipped to occupy the high office they sought. What were they doing there? Selling books? Pampering egos? Running for vice president? Some high-profile people only toyed with the idea of running, but never joined the race. Jon Huntsman, former governor of Utah and ambassador to China, who appeared by reason of experience and clear thinking to be most qualified, did not appeal to the conservative base because he had served as ambassador to China in the Obama Administration. He was stuck at or near the bottom of the pack, while a parade of candidates and pseudo-candidates struggled to be the anti-Mitt Romney contender. Ron Paul, a Texas Congressman with libertarian views had a loyal but narrow following. Rick Santorum, former senator from Pennsylvania, and Congresswoman Michele Bachmann of Minnesota articulated clear conservative ideas, but managed only temporary spikes in popularity. Former House Speaker Newt Gingrich carried a lot of heavy baggage that could be held against him. Herman Cain, an ex-pizza executive, stood out as uninformed on the issues, especially foreign policy. Romney—intelligent, articulate, and well prepared—was the favorite to win the nomination, but widely considered to be a liberal, flip-flopping opportunist not to be trusted by conservatives. These and other candidates engaged in several revealing debates carried on cable news channels and broadcast networks that alternated between high promise and low comedy.

With the Tea Party's anti-regulation, tax-cut gestalt firmly attached to the Republican Party brain, candidates began lining up to contend for the GOP nomination. At the start, some potential candidates only teased the faithful. Donald Trump, the New York real estate tycoon, was an early favorite. He had gained national name recognition by hosting "The Celebrity Apprentice" on television in which he fires people from their employment—all in good fun, of course, but a lumpish act in a presidential race where he would have to address the jobs issue. He did not actually declare his candidacy and spent most of his political energy bugging Obama about his place of birth, arguing that he was born in Kenya and therefore ineligible to hold the office of U.S. President—the so-called "birther" issue. Obama was actually born in Honolulu, the principal city of the fiftieth state, and because Trump and a few extreme Tea Partiers considered Obama a Muslim double agent in a conspiracy against America, the President went to the trouble of producing his original birth certificate. Without acknowledging his personal embarrassment, Trump took credit for "smoking out" the President.

With Trump in attendance at the 2011 White House correspondents' dinner in Washington, Obama, flashing a broad smile, displayed the birth certificate on a video screen and declared in words that dripped with sarcasm amid uproarious peals of laughter,

> No one is happier to put this birth certificate issue to rest than The Donald.... We all know, [Mr. Trump], about your credentials and breadth of experience. ... For example, in an episode of "Celebrity Apprentice" at the steakhouse, the men's cooking team did not impress the judges..., and there was a lot of blame to go around. But you, Mr. Trump, recognized that the real problem was a lack of leadership. So you didn't blame Little John or Meatloaf. You fired Gary Busey. But these are the kind of decisions that would keep me up at night. Well handled, sir. Well handled.

Then he displayed on the screen an image of how Trump might change things at the White House. It showed a large sign blocking out much of the White House that read,

Trump
The White House
Hotel Casino Golf Courses
Presidential Suite

It symbolized both Trump's bizarre qualifications for president and his outsized ego that inspires him to put his name up high at casinos and other real estate that he acquires. Shortly thereafter Trump announced that he would not seek the Republican nomination. But there is no reason to think that Obama's roast influenced Trumps withdrawal.

Sarah Palin, John McCain's Republican running mate in 2008 and a Tea Party darling, hung around to compete with other candidates for attention without dropping her hat in the ring. The former Alaska governor joined the Tea Party express in New Hampshire on the day that Mitt Romney formally announced his candidacy and appeared in Iowa when President Obama showed up. She did not enter the Iowa straw poll or participate in a candidates' debate, but she worked the crowds at the state fair. Comedian Jon Stewart mocked her "maybe" candidacy for squeezing contributions out of her supporters without committing herself—"Take the money and don't run," said the tag on the television screen. Finally, on the day that Governor Chris Christie of New Jersey rejected pleas for him to enter the race, Palin quietly announced that she would not run either.

Michele Bachmann was the other mama in the Republican melee. Remarkably, she has raised five children and twenty-three foster children in thirty-three years of marriage. A Congresswoman from Minnesota and another Tea Party favorite with far right Christian conservative credentials, she let it be known at the earliest debate in New Hampshire that she would enter the race. It was her favorite line (echoing Mitch McConnell) that Obama would be a one-term

President. She made it her first priority to repeal "Obamacare," the Republicans' sneering term for the Democrats' health care reform legislation. In her short time on Capitol Hill, she had managed to create an unfavorable image of herself. On June 26, 2011 before she formally announced her candidacy, Chris Wallace interviewed her on "Fox News Sunday." Referring to the "rap" against her in Washington based on comments she had made that some members of Congress were anti-American and that NATO forces had killed 30,000 innocent people in Libya, Wallace asked her if she was a flake. Bachmann replied that it was an insulting question and that she was a serious candidate for President. A day or two later, after a strong negative reaction from his viewing audience, Wallace apologized. Bachman neither accepted nor rejected the apology, but told ABC reporter Jonathan Karl that it was a small matter and she was focused on big issues. Wallace did right to apologize, but in that dust-up she came out ahead. When she won the Iowa straw poll with twenty-nine percent of the votes, she vaulted to the top of the heap, chasing former Minnesota Governor Tim Pawlenty out of the race. Bachmann's triumph, however, was short-lived.

On the day of the Iowa straw poll, third-term Governor Rick Perry of Texas chose to announce his candidacy for President in the early primary state of South Carolina. Riding a wave of remarkable job growth in Texas, Perry instantly took the lead in public opinion polls, but within days he demonstrated a knack for sticking his Texas-booted foot in his mouth. On the stump in Iowa, he had this to say about Federal Reserve Chairman Ben Bernanke: "If this guy prints more money between now and the election, I dunno what y'all would do with him in Iowa, but we would treat him pretty ugly down in Texas. Printing more money to play politics at this time in American history is almost treacherous, er, treasonous, in my opinion." Subsequently, Perry rejected the science of global warming, explained to a child his preference for creationism over evolution, and in a late September debate in Orlando, Florida, stumbled so badly describing Romney as a flip-flopper that Fox newsman

Brit Hume commented, Perry "threw up all over himself." The fallout was swift. In a straw poll of Florida Republican delegates two days later, Perry won only fifteen percent of the vote. The surprise winner was Herman Cain with thirty-seven percent. Romney received fourteen percent and Bachmann went down with a thud to one percent. She had attacked Perry for mandating as governor of Texas HPV vaccine for teenagers to prevent cervical cancer. She alleged, erroneously, that the vaccine caused mental retardation in children.

Cain, the only black in the race, had a style hinting of bravado. He was once CEO of Godfather Pizza, with no government or political experience except an unsuccessful run for the U.S. Senate in Georgia. His main campaign theme was tax reform, expressed as "nine—nine—nine," 9 percent sales tax, 9 percent income tax, and 9 percent corporation tax. He said it would create jobs, but it sounded more like a gimmicky campaign slogan than a serious proposal. Huntsman quipped that he thought Cain was quoting the price of a pizza. Up to the Florida straw poll, the pundits had paid little heed to Cain, but his victory there and his sudden rise in public opinion polls caught their attention. The Cain tax reform, liberals concluded, was no less regressive than the George W. Bush formula. It would raise taxes for the poor and middle class while lowering taxes for the wealthy. Conservatives panned it because it introduced a new form of federal taxation, the sales tax, and they feared that liberals would raise the rate above 9 percent at the first opportunity.

When it came to foreign affairs, Cain made Perry seem like the second coming of Socrates. Cain even lacked Bush's foresight to bone up on the subject before he began running for President. He told host David Gregory on NBC's "Meet the Press" that he was not familiar with the neoconservative movement that had promoted the unnecessary war in Iraq, which war Cain thought was "a good idea." In an interview with Judy Woodruff of PBS, he said that he knew China was seeking nuclear technology nearly a half century after China first tested an atomic bomb. At one point in the campaign, he staged a photo op with Henry Kissinger. But that did not seem to help him at a meeting with the *Milwaukee Journal Sentinel* editorial board shown on video released by the newspaper. Asked if he supported Obama's handling of the Libyan crisis, he stumbled badly. After pauses, false starts, and some shuffling in his seat as if reaching for an answer that kept eluding him, he finally asserted that he would have done a better job than Obama of assessing the nature of the opposition to Libyan dictator Muammar Qaddafi. Cain also disclosed at the meeting that Kissinger had turned down his offer to be secretary of state in his cabinet. (The only surprise there is that Kissinger even wasted his time meeting with Cain.)

Cain, showing a certain personal magnitude, used his sudden popularity to raise money and strengthen his organization. One source he sought out was the fabulously rich Koch brothers, generous sponsors of conservative causes and candidates. Cain expressed his love of them in a speech in Washington, D.C., to Americans for Prosperity, which was founded and is still funded by the Koch brothers. "I am the Koch brothers' brother from another mother," he declared to a receptive audience that included the Kochs. Cain flew high in the polls, challenging Romney at the top while the malaprop Perry fell far behind after committing more campaign gaffes, including an embarrassing "brain freeze" during a debate in which he couldn't remember one of three federal agencies (the Energy Department) he vowed to abolish as President.

But as much as conservative voters seemed to like him, Cain didn't stay at the top either. His decline began with a sex scandal dating back to the late 1990s. At first, it involved two women who filed sexual harassment charges against him while he was president of the National Restaurant Association (NRA). A third woman spoke out, and then a fourth. Finally, a fifth woman, Ginger White, revealed that she and Cain carried on a consensual thirteen-year sexual affair—unknown to Cain's wife. The pity from the standpoint of American politics is that Cain's alleged sexual dalliances distracted from his wholesale ignorance of the issues facing the nation. Cain's high standing in the polls did not collapse; it slid gradually over the following two or three weeks, but he was finished as a serious candidate. The butt of late night television jokes, he stood out as a larger-than-life con artist who knows next to nothing about policy. So what was he doing running for president? The very question exposes a flawed electoral system in the age of television.

Newt Gingrich became the next anti-Romney challenger. Gingrich, a Ph.D. and former professor, has authored both fiction and non-fiction works on historical subjects. He served in the House of Representatives for twenty years, the last four as Speaker. He is highly intelligent and skilful in debate. Ideas good and bad pour out of him like cascading water. He has taken an unwarranted share of credit for the defeat of communism and balancing the Clinton budget, but earned a legitimate place in history for something he might like to forget as a candidate for President. He introduced the politics of personal destruction in Congress. In 1983, he and Congressman Bob Walker of Pennsylvania began staying after the close of business to make speeches to an empty House chamber carried nationwide on C-Span castigating certain Democratic colleagues as "radicals" for criticizing the Vietnam War a decade after it ended for America. Then-Speaker Tip O'Neill blew his stack at what he considered a breach of House decorum for attacking members by name without giving them a chance to respond. O'Neill confronted Gingrich on the House floor and called his action "the lowest thing I have ever seen in my thirty-two years in Congress," but Republicans succeeded in having O'Neill's words stricken from the record.

Gingrich became a hero to many Republican members and subsequently led a fight to oust Jim Wright, O'Neill's successor as Speaker, on ethics violations. The GOP took over the House in the 1994 midterm election, ending four decades of Democratic control, and rewarded Gingrich by electing him Speaker in 1995. *Time* named him its 1995 Man of the Year. Four years later he resigned under a cloud of ethics charges at a time of Republican rancor over losing ground in the 1998 election.[7] The Gingrich experience left Congress locked in bitter partisan warfare that often puts the nation's real business in cold storage. Gingrich created chaos in the Congress. What would he do in the White House? What would he do to the image of a great nation?

Since leaving Congress he has made a ton of money serving special interests. The intellectual conservative columnist and author George Will called Gingrich the "classic rental politician" for using his clout in Washington to influence the powerful on behalf of corporate clients. It made him a multi-millionaire with a life-style that included travel by private jet and chauffeured limousines. His many business activities included a health-care think tank, consulting (i.e., lobbying), speeches at $60,000 a pop, media appearances, book writing with two co-authors focusing on historical fiction, a video production company that made documentaries on historical subjects, and a non-profit political operation called American Solutions for Winning the Future. His personal income in 2010 was $2.5 million, according to his financial disclosure form obtained by the *Washington Post*. He charged travel expenses, including the chartered jet and chauffeured limousine, to American Solutions.[8]

Gingrich has flip-flopped on major issues at least as much as Romney. He once supported the controversial individual health insurance mandate in Massachusetts, and then as presidential candidate, he criticized Romney for pushing it through. He blasted Rep. Paul Ryan's budget plan for funding Medicare through block grants to states as "right wing social engineering." Later, he backed off and expressed support for the Ryan budget proposal. After he left Congress, Freddie Mac hired Gingrich's consulting firm to influence his former conservative peers. *Bloomberg* reported that Gingrich personally made $1.6 million to $1.8 million off the Freddie Mac account over several years. He tried to say Freddie hired him for his knowledge of history, but that cock and bull story fell flat and he has admitted to contributing "strategy" advice. Then he had the gall to say that Democratic Senator Chris Dodd and Congressman Barney Frank should go to jail for being in bed with Freddie Mac. He denies that he ever lobbied for anyone.

Gingrich's double-dealing persona extends to his philandering private life. He has been married three times and divorced twice, and prior to each divorce he carried on with his future wife. He recently converted to Catholicism and repented his sins. Now he strives for redemption. Evangelical Christians, a large part of the conservative base, believe in redemption, which may offset their distress over his infidelity. They were not the least forgiving of former President Clinton who also engaged in sex outside of marriage and whose affair with Monica Lewinski led the House to vote for impeachment. Gingrich is on the side of the Evangelicals. He articulates their conservative values. But by their support of him, God's law gives way to tribal politics.

While Romney's more conservative opponents rose and fell in successive polls, the former Massachusetts governor usually polled at about 25 percent, meaning that seventy-five percent of those queried were against him, but divided on who they were for. Clearly, conservatives considered him a threat, not a hero. Their successive favorites momentarily lit up the sky and then faded—until in early December 2011 after the fall of Cain, Gingrich suddenly surged to the top while Romney's poll numbers dropped into the teens. Just as suddenly, Gingrich fell out of favor, but this time not from any of his campaign failings. In the days prior to the Iowa caucus, SuperPACs supporting Romney ran a series of negative ads reminding Iowa voters of Gingrich's uneven political past. The former Speaker's standing in the polls collapsed just as the Iowa caucuses approached.

Romney's pre-caucus blitz came with the compliments of the U.S. Supreme Court in its unprecedented *Citizens United* decision, which allows unlimited spending by SuperPACs immediately prior to balloting without identifying the individual, corporation, or organization that puts up the money. An obvious blunder by the Supreme Court that overturned existing law, the decision served as a preview of things to come in the Republican primaries and the 2012 general election. None other than President George W. Bush shaped the court with the appointment of two conservative justices, including the chief justice, which made the *Citizens United* ruling. The conservative court claimed to be non activist, or strict constructionist, but has proved to be activist on conservative issues. Past rulings that corporations are people and that money in political campaigns is a form of free speech set the groundwork for allowing the rich to speak orders of magnitude louder than the poor.

Santorum was next to rise on the very eve of the Iowa caucuses. He had waged a vigorous low budget, highly personal campaign, visiting every county in the state and talking to people on Main Street, in their homes, and at small neighborhood gatherings. With his laudable work ethic, he peaked at just the right time, but pundits did not believe that he had the magnetism, money, or organization to win the nomination.

It appears from the ups and downs of the 2011 preseason that Tea Party conservatives don't know who they want among available candidates for president, but they know who they don't want, Barack Obama. Yet, it's not clear why. They seem very passionate in their hatred of him for reasons that dwell deep inside but may be for many of them no more than skin deep. To be sure, no one is perfect, but Obama has been a competent President with compassion for his fellow Americans and a desire to compromise. He stands tall against the record of his predecessor.

George W. Bush brought America unnecessary war, income inequality, serious debt, and deep recession. The voters in 2012 should think carefully whether they want to elect a Republican spouting the same Bush nostrums that took the nation to the brink of disaster. Some of the Republican candidates seem unable to escape the Bush shadow even as they try to ignore it. Every one of the Republican candidates proposes to lower taxes for the rich as the national debt continues to grow. They advocate further deregulation, a thirty-year failure that presidential aspirants still promote as the solution to the nation's economic woes. All but Ron Paul and Jon Huntsman talk like imperialist bullies about waging war against Iran. They condemn Freddie Mac and Fannie Mae without mentioning that Bush pressured them to encourage homeownership for poor people who could not afford it. In Republican campaign debates Bush's name rarely comes up, as if the candidates would like the voters to forget those traumatic years.

Many conservatives have correctly pegged one major issue: the deficit needs fixing. Obama has the power to make a big impact without the involvement of Congress. At the end of this year, win or lose the election, he can simply let the Bush tax cuts expire—the whole kit and caboodle. Everyone would sacrifice. The economy would most likely decline, and the administration would have to work harder to create jobs. Obama can make it happen by doing nothing; just let the tax cuts expire. If Congress should try to extend them, he need only veto the bill. Tax collections would revert automatically to the level by which Clinton balanced the budget. The additional revenues going forward, while not entirely solving the problem would eat into the Bush- and Obama-created deficit over the next decade. Some of these revenues might even be used to tweak the economy. In a worst-case scenario, Republicans could win control of the White House, House of Representatives and the Senate with a sixty-vote, filibuster-proof majority. Short of that, Democrats with possible help from Republican deficit hawks could hold the line even if Obama lost. Republicans want to shrink the deficit by privatizing Social Security and transferring Medicare and Medicaid to the states' control. These would be steps backward. The elderly, disabled, and poor would suffer grievously. Undoubtedly, Obama's campaign advisors would urge him not to speak of restoring the Clinton taxes before the election. Instead, he could make it a November or December surprise. And whatever the outcome of the presidential election, it will have been his last, so he will not suffer any personal political consequences for doing the right thing.

The thought of returning far right conservatives to executive power only raises the prospect of another damaging period of reckless governance. If the voters should return a divided government, gridlock and bitterness in Washington will continue. Obama's poll numbers were low as the Republicans entered the primary/caucus season. Despite the hi-jinks of the clowns, the preseason had afforded the Republican candidates the opportunity to hammer Obama and his policies in a series of TV debates without a direct on-site response from Democrats. In short, they defined Obama's leadership with their often distorted rhetoric. Once a Republican nominee emerges and debates boil down to the Democratic or Republican vision, and possibly that of a third or even fourth party, the voters will see the issues more distinctly. Elections, however, are not always decided on a rational evaluation of the issues. Emotions are often more dominant. Voters on the far right tend to be emotionally tied to wedge issues growing out of their religious and patriotic values. The extent to which these feelings spread to the center may determine the outcome of the upcoming election.

One thing can be predicted with complete confidence. Whether Obama winds up a one- or two-term president, the majority of historians are certain to judge his presidency more favorably than that of George W. Bush. Just check their records. Given another term and more time to turn things around, he might even rank high among American presidents.

Notes

INTRODUCTION

1 Robert S. McElvaine, "Historians vs. George W. Bush," *History News Network*, George Mason University (December 5, 2005).

2 McElvaine, "HNN Poll: 61% of Historians Rate the Bush Presidency Worst," *History News Network*, George Mason University (April 1, 2008).

3 Kenneth T. Walsh, "Historians Rank George W. Bush among Worst Presidents," *U.S. News and World Report* (February 17, 2009).

4 Tom Kelly and Douglas Lonnstrom, co-directors, *American Presidents: Greatest and Worst*, Siena Research Institute (July 1, 2010). In a similar poll taken by Siena in 2003, George W. Bush was ranked twenty-third. In the 2010 poll, Bill Clinton was ranked thirteenth and Barack Obama, fifteenth.

5 McElvaine, "HNN Poll."

6 Molly Ivins, "The Uncompassionate Conservative," *Mother Jones*, November/December 2003.

7 Jeffrey Goldberg, "Letter From Washington: Breaking Ranks," *New Yorker*, October 31, 2005.

8 "Fox News Sunday," February 11, 2008.

9 McElvaine, "HNN Poll."

10 Robert Draper, *Dead Certain: The Presidency of George W. Bush* (New York: Free Press, 2007). 9, 50.

11 Craig Unger, *The Fall of the House of Bush: The Untold Story of how a Band of True Believers Seized the Executive Branch, Started the Iraq War, and Still Imperils America's Future* (New York: Scribner, 2007), 84-5.

12 Ibid, 80.

13 David Corn, *The Lies of George W. Bush: Mastering the Politics of Deception* (New York, Three Rivers Press, 2003), 21-2.

14 Corn, 1.

15 George W. Bush, *Decision Points* (New York: Crown, 2010), 440.

16 "Morning Edition," NPR, May 25, 2001.

CHAPTER 1

1 Joseph Cummins, *Anything for a Vote: Dirty Tricks, Cheap Shots, and October Surprises in U.S. Presidential Campaigns* (Philadelphia: Quirk Books, 2007), 26-7, 124-26.

2 Cummins, 226, 229, 242-44.

3 James Moore and Wayne Slater, *Bush's Brain: How Karl Rove Made George W. Bush Presidential* (Hoboken, New Jersey: John Wiley & Sons, 2003), 113-31.

4 Projections based on the Consumer Price Index, www.measuringworth.com.

5 Moore and Slater, 130-31.

6 Moore and Slater, 149.

7 Draper. 48-9.

8 Draper, 57.

9 Unger, 173-74.

10 Nancy Snow, "The South Carolina Primary: Bush Wins, America Loses," CommonDreams.org (February 21, 2000).

11 David Corn, *The Lies of George W. Bush: Mastering the Politics of Deception* (New York: Three Rivers Press, 2004), 34.

12 Draper, 65.

13 Snow, "South Carolina Primary"; Draper, 73-8.

14 Evgenia Peretz, "Going After Gore," *Vanity Fair* (October, 2007).

15 Jeffrey Toobin, *Too Close to Call: The Thirty-six Day Battle to Decide the 2000 Election* (New York: Random House, 2001), 193.

16 Toobin, 149-57.

17 Open Secrets.org, Swift Boat Veterans for Truth: 2004 Election Cycle,

Top Donors, http://opensecrets.org/527s/527cmtedetail_contribs. php?cycle=2004&ein=201041228.

18 "Vietnam Veteran John Kerry's Testimony before the Senate Foreign Relations Committee," April 22, 1971.

19 John E. O'Neil and Jerome R. Corsi, *Unfit for Command: Swift Boat Veterans Speak Out Against John Kerry* (Washington, D.C.: Regnery Publishing, Inc., 2004), 31-41, 77-93.

20 "Republican-Funded Group Attacks Kerry's War Record," Fact Check.Org (August 6, 2004, updated August 22, 2004), http://www.factcheck.org/article231.html.

21 Joe Conason, "Republicans' Dishonorable Charge," *Salon.com* (August 6, 2004), http://www.salon.com/news/opinion/joe_conason/2004/08/06/mccain_on_swift_boat_veterans/index.

22 Paul Taylor, "Wedge Issues on the Ballots," Pew Research Center Publications, July 26, 2006, Windows Internet Explorer.

23 Daniel A. Smith, Matthew DeSantis, and Jason Kassel, "Same-Sex Marriage Ballot Measures and the 2004 Presidential Election," State and Local Government Review, Vol. 38, No. 2 (2006), 78-91, http://www.clas.ufl.edu/users/dasmith/SLGR2006.pdf.

24 Draper, 90.

25 Glenn Kessler, "Revisiting the cost of the Bush Tax Cuts," Washington Post, May 10, 2011, http://www.washingtonpost.com/blogs/fact-checker/post/revisiting-the-cost-of-the-bush-tax-cuts/2011/05/09/AFxTFtbG_blog.html. The tax figures are estimated costs at the time the bills were passed.

CHAPTER 2

1 Quoted by Bruce Bartlett, "Money and Politics: Why spending millions on personal campaigns might help you lose," *Forbes.com,* June 12, 2009, http://www.forbes.com/2009/06/11/terry-mcauliff-virginia-primaries-opinions-columnists-fundraising.html.

2 Joseph Cummins, *Anything for a Vote: Dirty Tricks, Cheap Shots, and October*

Surprises in U.S. Presidential Campaigns (Philadelphia: Quirk Books, 2007), 141-44.

3   Richard A. Oppel, Jr., "Campaign Documents Show Depth of Bush Fund-Raising," *New York Times*, May 5, 2003, Windows Internet Explorer.

4   Jim Drinkard and Laurence McQuillan, "'Bundling' contributions pays for Bush campaign," *USA Today*, October 16, 2003, http://www.usatoday.com/news/politicselections/nation/2003-10-15-cover-bundlers_x.htm.

5   John Cheves, Texans for Public Justice, August 29, 2004, http://info.tpj.org/page_view.jsp?pageid=680&pubid=442.

6   Texans for Public Justice, http://info.tpj.org/docs/pioneers/pioneers_table.jsp.

7   Ken Herman, "Bush to Give Away Political Donation from Abramoff," Austin American-Statesman, January 5, 2006, Archives | Austin American-Statesman | Statesman.com – Windows Internet Explorer.

8   Conor Kenny, "Jack Abramoff: Captain Jack," In These Times blog, July 31, 2006, http://www.inthesetimes.com/article/2752/.

9   Kim Geiger, "Television advertising in 2012 election could top $3 billion," *Los Angeles Times*, October 6, 2011, http://www.latimes.com/news/politics/la-pn-2012-ads-could-top-$3-billion-20111006,0,3667624.story. The figures are based on research by the Campaign Media Analysis Group and apply only to political advertizing in large markets. They would be higher if small market advertizing had been included in the survey.

10   Draper, 237-38.

11   Corn, 13. Corn cites the *New York Times* and *Time* magazine as his sources.

12   Lobbying Database, Open Secrets.org, http://www.opensecrets.org/lobby/.

13   Robert G Kaiser, *So Damn Much Money: The Triumph of Lobbying and the Corrosion of American Government* (New York: Alfred A. Knopf. 2009), 61-164.

14   Kaiser, 331-33.

15   Hollywood has produced a documentary, "Casino Jack and the United States of Money," and a full-length movie, "Casino Jack," starring Kevin Spacey.

16   Bill Moyers, "DeLay, Abramoff, and the Public Trust," *Huffington Post*, February 28, 2006, Windows Internet Explorer.

17 James V. Grimaldi and R. Jeffrey Smith, "Gambling Interest Funded DeLay Trip," *Washington Post*, March 12, 2005, Windows Internet Explorer.

18 R. Jeffrey Smith, "The DeLay-Abramoff Money Trail," *Washington Post*, December 31, 2005, Windows Internet Explorer.

19 Minority Staff Report, "Investigation of Jack Abramoff's Use of Tax-Exempt Organizations," Senate Committee on Finance, October 2006, 20, prb101206[1]. pdf-Adobe Reader.

20 Final Report, "'Gimme Five,' Investigation of Tribal Lobbying Matters," Senate Committee on Indian Affairs, June 22, 2006, 15-38, Report [1].pdf – Adobe Reader.

21 "Gimme Five," 40-58.

22 "Gimme Five," 147-80.

23 Kaiser, 341.

24 Stephen Slivinski, "A Reality Check on Earmark Reform," Cato Institute, January 22, 2007, http://www.cato.org/pub_display.php?pub_id=6955.

25 "Earmarks Executive Order: Legal Issues," Congressional Research Service, February 13, 2008, RL34373[1].pdf – Adobe Reader.

26 Molly K. Hooper, "President Obama calls for earmark reform as GOP issues challenge," *The Hill*, November 13, 2010, President Obama calls for earmark reform as GOP issues challenge – TheHill.com – Windows Internet Explorer.

27 Jeffrey Young, "Lobbying Regulated to Prevent Abuse in US," Voice of America, August 24, 2010, Windows Internet Explorer.

Chapter 3

1 Bob Woodward, *Bush at War* (New York: Simon & Schuster, 2002), 34-5.

2 "The 9/11 Commission Report: Final Report of the National Commission on Terrorist Attacks upon the United States," Authorized Edition (New York: W.W. Norton, undated), xvi, hereafter "9/11 Report."

3 "9/11 Report," 340-41.

4 "9/11 Report," 259, 261-62.

5 One unnamed lawyer in the Justice Department actually did envision a scenario

in which terrorists on a suicide mission hijacked a jumbo jet loaded with fuel and used it as a weapon that could destroy any building in the world. He was exploring the legal issues that would be involved in shooting the plane down. "9/11 Report," 346, 561, note 21.

6   The threats enumerated here are contained in the "9/11 Report," 256-59.

7   Richard Clark, *Against All Enemies: Inside America's War on Terror* (New York: Free Press, 2004), 236.

8   Robert B. Stinnett, *Day of Deceit: The Truth about FDR and Pearl Harbor* (New York: Free Press, 2000), 145. The exercise was called back by higher naval authority in Washington. Stinnett argues that President Roosevelt tacitly invited the Japanese attack on Pearl Harbor in a conspiracy to get America involved in the war.

9   Woodward, *Bush at War*, 39.

10   Condoleezza Rice, "Transcript of Rice's 9/11 commission statement," (May 19, 2004), http://articles.cnn.com/2004-04-08/politica/rice.transcript_1_terrorist.

11   James Gannon, *Stealing Secrets, Telling Lies: How Spies and Codebreakers Helped Shape the Twentieth Century* (Washington, D.C.: Brassey's, 2001), 195.

12   "9/11 Report," 261-62.

13   President George W. Bush, speech at National Defense University, Washington, D.C. (May 1, 2001), White House transcript.

14   Clarke, 229.

15   Clarke, 228-34.

16   George Tenet, with Bill Harlow, *At the Center of the Storm: My Years at the CIA* (New York: HarperCollins, 2007), 130-31, 143-44.

17   Clarke, 237-38.

18   Rice, "9/11 commission statement."

CHAPTER 4

1   Scott McClellan, *What Happened: Inside the Bush White House and Washington's Culture of Deception* (New York: Public Affairs, 2008), 142, 144-45.

2   Terry Gross, "Fresh Air," *NPR* (March 17, 2010).

3   Unger, 35-6.

4   William Kristol and Robert Kagan, "Toward a Neo-Reaganite Foreign Policy," *Foreign Affairs* (July/August, 1996).

5   Michael Isikoff and David Corn, *Hubris: The Inside Story of Spin, Scandal, and the Selling of the Iraq War* (New York: Crown Publishers, 2006), 70.

6   Laurie Milroie, *Study of Revenge: The first World Trade Center Attack and Saddam Hussein's War Against America* (Washington, DC: AEI Press, 2001), 251. The main title, *Study of Revenge*, was the same in both editions. The first edition in 2000 was subtitled, *Saddam Hussein's Unfinished War Against America*; the second in 2001, as spelled out here with a forward by James Woolsey that acknowledged the 9/11/01 attack. Both editions were published by the American Enterprise Institute.

7   Zalmay Khalilzad and Paul Wolfowitz, "Overthrow Him," *Weekly Standard* (December 1, 1997), 14.

8   Isikoff and Corn, 78.

9   Seymour Hersh, "Lunch With the Chairman: Why Was Richard Perle Meeting with Adnan Khashoggi?" *New Yorker* (March 17, 2003).

10 Dick Cheney, Soref Symposium speech (April 29, 1991).

11 Leslie Stahl, "60 Minutes," *CBS News* (March 22, 2004).

12 Clarke, 32.

13 Bob Woodward, *Plan of Attack* (New York: Simon and Schuster, 2004), 2.

14 David Wurmser was the principle author, but Perle's name appeared first, followed by seven other names in alphabetical order, Wurmser's next to last ahead of his wife, Meyrav. David Wurmser went on to write a book, *Tyranny's Ally*, which expanded on the "Clean Break" theme. See James Gannon, *Military Occupations in the Age of Self-Determination* (Westport, CT: Praeger Security International, 2008), 15.

15 Douglas Feith, "Inside the Inside Story," *Wall Street Journal* (February 4, 2007). Feith expressed this judgment that the secular Baathists and the Islamist fanatics had banded together to fight the American occupation at about the time the Baathists had joined the American side to fight al-Qaida.

16 James Risen, "How Pair's Finding on Terror Led to Clash in Shaping Intelligence," New York Times, (April 28, 2004), Windows Internet Explorer.

17 John Prados, *Hoodwinked: The Documents That Reveal How Bush Sold Us a War* (New York: New Press, 2004), 306.

18 9/11 Report, 228-29.

19 Isikoff and Corn, 110.

20 Isikoff and Corn, 50-51; GAO-04-559, State Department: Issues Affecting Funding of Iraqi National Congress Support Foundation (May 20, 2004).

21 Isikoff and Corn, 110-11.

22 Robert Dreyfuss and Jason Vest, "The Lie Factory," Mother Jones, (January/ February, 2004), Windows Internet Explorer.

23 Karen Kwiatkowski, "The New Pentagon Papers," *Salon* (March 10, 2004).

24 Kwiatkowski, "New Pentagon Papers."

25 Michael Rubin, "Web of Conspiracies," *National Review Online* (May 18, 2004).

26 Rubin, "Web of Conspiracies."

27 Marc Cooper, "Soldier for the Truth: Exposing Bush's Talking Points War," *LA Weekly* (February 20-26, 2004), reprinted in *Common Dreams.org* (http://www.commondreams.orf/views04/0220-03.htm).

28 See "Fox News Sunday with Chris Wallace" (February 11, 2007).

29 Ibid.

30 See Moore and Slater, 301-22.

31 Walter Pincus, "British Intelligence warned of Iraq War," *Washington Post* (May 13,2005), A18, online edition.

32 Prados, *Hoodwinked*, 23-4.

33 Joseph C. Wilson, "What I didn't Find in Africa," *New York Times* (July 6, 2003), online at http://www.nytimes.com/2003/07/06/opinion/06WILS.html?pagew anted=1&pagewanted=... Valerie Plame worked undercover at the CIA. After her husband published this article in the *New York Times* contradicting the administration's version of the yellowcake affair, her identity was exposed. An investigation ensued over whether someone in the administration had leaked her identity to the news media. It became a loud, highly contentious side issue damaging to Plame that helped to distract the media from the real issue of government disinformation and prevarication. Ultimately it resulted in the indictment of

Scooter Libby for perjury. The leaker turned out to be Richard Armitage, the deputy secretary of state.

34 Prados, *Hoodwinked*, "Document 1: The CIA White Paper on Iraq's Weapons of Mass Destruction Programs," (October 2002), 50 seq., 78.

35 Unger, 247-48.

36 *Iraq on the Record: The Bush Administration's Public Statements on Iraq*, House Committee on Government Reform—Minority Staff (March 16, 2004).

37 Joseph Cirincione, "Not One Claim Was True," *Bulletin of the Atomic Scientists* (January/February 2005). Cirincione became president of the Ploughshares Fund, which advocates for a nuclear-free world, in March 2008.

38 See, for example, Jim Lobe, "The Chicken Hawk Factor," *PeaceOnEarth.net* (September 9, 2002).

39 Unger, 164-65.

40 "Fox News Sunday" (February 11, 2007).

41 Richard Perle, "Ambushed on the Potomac," *National Interest Online* (January 21, 2009).

42 "Fox News Sunday" (July 6, 2008); Peter Baker and Jonathan Weisman, "A Plea from Petraeus," *Washington Post* (April 9, 2008).

43 Richard N. Haass, *War of Necessity, War of Choice: A Memoir of Two Iraq Wars* (New York: Simon & Schuster, 2009), 1-16. Haass served in foreign policy advisory positions in both Bush administrations.

44 Trudy Rubin, *Willful Blindness: The Bush Administration and Iraq* (Philadelphia: The Philadelphia Inquirer, 2004).

Chapter 5

1 Bush, *Decision Points*, 88-9.

2 Salon staff, "Introduction: The Abu Ghraib Files," *Salon.com*, March 14, 2006, http://www.salon.com/news/abu_ghraib/2006/14/06/introduction/. Since the first pictures from Abu Ghraib were shown on CBS's *60 Minutes II* on April 28, 2004, these and many others are available at multiple sites on the internet. Simply call up a search engine and type in "Abu Ghraib pictures" and log onto the site of your choice.

3   Michael Scherer and Mark Benjamin, "Other government agencies," *Salon.com*, November 4-5, 2006, http://www.salon.com/news/abu_ghraib/2006/03/14/ chapter_5/index.html.

4   Ibid.

5   Ibid.

6   "Prosecutions and Convictions," The Abu Ghraib Files, *Salon.com*, March 14, 2006, httb://www.salon.com/news/abu_ghraib/2006/03/14/ prosecutions_convioctions/.

7   "US army rejects court martial of Abu Ghraib commander," *Guardian*, from *Associated Press*, January 11, 2008, http://www.guardian.uk.co/world/2008/ jan/11/iraq.usa.

8   "Prosecutions and Convictions," Salon.com.

9   Warren P. Strobel, "General Who Probed Abu Ghraib Says Bush Officials Committed War Crimes," *McClatchy Newspapers,* June 18, 2008, http://www. mcclastchydc.com/2008/06/18/41514/general-who-probed-abu-ghraib.html.

10 Barton Gellman and Jo Becker, "A Different Understanding With the President," *Washington Post,* June 24, 2007, http://voices.washingtonpost.com/cheney/ chapters/chapter_1/; Barton Gellman, *Angler: The Cheney Vice Presidency*, (New York: Penguin, 2008), 114-30.

11 "Authorization for Use of Military Force," September 18, 2001, attachment in Gellman and Becker, "A Different Understanding," op.cit. This resolution has also been cited as justification for the interception of communications to and from the United States without prior court authorization.

12 Presidential Order, September 25, 2001, attachment in Gellman and Becker, "A Different Understanding," op. cit.

13 This account of the events leading up to Abu Ghraib is taken from the Executive Summary of the Senate Armed Services Committee report, "Inquiry into the Treatment of Detainees in U.S. Custody," November 20, 2008, xii-xxix. (Hereafter, "Senate Report.")

14 Gellman and Becker, "A Different Understanding."

15 "Senate Report," xiv.

16 Karl Vick, "Amid Outcry on Memo, Signer's Private Regret," *Washington Post*,

April 25, 2009, http://www.washingtonpost.com/wp-dyn/content/article/
2009/04/24/AR2009042403888html?hpid=topnews.

17 Vick, "Amid Outcry." It would be speculative, but not preclusive to suggest that
Bybee was set up for his role in the torture memos. He had approached Gonzales
to let him know of his availability for a seat on the Ninth Circuit Court of
Appeals. No vacancy existed at the time, but Gonzales offered him the Justice
Department job in the meantime. He is reported by friends to have been under
tremendous pressure to sign the documents, and to have expressed regret later at
the way the memos were used to justify the harsh interrogations that unfolded.

18 Jay Bybee, "Memorandum for Alberto R. Gonzales, Counsel to the President,"
August 1, 2004.

19 "Senate Report," xxii.

20 Philippe Sands, *Torture Team: Rumsfeld's Memo and the Betrayal of American
Values* (New York: Palgrave MacMillan, 2008), 2-6.

21 "Al Qahtani v. Bush, al Qahtani v. Gates," Center for Constitutional Rights,
http://ccrjustice.org/ourcases/current-cases/al-Qahtani-v.-bush%2C
-al-Qahtani-v.-gates.

22 Ibid.

23 "Senate Report, xix"; "Al-Qahtani v. Bush, al-Qahtani v. Gates."

24 "Senate Report," xxi.

25 "Senate Report," xv.

26 The distinction between rendition and extraordinary rendition was made by
Scott Horton, "Renditions Buffoonery," *Harper's Magazine* (February 2, 2009),
http://www.harpers.org/archive/2009/02/hbc-90004326. Horton helped
prepare a report on renditions issued jointly by New York University Law School
and the New York City Bar Association and was an expert witness in hearings
leading to a report on renditions for the European Parliament. For a different
definition of extraordinary rendition, see "Fact Sheet, Extraordinary Rendition,"
American Civil Liberties Union, December 6, 2005, http://aclu.org/safefree/extr
aordinaryrendition/22203res200512; Peter Berger and Katherine Tiedemann,
"Disappearing Act: Rendition by the Numbers," *New American* Foundation,
2008, http://www.newamerica.net/publications/articles/2008/disappearing...;
published in *Mother Jones*, March 3, 2008.

27 Craig Whitlock, "Jordan's Spy Agency: Holding Cell for the CIA," *Washington Post* (December 1, 2007), A01, http://www.washingtonpost.com/wp-dyn/content/article/2007/11/30/AR2007113002484_p...

28 Erik Eckholm, "Pakistanis Arrest Qaeda Figure Seen as Planner of 9/11," *New York Times* (March 2, 2003), 1.

29 Josh White, "Al-Qaeda Suspect Says He Planned Cole Attack," *Washington Post* (March 20, 2007), A01, online at http://www.washingtonpost.com/wp-dyn/content/article/2007/03/19/AR2007031900653_p...

30 Simon Elegant, "The Terrorist Talks," *Time* (October 5, 2003).

31 For a more detailed report on the capture of Islamist terrorists and the extraordinary rendition program see, James Gannon, *Obama's War: Avoiding a Quagmire in Afghanistan*, (Washington, DC: Potomac Books, 2011), 115-120.

32 Dana Priest, "Wrongful Imprisonment: Anatomy of a CIA Mistake," *Washington Post* (December 4, 2005), http://www.washingtonpost.com/wp-dyn/content/article/2005/12/03...

33 Bush, *Decision Points*, 168-69.

34 Evan Wallach, "Waterboarding Used to Be a Crime," *Washington Post* (November 4, 2007), B01.

35 Scott Shane, "Waterboarding Used 266 Times on 2 Suspects," *New York Times* (April 19, 2009), 1. Shane cites Marcy Wheeler of the blog *emptywheel* for the discovery, and notes, "The sentences in the [DOJ] memo containing that information appear to have been redacted from some copies but are visible in others."

36 Jane Mayer, "Outsourcing Terror: The secret history of America's 'extraordinary rendition' program, *New Yorker* (February 14, 2005), http://www.newyorker.com/archive/2005/02/14/050214fa_fact6?pri...; Michael Bilton, "Post-9/11 Renditions: An Extraordinary Violation of International Law," *Center for Public Integrity* (May 22, 2007), http://projects.publicintegrity.org/militaryaid/report.aspx?aid=855&g...;

37 Priest, "Wrongful Imprisonment."

38 Peter Bergen, "Exclusive: I Was Kidnapped by the CIA," *Mother Jones* (March 3, 2008), http://www.motherjones.com/print/15664.

39 "Court convicts 23 ex-CIA agents in imam kidnapping trial," *Agence*

France Presse (November 4. 2009), online at http://www.france24.com/en/20091104-italy-convicts-23-ex-cia-agents-imam-kidnapping-trial-justice-pr.

40 "Al Shimari v. CACI et al," Center for Constitutional Rights, http://ccrjustice.org/ourcases/current-cases/al-shimari-v.-CACI-et-al.

41 "Universal Jurisdiction: The Case Against Rumsfeld and Accountability for U.S. Torture," "German War Crimes Case Against Donald Rumsfeld, et. al," Center for Constitutional Rights, http://ccrjustice.org/case-against-rumsfeld.

Chapter 6

1 David Cay Johnston, "Income Gap Widening, Data Shows (cq)," *New York Times*, March 29, 2007, Windows Internet Explorer.

2 David Leonhardt, "Income Inequality," *New York Times*, September 22, 2011, http://topics.nytimes.com/top/reference/timestopics/subjects/i/income_inequality/i...

3 Richard Wilkinson and Kate Pickett, *The Spirit Level: Why Greater Equality Makes Societies Stronger* (London: Bloomsbury Press, 2009), 3-5.

4 Wilkinson and Pickett, 19.

5 Wilkinson and Pickett, 173-74.

6 Grover Norquist, *Leave Us Alone: Getting the Government's Hands off Our Money, Our Guns, Our Lives* (New York: HarperCollins, 2008), 234-41.

7 Norquist, 253-54.

8 D. Wilson and William Beach, "The Economic Impact of President Bush's Tax Relief Plan," *Heritage Foundation*, April 27, 2001, Windows Internet Explorer.

9 "Year-by-Year Analysis of the Bush Tax Cuts Shows Growing Tilt to the Very Rich," *Citizens for Tax Justice*, June 12, 2002, Windows Internet Explorer.

10 See the discussion in Jacob S. Hacker and Paul Pierson, *Off Center: The Republican Revolution and the Erosion of American Democracy* (New Haven, CT: Yale University Press), 55-62.

11 "Here We Go Again: Bush Exaggerates Tax Cuts," FactCheck.org, February 20, 2004, http://www.factcheck.org/here_we_go_again_bush_exaggerates_tax.html.

12 Martin A. Sullivan, "The Decline and Fall of Distribution Analysis," *Tax Notes*, June 30, 2003, cite_tn_063003.pdf-Adobe Reader.

13 *PolitiFact.com*, "John Boehner says tax cuts created 8 million jobs over 10 years," article generated by Boehner statement on NBC "Today," May 10, 2011, Windows Internet Explorer.

14 Statistical backup is available at Historical Tables, Budget of the United States, 2011, http://www.goaccess.gov/usbudget/fy11/pdf/hst.pdf.

15 Jonathan Chait, "Pat Toomey's Epistemic Closure," *New Republic*, October 11, 2010, http://www.npr.com/blog/jonathan-chait/78304/pat-toomey's-epemistic-closure..

16 An Economic Analysis of the Tax Payer Relief Act of 1997, Congressional Budget Office, April 2000, http://www.cbo.gov/doc.cfm?index=1959&type=0 &sequence&2.

17 Edmund L. Andrews, "Bush Budget Cuts a Variety of Programs," *New York Times*, February 4, 2004, http://www.nytimes.com/2004/02/04/politics/04BUDG.html.

18 David Sirota, "Hurricanes rain on Bush's Tax Cut Parade," *In These Times*, September 27, 2005, Windows Internet Explorer.

19 John Schwartz, "New Study of Levees Faults design and Construction," *New York Times*, May 22, 2006, http://www.nytimes.com/2006/05/22/us/22corps.html.

Chapter 7

1 George Orwell, *Nineteen Eighty-Four*, Part 2, Chapter 9, from *Oxford Dictionary of Quotations* (New York: Oxford University Press, 1999), 558.

2 U.S. House of Representatives, *Political Interference with Climate Change Science under the Bush Administration*, Committee on Oversight and Government Reform, December 2007, I, political-interference.pdf, hereafter, "Political Interference."

3 Robert F. Kennedy, Jr., *Crimes Against Nature: How George W. Bush and His Corporate Pals Are Plundering the Country and Hijacking Our Democracy* (New York: HarperCollins, 2004), 94; "Scientists' Report Documents ExxonMobil's Tobacco-like Disinformation Campaign on Global Warming Science," Union of Concerned Scientists, January 3, 2007, Windows Internet Explorer.

4 Political Interference.

5 Oil and Gas, OpenSecrets.org, http://www.opensecrets.org/industries/indus.php?ind=e01.

6 Political Interference, 16-17.

7 Political Interference, 9-11.

8 Laura Flanders, *Bushwomen: Tales of a Cynical Species* (New York: Verso, 2004), 212.

9 Testimony of James R. Mahoney, Ph.D., Assistant Secretary of Commerce for Oceans and Atmosphere, before the United States Senate Committee on Commerce, Transportation, and Science, Subcommittee on Global Climate Change and Impacts, July 20, 2005.

10 Political Interference, 5-6.

11 Political Interference, 7-8.

12 Political Interference, 12.

13 Political Interference, 11-12.

14 Kennedy, *Crimes Against Nature*, 83-4.

15 Political Interference, 16.

16 Rick S, Piltz, "The Denial Machine: Science, Censorship and the White House," Index on Censorship, Vol. 37, November 4, 2008, 76, The_Denial_Machine_-_Index_on_Censorship.pdf-Adobe Reader.

17 Flanders, *Bushwomen*, 202.

18 Flanders, *Bushwomen*, 190.

19 "N.J. DEP Employees Say Whitman Administration Soft on Polluters," Public Employees for Environmental Responsibility, Press Release, December 20, 2000, http://www.peer.org/news/news_id.php?row_id=63. PEER claims that it sent questionnaires to all 3,142 employees of the New Jersey DEP and received 711 responses, or 23.5 percent.

20 Kennedy, *Crimes Against Nature* 48-52.

21 Sarah Cottrell, Elaine Farber, Andrew Kovacs, and Danielle Osler, "Dangerous Waters: EPA Administrator Whitman and the Arsenic in Drinking Water Standard," *New York Times Magazine*, August 19, 2001.

22 Environmental Protection Agency, Office of the Inspector General, *EPA's Response to the World Trade Center Collapse: Challenges, Successes, and Areas for Improvement*, Report No. 2003-P-00012, August, 21, 2003, 17, http://www.epa. gov/oig/reports/2003/WTC_report_20030821.pdf (hereafter OIGEPA).

23 OIGEPA, 16.

24 Julia Preston, "Public Misled on Air Quality After 9/11 Attack, Judge Says," *New York Times*, February 3, 2006,

25 Flanders, *Bushwomen*, 188-89.

26 OIGEPA, 2.

27 Anthony DePalma, "Illness Persisting in 9/11 Workers, Big Study Finds," *New York Times*, September 6, 2006, http://www.nytimes.com/2006/09/06/ nyregion/06health.html?pagewanted=all.

28 "WTC Responder Fatality Investigations," New York State Department of Health, June 2010, http://www.health.state.ny.us/environmental/investigations/ wtc/health_studies/fatality_inves.

29 Kitty H. Gelberg, Final Report, World Trade Center Responders Fatality Investigation Program, New York State Department of Health, September 19, 2011.

30 Mark Hertsgaard, "Conflict of Interest for Christine Todd Whitman?" *Salon. com*, January 14, 2002, Windows Internet Explorer.

31 Flanders, *Bushwomen*, 214; "Profile: Christine Todd Whitman," History Commons, Windows Internet Explorer.

32 Shankar Vedantam, "Senate Impasse Stops 'Clear Skies' Measure," *Washington Post*, March 10, 2005, http://www.washingtonpost.com/wp-dyn/articles/ A20314-2005Mar9.html.

33 Bruce Barcott, "Changing All the Rules," *New York Times Magazine*, April 4, 2004, http://www.nytimes.com/2004/04/04/magazine/04BUSH.html? pagewanted=print.

34 Barcott, "Changing All the Rules."

35 Flanders, *Bushwomen*, 216; Robert F. Kennedy, Jr., "Crimes Against Nature," *Rolling Stone*, December 11, 2003, http://www.rollingstone,com/features/ nationalaffairs/featuregen.asp?pid=2154; Eric Schaeffer and Zachary Frankel,

"When Nice Words Hide a Bad Environmental Record," *Salt Lake Tribune*, September 28, 2003, http://www.environmentalintegrity.org/pdf/publications/Article_-_Salt_Lake_Tribune_-_Leavitt.pdf..

36 Michael Janofsky, "E.P.A. Nominee Gets an Earful from Committee Democrats," *New York Times*, April 6, 2005, Windows Internet Explorer.

37 John Shiffman and John Sullivan, "Eroding Mission at the EPA," *Philadelphia Inquirer*, December 7, 2008, http://articles.philly.com/2008-12-07/news/24992895_1_climate-change-climate-change-deputy-administrator-jason-burnett.

38 John M. Broder and Felicity Barringer, "E.P.A. Says 17 States Can't Set Emission Rules," *New York Times*, December 20, 2007, http://www.nytimes.com/2007/12/20/washington/20epa.html?_r=slogin&oref=slogin.

39 Shiffman and Sullivan, "Eroding Mission."

40 Kennedy, *Crimes Against Nature*, 103.

41 Kennedy, *Crimes Against Nature,* 99.

42 "Summary of 2005 Energy Bill," Union of Concerned Scientists, Windows Internet Explorer.

43 Jim VandeHei and Justin Blum, "Bush Signs Energy Bill, Cheers Steps Toward Self-Sufficiency," *Washington Post*, August 8, 2005, Windows Internet Explorer.

44 Daniel Whitten, "Bush Signs Energy Bill Mandating Tougher Efficiency Standards," *Bloomberg*, December 19, 2007. Windows Internet Explorer.

45 John M. Broder, "Bush Signs Broad Energy Bill," *New York Times*, December 19, 2007, Windows Internet Explorer.

CHAPTER 8

1 Debate Transcript, Commission on Presidential Debates, October 17, 2000.

2 2000 Annual Report, Old-Age and Survivors Insurance and Disability Insurance Trust Funds, March 30, 2000, Adobe Reader.

3 Corn, The Lies of George W. Bush, 43.

4 Andres Louise Campbell and Kimberly Morgan, "The Shifting Line between Public and Private: The Politics of the 2003 Medicare Modernization Act and Prescription Drug Reform," Paper Prepared for the Social Science History

Association Annual Meeting, November 3-6, 2005, http://www.gpcal.org/documents/medicarereport.html.

5   Melissa Ganz, "The Medicare Prescription Drug, Modernization, & Improvement Act of 2003: Are We Playing the Lottery with Health Care Reform?" *Duke Law & Technology Review*, October 1, 2004, paragraph 38, Windows Internet Explorer.

6   Ceci Connolly and Mike Allen, "Medicare Drug Benefit May Cost $1.2 Trillion," *Washington Post*, February 9, 2005, Windows Internet Explorer.

7   Ganz, "Lottery with Health Care Reform?"

8   "A Detailed Description of CBO's Cost Estimate for the Medicare Prescription Drug Benefit," Congressional Budget Office, July 2004, Windows Internet Explorer.

9   Dean Baker, "The Origins of the Doughnut Hole: Excess Profits on Prescription Drugs," *Center for Economic Policy Research*, August 2006, http://www.cepr.net/documents/part_d_drug_profits_2006_08.pdf.

10 Robert A. Berenson and Melissa M. Goldstein, "Will Medicare Wither on the Vine? How Congress has Advantaged Medicare Advantage—and What's a Level Playing Field Anyway?" *Saint Louis University Journal of Health and Policy*, Vol. 1:5, http://law.slu.edu/healthlaw/journal/archives/berenson_and_goldstein.pdf.

11 Government Accounting Office, "Medicare Advantage Expenses," Letter of Transmittal to Representative Pete Stark, December 8, 2008, http://www.gao.gov/new.items/d09132r.pdf.

12 Quoted by Sarah Rubenstein, "Private Medicare Advantage Plans Take Heat for Profits," *Wall Street Journal*, December 11, 2008, http://blogs.wsj.com/health/2008/12/11/private-medicare-advantage-plans-take-heat-for-profits/.

13 United States House of Representatives Committee on Energy and Commerce Majority Staff, "Profits, Marketing, and Corporate Expenses in the Medicare Advantage Market," December 2009, http://democrats.energycommerce.house.gov/Press_111/20091209/MedicareAdvantageReport120909.pdf; House Committee on Energy and Commerce, "New Report Highlights Medicare Advantage Insurers' Higher Administrative Spending," December 8, 2009, http://democrats.energycommerce.house.gov/index.php?q=news/news-report-highlights-medicare-advantage-insurers-administrative-spending.

14 Larry DeWitt, "The Social Security Trust Funds and the Federal Budget," Social Security Administration Agency History, Research Note #20, March 4, 2005, updated June 18, 2007, Windows Internet Explorer.

15 Actuarial Publications, "Old Age and Survivors Insurance Trust Fund, 1937-2010," Social Security Administration, http://www.ssa.gov/oact/STATS/table4a1.html. A separate fund was set up for disability insurance in 1957, and a separate table shows a combined surplus $3 billion higher in 1968.

16 DeWitt, "Trust Funds."

17 "Trust Fund, 1939- 2010."

18 David John, "Misleading the Public: How the Social Security Trust Fund Really Works," Heritage Foundation, September 2, 2004, http://www.heritage.org/research/reports/2004/09/misleading-the-public-how-the-social-security-trust-fund-really-works.

19 Bush, *Decision Points*, 296.

20 Ibid, 296-97.

21 Draper, 296-304.

22 Paul N. Van de Water, "Ryan Plan Makes Deep Cuts in Social Security," Center on Budget and Policy Priorities, October 21, 2010, Windows Internet Explorer.

CHAPTER 9

1 Paul Krugman, *The Great Unraveling: Losing Our Way in the New Century* (New York, W.W. Norton, 2005), 406.

2 Paul Krugman, *The Return of Depression Economics and the Crisis of 2008* (New York: W.W. Norton, 2009),154-57.

3 This account of deregulation follows the timeline and facts laid out by Matthew Sherman's brief volume, "A Short History of Financial Deregulation in the United States" (Washington, DC: Center for Economic and Policy Research), July 2009, http://www.openthegovernment.org/otg/dereg-timeline-2009-07.pdf.

4 Stephen Pizzo, Mary Fricker, and Paul Muolo, *Inside Job: The Looting of America's Savings and Loans* (New York: McGraw-Hill, 1989).

5   Lawrence J. White, *The S&L Debacle: Public Policy Lessons for Bank and Thrift Regulation* (New York: Oxford University Press, 1991), 117.

6   White, 75.

7   Pizzo, Fricker, and Muolo, 18-19.

8   Ibid, 86.

9   Leonard Buder, "Two Are Charged with Stealing Union Funds, *New York Times*, June 17, 1987, http://www.nytimes.com/1987/06/17/nyregion/2-are-charged-with-stealing-union-funds.html.

10 Pizzo. Fricker, and Muolo, 87.

11 Pizzo. Fricker, and Muolo, 92-5.

12 Pizzo. Fricker, and Muolo, 290-94.

13 Pizzo. Fricker, and Muolo, 328-31.

14 James S. Granelli, "Keating Ordered Freed From Prison on Bond," *Los Angeles Times*, October 4, 1996, httb://articles,latimes.com/1996-10-04/business/fi-50432_1_federal-trial.

15 Timothy Curry and Lynn Shibut, "The Cost of the Savings and Loan Crisis: Truth and Consequences," FDIC Banking Review, December 2000,.

16 Ibid.

17 Ginnie Mae Report to Congress, November 13, 2007, https://www.ginniemae.gov/about/ann_rep/ReportToCongress07.pdf.

18 Souphala Chomsisengphet and Anthony Pennington-Cross, "The Evolution of the Subprime Mortgage Market," *Federal Reserve Bank of St. Louis Review*, January/February 2006, subprime.pdf – Adobe Reader.

19 "US Elections, How Groups Voted in 2000," Roper Center, Public Opinion Archives, University of Connecticut, http://www.ropercenter.uconn.edu/elections/how_groups_voted_00.html.

20 "G.W. Bush on the Housing Boom," Text of Bush Speech, October 2002, Ron Paul.com.

21 Bush, 449.

22 U.S. Census Bureau, Homeownership Rate Since 1960.

23 Robert Weissbourd and R.W. Ventures, "Understanding a Dynamic Decade:

Trends in Housing and Foreclosures," School of Social Service Administration, University of Chicago, February 26, 2010, http://www.ssa.uchicago.edu/aboutss a/2010censusconference/20100226_Census-W4_WeissbourdT.pdf.

24 Jo Becker, Sheryl Gay Stolberg, and Stephen Labaton, "White House Philosophy Stoked Mortgage Bonfire," *New York Times*, December 20, 2008, httb://www. nytimes.com/2008/12/21/business/21admin.html?emc=etal&pagewanted=all.

25 Krugman, *Return of Depression Economics*, 163.

26 Kevin Phillips, *Bad Money: Reckless Finance, Failed Politics, and the Global Crisis of American Capitalism* (New York, Penguin, 2008, 107-08.

27 James R. Hagerty and Ken Gepfert, "One family's Journey into a Subprime Trap, *Wall Street Journal*, August 16, 2007, http://wwwonline.wsj.com/article/ SB11872207270749901.html.

28 Warren Buffett, Berkshire Hathaway Annual Report, 2002. In fact, Berkshire's portfolio contained derivative contracts worth billions of dollars. In some of them, Berkshire assured clients that the stock market would not be lower fifteen or twenty years later. In exchange, Berkshire collected premiums up front to use for investing. If the market should tank and he lose these bets, Berkshire would be on the hook for huge payouts. Buffett rationalized his apparent double standard by explaining that he was not out to destroy the derivatives market, but to have it regulated—but regulation for the future, not for the past. In 2010, while Congress prepared a new financial regulation law, Buffett lobbied successfully for a grandfather clause that would exempt companies like his from putting up more collateral on previously written long-term derivatives. Otherwise, Berkshire profits would have taken a big hit, so it was necessary to keep the tax man away and let the little people pay for corporate greed.

29 Andrew Ross Sorkin, *Too Big to Fail: The Inside Story of how Wall Street and Washington Fought to Save the Financial System—and Themselves* (New York: Viking Penguin, 2009), 90.

30 Matthew Philips, "The Monster that Ate Wall Street," *Newsweek*, September 27, 2008, http://www.newsweek.com/2008/09/26/the-monster-that-ate-wall-street.html.

31 Michael Lewis, *The Big Short: inside the Doomsday Machine* (New York: Norton, 2010), 228.

32 Jia Lynn Yang, "How Uncle Sam Will Profit from TARP," *CNN*, January 27, 2010, http://money.cnn.com/2010/01/27/news/economy/tarp_profit.fortune/index.html.

33 Sorkin, 446.

34 Michael Corkery, "Ratings Firms Notch Key Victory," *Wall Street Journal*, May 12, 2010, http://online.wsj.com/article/SB10001424052748704681904576317693173069976.html.

35 Becker, Stolberg, and Labaton, "White House Philosophy."

36 Gregory Zuckerman, *The Greatest Trade Ever: The Behind-the-Scenes Story of How John Paulson Defied Wall Street and Made Financial History* (New York: Broadway Books, 2009), 2.

37 Lewis, 246.

38 Hugo Lindgren, "No More Heroes," *New York Magazine Book Review*, March 5, 2010.

39 Lewis, 263-64.

CHAPTER 10

1 Neil Irwin and Nia-Malika Henderson, "Obama answers skeptics after recession is declared officially over," *Washington Post*, September 21, 2010, http://www.washingtonpost.com/wp-dyn/content/article/2010/09/20/AR2010092005999.html.

2 Robert Pear, "Recession Officially Over, U.S. Incomes Keep Falling," *New York Times*, October 9, 2011, http://www.nytimes.com/2011/10/10/us/recession=officially-over-is-incomes-keep-falling.html?_r=1&nl=todaysheadlines&emc=tha2.

3 Barack Obama, *Dreams From My Father: A Story of Race and Inheritance* (New York: Times Books, 1995), 44.

4 Report on the Troubled Asset Relief Program, Congressional Budget Office, March 2011, http://www.cbo.gov/ftpdocs/121xx/doc12118/03-29-TARP.pdf. The Office of Management and Budget estimated a $64 billion loss, not $19 billion.

5 Jackie Calmes, "TARP Bailout to Cost Less Than Once Anticipated," *New*

York Times, September 30, 2010, http://www.nytimes.com/2010/10/01/business/01tarp.html.

6 Daniel Gross, "Exclusive: Treasury's TARP, AIG Bailout Costs Fall to $30 billion," Yahoo Finance, October 5, 2010, Windows Internet Explorer

7 Business Day. "American International Group. Inc.," *New York Times*, November 1, 2011, http://topics.nytimes.com/top/news/business/companies/american_international_group/index.html.

8 Alan Zibel, "Obama Foreclosure Efforts Still Falling Short," *Wall Street Journal*, May 6, 2011, http://financialservices.house.gov/News/DocumentSingle.aspx?DocumentID=242018.

9 Renae Merle and Dina El Boghdady, "Obama administration announces effort to slash mortgages for unemployed borrowers," *Washington Post*, March 26, 2010, http://www.washingtonpost.com/wp-dyn/content/article/2010/03/26/AR2010032602031.html.

10 Don Lee, "Obama administration ramps up mortgage refinancing effort," *Los Angeles Times*, October 24, 2011, http://articles.latimes.com/2011/oct/24/business/la-fi-obama-housing-20111024.

11 James Surowiecki, "Second Helpings," *New Yorker*, September 20, 2010.

12 Michael Grunwald, "How the Stimulus is Changing America," *Time*, August 26, 2010, http://www.time.com/time/magazine/article/0,9171,2013826-1,00.html.

CHAPTER 11

1 Faiz Shakir, "Mitch McConnell: I Want To Be Senate Majority Leader in Order To Make Obama a One-Term President," *ThinkProgress*, October 25, 2010, http://thinkprogress.org/politics/2010/10/25/126242/mcconnell-obama-one-one-term/?mobile=nc.

2 PolitiFact.com, "President Barack Obama claims Mitch McConnell says his main goal is for GOP to regain the White House," St. Petersburg Times, http://www.politifact.com/truth-o-meter/statement/2010/oct/30/barack-obama/president-barack-obama-claims-mitch-mcconnell-says/.

3 Kate Zernike, "Unlikely Activist Who Got to the Tea Party Early," *New*

York Times, February 27, 2010, http://www.nytimes.com/2010/02/28/us/politics/28keli.html.

4   Ryan J. Donmoyer and Mike Dorning, "Obama Confronts Resistance from Democrats over Deal to Adopt Bush Tax Cuts," *Bloomberg*, December 7, 2010, http://www.bloomberg.com/news/2010-12-06/payroll-tax-on-the-table-as-negotiators-debate-bush-rate-extension.html.

5   Infoplease, http://www.infoplease.com/ipo/A0005148.html.

6   PoliFact.com, "John Kerry Says Simpson-Bowles proposal raised $2 trillion in new revenue," St. Petersburg Times, http://www.politifact.com/truth-o-meter/statements/2011/nov/21/john-kerry/john-kerry-says-simpson-bowles-proposal-raised-2t/.

7   Kaiser, So Damn Much Money, 206-214.

8   Karen Tumulty and Dan Eggen, "Newt Gingrich Inc.: How the GOP hopeful went from political flameout to fortune," *Washington Post*, November 26, 2011, http://www.washingtonpost.com/politics/newt-gingrich-and-how-he-got-rich/2011/11/21.

Index